IN CITE

IN CITE

Epistemologies of Creative Writing

CAMELIA ELIAS

EYECORNER PRESS

In Cite: Epistemologies of Creative Writing © Camelia Elias 2013
Published by EyeCorner Press, March 2013
Roskilde, Denmark
Typography and design by Camelia Elias
Set in Candara and Monotype Corsiva

ISBN 978 87 92633 33 0

All rights reserved.
No part of this book may be reproduced in any form, without written permission from the publisher and the copyright holder.

NÅR DET KJEM TIL STYKKET

År ut og år inn har du site bøygd yver bøkene,
du har samla deg meir kunnskap
enn du treng til ni liv.
Når det kjem til stykket, er det
so lite som skal til, og det vesle
har hjarta alltid visst.
I Egypt hadde guden for lærdom
hovud som ei ape.

– Olav H. Hauge, Janglestrå, 1980

WHEN ALL IS SAID AND DONE

Year in, year out, you've bent over books.
You've gathered more knowledge
than you'd need for nine lives.
When all is said and done,
so little is needed, and that much
the heart has always known.
In Egypt the god of knowledge
had the head of an ape.

– Trans. from the Norwegian by Robert Hedin

ACKNOWLEDGEMENTS

Some of the material presented here is based on peer-reviewed articles. I thank the following for permission to republish in revised form:

"Composing Mystics: Gertrude Stein between Zen and Zeit." *PsyArt: Journal for the Psychological Study of the Arts.* June, 2012.

"Double-Forked Artifice: Nietzsche's Dynamite." *Sensual Experience and Critical Thinking. Nietzsche Studies on the 140th Anniversary of the Birth of Tragedy.* Kristóf Fenyvesi and Jolán Orbán, eds. Pecs: Jelenkor Publishing, 2012.

"Meanwhile, some Math: Brian Rotman's Becoming Beside Ourselves: The Alphabet, Ghosts, and Distributed Human Being." *Parallax, Vol. 16, Nr. 2, 2010.*

"The Nothing That Is: Epistemologies of Creative Writing." *Kritikos: Journal of Postmodern Cultural Sound, Text and Image.* Volume 7, January-February 2010.

"The Body 'Prefers Not to': Nietzsche on Ethereal Run in Melville and Acker." *Hyperion: On the Future of Aesthetics.* Vol. II. Nr. 3. 2007. New York: The Nietzsche Circle.

"Unbeginnings: The Fragment as a Round Space." *Forma Breve 4: O Fragmento.* Ed. António Manuel Ferreira. Aveiro: Universidade de Aveiro, Centro de Linguas e Culturas, 2006

"Stumbling unto Grace: Invention and the Poetics of Imagination in Hofstadter's Gödel, Escher, Bach." *Janus Head: Interdisciplinary Journal of Continental Philosophy, Literature, Phenomenological Psychology, and Art.* Summer/Fall 9.1, 2006.

"Clowns of Potentiality: Repetition and Resolution in Gertrude Stein and Emile Cioran." *Cercles: Interdisciplinary Journal of Anglo-American Literature. Nr. 14. Style in the Making.* Ed. Mireille Quivy and Philippe Romanski. October 2005

"The Graveyard of Genre: David Markson's Postmodern Epitaphs." *Reconstruction. Studies in Contemporary Culture.* Ed. Davin Heckman and M. Wolf-Meyer. Winter 2004/2005. Vol 5.1

On the private front, I thank my family and friends for believing that such a book is needed, even as it tackles the idea that it is significant to pay attention to what is useless in writing, and take it as such, rather than try to exorcise it in the name of academic relevance, or lie and pretend that the useless is useless and therefore of no value. I thank them for encouraging me to take a political stance somewhere between the lines, and thus advance the claim that what we ought to pay attention to is precisely the usefulness of all that which presents itself to us intentionally as useless.

I thank Manna for saying: 'You can do it.'
I thank Bent for saying: 'In a week, if need be.'
I thank Søren for saying: 'Even if you don't need to, do it.'
I thank Anthony for saying: 'Your secret name is Alogon.'
I thank Enrique for saying: 'A sentence is a distance.'
I thank Patrick for saying: 'Remember, 300 + is beautiful.'
I dedicate this book to all the lovers of axioms in my life.

CONTENTS

1
EPISTEMIC ADVENTURES
COOL CREATIVE WRITING / 11

2
NO-CITE, CRITI-CITE
BECKETT AND FEDERMAN / 43

3
MYSTICAL SITE
A STONE FOR STEIN / 77

4
GRACE IN SIGHT
LACAN, O'HARA, HOFSTADTER, ROTMAN / 133

5
I CITE CYBORGS
NIETZSCHE, MELVILLE, ACKER, ZARATHUSTRA / 177

6
EPISTEMOLOGISTS OF SITE
MARKSON AND CODRESCU / 215

7
EPISTEMOLOGIES OF CREATIVE WRITING
AXIOMATIC REDUX / 271

BIBLIOGRAPHY / 294
ABOUT THE AUTHOR / 305

1

EPISTEMIC ADVENTURES
COOL CREATIVE WRITING

> *I very recently met a man who said how do you do. A splendid story.*
> — Gertrude Stein

There is one obvious thing that academic writing and creative writing have in common: the fact that they are prompted by occasion. But whereas the first has research at its basis, the second relies more on inspiration. And whereas research has the formulation of what is found and the dissemination of knowledge as its primary aim, inspiration adds a poetic touch to how knowledge is formulated. The writer who does research and is not afraid of inspiration thus seeks to strike a symmetrical balance between reflective thought and creative thought, between belief in the power of the text and love of words. The best practitioners of academic creative writing are the ones who can devise strategies for entangling institutionalized formalism with inspiration. What is achieved in this endeavor is a kind of continuous symmetry which ties knowledge to beauty. What mediates the passage from knowledge to beauty, or some other hierophantic manifestation which beauty also is, is an intuitive idea corresponding to the concept of viewing some symmetries as motion as opposed to viewing symmetry as reflection, which enhances the flipping of thought from one state to another, say, from analysis to inspiration. In fields other than mathematics, where these concepts are thoroughly formalized, the understanding of how an academic writer writes creatively can be formulated along similar lines where we can see epistemic inquiry as aiming for symmetry in motion, whereas the ontological status of text and writer can be perceived as a kind of reflection symmetry. The text mirrors the author who mirrors the text in a time and space continuum. Thus, where reflection in general can be considered a response to a writer's question of representation, motion represents the represented, all according to how knowledge is formulated in the way: as attitude, ability, belief, or something else.

Donald Barthelme, a prominent postmodernist and an influential critic has this to say on writing, which further illustrates the relation of creative representation to states of knowing and not-knowing as they are deployed in both motion and reflection:

> Writing is a process of dealing with not-knowing, a forcing of what and how [...] The not-knowing is crucial to art, is what permits art to be made. Without the scanning process engendered by not-knowing, without the possibility of having the mind move in unanticipated directions, there would be no invention [...] The not-knowing is not simple, because it's hedged about with prohibitions, roads that may not be taken. The more serious the artist, the more problems he takes into account and the more considerations limit his possible initiatives (Barthelme, 1991: 486-497).

What Barthelme does here that is also of primary interest in this book is to suggest that not-knowing in creative writing is precisely a strategy to be employed in academic creative writing, as the latter is particularly about the juncture between the occasion of writing, the ethics of writing, autobiography as motivated by inspiration and not always by fact, the embodiment of writing through words which can be hurled at people, the form of writing, axiomatic writing – 'keep it simple, but not that simple' is an example – the beauty of writing when writing is considered loss, and the metaphysical death of writing – 'a long sentence is a death sentence' is also a good example.

The paradox of creative writing, a paradox opposing popular belief, is that although as the very adjective 'creative' indicates, creative writing is in fact more the result of skill and analytical reflection than pure inspiration. All good poets have valuable things to say about their craft, which already suggests, quite persuasively, that if creativity can be taught in the academia, or rather regimented, then it is not less worthy than math or English studies.

In light of this commonsensical observation, why academic institutions still insist that research be devoid of what they refer to as too much embellishing is already quite mind boggling, as the very insistence on objectivity can itself be considered as emotional and not the result of any thinking that truly legitimizes the prohibition against being creative. Being creative does not mean not-knowing. Any writing thus begins with taking suggestions from those who know better, have tried it themselves, and are not afraid of being surpassed. No master is a master if he cannot tolerate the fact that what he needs to teach is also how to bow when the student takes over. Academic writing and creative writing thus share the same premise of following advice.

Here is a favorite of mine, Basil Bunting sharing his knowledge by way of a poem wittily titled, "I Suggest":

1. Compose aloud; poetry is a sound.
2. Vary rhythm enough to stir the emotion you want but not so as to lose impetus.
3. Use spoken words and syntax.
4. Fear adjectives; they bleed nouns. Hate the passive.
5. Jettison ornament gaily but keep shape; Put your poem away till you forget it, then:
6. Cut out every word you dare.
7. Do it again a week later, and again. Never explain - your reader is as smart as you.
(Bunting, in Schmidt, 2006: 97)

"I write for myself and strangers," Gertrude Stein, famously proclaimed anticipating both Barthelme and Bunting, suggesting that the authentic writer will always write out of a completely disinterested impetus. He does not write for a target audience, for an agenda that fits a publisher, and nor is he interested in knowing how many copies his book will sell. Writing for strangers means writing for yourself, but with the hope, rather than the intent to strike a chord in the reader. Good writing is disinterested writing that resonates and that has the potential to instruct and to help the reader know more about himself. On the other hand, as soon as consecration to instruction is articulated, there goes the notion of disinterestedness.

Writers such as Stein understood that writing for yourself and for strangers means writing both in a personal and impersonal voice at the same time. A writer of Stein's caliber, then, can be said to be consecrated to the idea that one begins with instructing oneself, first, in how to be not only a writer, but second, how to also be a reader at the same time. It is also for this reason that one ends up reading Gertrude Stein not with the intent to know more about Gertrude Stein, unless it's her biography or autobiography that one reads, but with the intent to learn about oneself, and how that self can embody several states.

Creative writing thus, at its highest potential, begins with lessons in epistemology. Creative writing *is* epistemology. And the epistemology of creative writing is an acute awareness of the act of writing plus enunciation: 'Now I write.' This means that the epistemology of creative writing is first grounded in a programmatic aspect that entangles creativity with epistemic rules that one devises for oneself. The motivation for 'now I write' may well have to do with the fact that, insofar as one doesn't have a clue as to what one is thinking, one needs to simply sit down and formulate something by force. Something is bound to come out of the endeavor, which already has the potential to be the kind of writing that creates knowledge of self, others, the world, or wherever the writing leads.

The best strategy to identify whether there is even such a thing as an epistemology of creative writing is to look at avantguard writers who have been known to draft manifesto after manifesto. The Surrealists and the Dadaists did a good job at suggesting that writing, even when intended as the result of some automation, is epistemic. Epistemic writing basically follows the rules of making sense, yet, in the hands of avantguardists the epistemic perspective becomes collaborative, and not always the result of self-reflection, bat rather the result of 'other-reflection.'

Traditionally speaking, epistemic writing has been defined via epistemology and the need for self-reflection, and it is interesting to note that the concept is used with some degree of popularity also in classes other than creative, namely college teaching and business schools. It appears that thinking independently is not always a given, hence many believe that self-reflective epistemic writing is a powerful learning tool. As Chiaramonte argues: "Epistemology is the theory of the methods of knowledge. Therefore epistemic writing is writing that aids in thinking, learning, and self-knowledge" (Chiaramonte 1992: 4). My contention here is that an epistemology of creative writing is more inclusive, as it takes into account not only what we call epistemic writing but also inspiration. The reason why I mentioned the example with the Surrealists and the Dadaists is because they were among the first to understand the relation between dense formulations, which dreams and cut-outs contribute to, and clarity of vision that creative ingenuity always opens a door for.

We can thus take our cue from writers who are particularly conscious of their craft, especially as it relates, on the one hand, to how writing disturbs the silence of the white page – here Beckett is a prime example – and on the other hand, to how epistemic creative writing has the potential to create knowledge. But not any knowledge. Creative knowledge. When Tristan Tzara cut his poem to pieces and then rearranged the fragments randomly at a poetry performance gathering, he was not only making new poetry but also a new statement. And with the new statement he created a poetics of poetry criticism and a new school, the Dada school. And what have we learned from that ever since? Among other things that there are always many more signs we have the capacity to mobilize than we know.

This learning is quite beautiful in itself as it says something about the way in which an epistemology of creative writing can be perceived not only in terms of epistemic acts, but also in terms of transgressive acts. Tzara's act of cutting another's genius, as it were, almost traumatized the audience at the time, but there are some things that we can extrapolate from this example that may emphasize how an epistemology of creative writing can enhance what good writing ultimately is and what it can teach apart from appalling conservative audiences.

Some critics have made the observation that powerful writing goes through four movements in relation to the way in which it depicts the trauma that a creative act necessarily involves: intensity, sexual content, nonsense and silence, and repetition (Anne-Maria Mazzega-Bachelet in an unpublished conference paper). On this list I particularly like the last two: when the author establishes intensity by reference to sexual symbolism, 'nonsense' takes over and articulates itself forcefully, which necessarily brings forth silence: characters and readers alike are baffled, so they 'say' nothing. Because silence is instituted, there is thus a need for the repetition of all the other movements. This repetition is what constitutes transgression. While this transgression often comes close to being interpreted as a form of obsession, it also ensures that something interesting happens between the author of the stories, the protagonists in the story and the readers of the story.

The brilliant insight is that because transgression is what it is, a site of struggle and tension with language and ideas, it cannot *per se* also be the vehicle for communication as a result of precise readings (across and between the agents involved). In other words, everybody misreads everybody else – but not entirely. An author may estimate a reader's response quite accurately, but not because she is able to read her opponents (characters and readers alike) with infallible precision, but because there is always a chance that she is wrong precisely and inasmuch as she is also right. I like this idea, especially as it relates to an ethical question: how much responsibility do writers have to show to their readers? (the sources of inspirations are included). Here the correct answer must be this one: none, if creativity is to stand a chance of survival in its intense, ravishing, illuminating, and for the most part violent mode.

Words are bodies, poststructuralists such as Judith Butler have taught us. They can be hurled at others; they can be made to caress others; they can be served as dishes for others to swallow, enjoy, or vomit; they can be made to transgress others' limits of being in the world by enhancing their eloquence, craft, articulation, calculation, communication, and creativity. When Tzara declared: "Any work of art that can be understood is the product of journalism [...] The rest, called literature, is a notebook of human imbecility to aid future professors," he was creating epistemology. But when he continued immediately in the next line, "The poem pushes or digs a crater, is silent, murders," he created an epistemology of creative writing (Tzara, 1973: 169).

Good writing thus creates a hypothetical world for the reader, which runs parallel with the reader's real life. An inspired reader might say about some writing: 'yes, I can also do this,' or 'no, I could never do it like that, but I admire what I see here.' This hypothetical world – insofar as it produces emotions that are both the result of invented narratives and also of instinctual drives (fear, pride, etc.) – converges with the real world and thus becomes truthful. Truth in fiction can be said to be on a par with truth in reality. Invented or not, the hypothetical world, or the alternative world of thought, in fact, even has the potential to become more truthful than the real world.

Computer game theorists have already formulated ideas that draw on the way in which consistency with truth (fictionally based, and also anchored in reality) can be said to form the basis for the condition of any epistemology of creativity (Caillois, 1961). The interactive human gains knowledge from thinking (about playing). Culture theorists have also emphasized how conceptions of knowledge are always mediated. Thus we deal with conceptions of knowledge based on knowledge as representation, knowledge as ability, knowledge as attitude, knowledge as belief.

As the best knowledge stems from inquiry and the interplay between an agent and the positions available to him or her, knowledge can also be said to dynamically converge to limit points. The formulation, 'now I know everything,' only works, however, when it is clearly context-situated and time-bound. When a lover tells the other in a relationship: 'now I know why you left me. Because you fell in love with someone else,' the lover does not make a metaphysical statement, but a factual one. If there is any transcendence in this, as the pain involved in that act of recognition might indicate, then it is the manifestation of a potential lament that the lover doesn't know all the details that brought about the misfortune. The knowing of everything converges precisely to the limit of here and now, and it is based precisely on this or that contextual evidence.

Everyone wants to know everything and understand everything. This is fair enough, particularly as this desire is quite democratic and ranges between high and low, narrow and wide.

When Bush invaded Iraq, he did so because he claimed that now he knew everything and understood everything. So did Osama bin Laden when he sent his martyrs out on a mission. In this context politicians are the easiest to figure out. It gets more interesting with writers and academics who have their desire to know everything about their fields mediated by a good dose of skepticism. What if knowing everything amounts to this statement: all I know is that I know nothing? If Socrates' discovery is not still revered because of what it means, many a writer apply it because it suggests modesty. The implicit call here is one of weighing one option against the other: you should know things as you see them reveal themselves unto you – "write what you know," Hemingway said convincingly – but you should not be too creative where the process of telling how you arrived at what you know is concerned. There is thus already a tension at work between fact and fiction, especially as this tension is wrung through the tall order of keeping it simple.

Now, all this is quite commonplace, as the distinction between fact and fiction has been debated since old times. And yet, however, the way in which this relates to the distinction between academic and creative writing is more interesting, for it is not always obvious that this distinction is further maintained by another distinction, namely the one between personal and impersonal voice. An academic is trained to exercise the impersonal voice in relation to communicating knowledge, yet the case is more often than not that the academic cannot dissociate his thoughts from that which inspires them, that which bends the impersonal design to including, if not fiction, then certainly ambiguity. This book, although adopting the Arnoldian injunction that criticism must be disinterested, also flaunts the very idea that forms the core of objective criticism, namely the notion that the more objective the criticism, the more it relies on drawing on others' thoughts. There is thus a strong sense of a community which informs individual creativity, a sense that interacts with both factual knowledge and invented knowledge.

The trajectory followed in this vein is quite straightforward: one researches, one acknowledges influences, and one exercises a personal voice against the background of the impersonal institution. This is no breaking methodology in itself where the composition of academic books is concerned, but here I want to add that if the academic writer allows himself to acknowledge loudly rather than silently, as has been the case, the presence of creativity within the very institutionalized production of regimented meaning, then he must make recourse to quoting, if he does not want to get fired, that is. Quite simply, here, I am interested in looking at the shielding effect that quoting texts has for the way in which academics go on with being academics while privately exhibiting behavior akin to that of being horses galloping for the race that would win them recognition also the creative way. Guy Davenport once described the Finnish philosopher Jaakko Hintikka in a single line which creates an image that is both lasting, in the sense that one relies entirely on its visual message, one that also invites to the decoding of a hidden meaning: "Jaako Hintikka: philosopher and critic of Wittgenstein. In private life a reindeer" (Davenport, 1997: 228).

Davenport, who was a professor of classics and had many prized translations from the Greek, was also a creative writer of fine sensibility. His book, *The Hunter Gracchus*, a collection of creative/academic essays, from where the line above is taken, is a modern example of how academic knowledge entangled with creative manifestation is more powerful, insofar as it is freed from the constraints of being merely objective. One could say that what academic creative writers are concerned with is not how to refute objectivity, but how to be even more objective, particularly in the face of current discursive trends that either claim that all writing is purely subjective or that it is the result of neuro-biological functions.

Davenport is an example of a writer who is in fact more than merely objective when he allows himself to become personal with the writers he writes about, and to ask them questions directly to their faces. Thus he has no problem identifying Hintikka with the roaming animal that is after Wittgenstein, nor does he have a problem with imagining that he eats barbecue with Heraclitus. Things do tend to become clearer by the illuminating fire. And the reader gets the message. If not, there is always the image, and that often can stand on its own, making its own aesthetic statement or judgment. Where I am concerned, I must confess: the tableau of the pioneer of game-theoretical semantics in logic, Hintikka, as a reindeer, makes me exclaim, 'how wonderful!' – and nothing else. My calculations about what is going on are brought at a standstill, and I advance with my eyes closed, but my gut open. Open to spatial logics, in this case.

Now, what writers such as Davenport do, that is of relevance to this study, is probe the territory between impact and effect. When the writing is personal, it is more likely than unlikely that it is also hot, snappy, and vigorous. It thus makes an impact. When the writing is impersonal, it is more likely than unlikely that it is crisp, cold, and conservative. It thus creates a calculated effect. Consequently, we are back to symmetries and how to strike the balance between relations: the relation between knowledge and invention, personal and impersonal voice, fact and fiction, the individual and the community.

Put more frankly, and if I'm allowed to assign agency to creative writing and knowledge respectively, or see them anthropomorphized, I would say that I'm interested particularly in what happens when creative writing allows itself to formulate strategies of telling institutionalized knowledge to go fuck itself. So I cite. Here, the poet Charles Olson who in 1951 theorized the implications of writing poems that are always specifically addressed, yet not necessarily to specific people – even though this was the very backbone of occasional writing – but to occasion itself.

In a letter to Robert Creely, which developed later into several volumes, Olson laments without a breath, or a full stop: "all this damn funny recent verse – *all* of it, if you will notice, directed to actual persons, composted, actually by and for OCCASION" (Olson in Butterick, 7: 79). And then the ax falls on concluding what impact such writing has for the community of both poets and critics, as it produces at least two necessary changes:

> (1) that you and I restore society in the act of communicating to each other… & (2) that what I mark about this correspondence is something I don't for a moment think is peculiar to thee et me— that the function of critique is more than the mere one of clarities (as, say, Flaubert, &, Mme Sand) it is even showing itself in the very form of our address to each other, and what work goes along with it […] I put it as of us, but, we do say to the Great Society go fuck yrself […] and quietly create a society of our wives and friends (George Butterick complete correspondence, 7:79).

In this book I am attracted to the idea of a community of wives and friends, which means that I am interested in pursuing a twofold aim: first, I want to look at writers who are acutely conscious of creating knowledge. This knowledge is often produced as the result of philosophizing not only generally on what the meaning of life is, as it were, but also on what it means to see oneself as a relational self, which is to say that one that learns from others what the Self is. Second, I want to know how this knowledge is formulated, more often than not, as a very individual statement, but one statement that does not veer off acknowledgement. In other words, one credits a collective body for one's ideas, and thus pays tribute to it by turning those forming it into first order agents that get to populate one's own creative writing. Beckett did it by negating everything. Federman took it to extremes. Gertrude Stein became her partner, Alice Toklas, in recognition of her, Lacan went to Freud for permission to call himself a Freudian in his Lacanian psychoanalytical practice, Nietzsche took to the Greek road, Hofstadter and Rotman credited the mathematician Georg Cantor for their literary and writerly ideas, Kathy Acker looked at the vampirism of others, Melville at the creative impossibility of others, Markson at the voice of the dead, and Codrescu at all those who say 'fuck' and 'God' in one sentence. These writers, who I will turn to for guidance in this book, were all into occasional writing even before the New American poets theorized on it. They created not only a poetics of writing, but, most importantly, an epistemology of creative writing.

In the context of the democratization of writing, which started after the second world war when creative writing programs were implemented in academia both in the UK and the US, charting the notion of an epistemology of creative writing becomes central, as it poses some essential concerns that take issue with the shifting figurations of the academic poet/writer's role in relation to the university. The questions of relevance here are both, first related to genre and poetics, and then to method, thus extending an argument about the use of various strategies of creative writing within the academy. For instance: must the poet be a practitioner of a 'poetry of knowledge' in order for him to gain teaching credentials and legitimation? How is erudition perceived in relation to other cognitive and emotional factors, such as interpretation, creativity, imagination, inspiration? In other words, what does it mean to say: 'I write as an academic, and I'm allowed to not only exercise my poetic genius but also teach it. Yet however, I also ask myself: 'do I excite my partner and friends as well with my intention to disseminate knowledge, perhaps also about that which one would do best to remain silent about?'

As historians have already done a good job at charting the rise of creative writing in the academy, my own aim here is not to repeat what was said, but by glancing at the matter sideways, I want to put into perspective what epistemic creative writing means for writers such as Samuel Beckett, Raymond Federman, Gertrude Stein, Jacques Lacan, Frank O'Hara, Doulgas Hofstadter, Brian Rotman, Herman Melville, Kathy Acker, Friedrich Nietzsche, David Markson, Andrei Codrescu, and a few others who get a passing, but significant mention.

Some of these authors are either taught in the university – they populate various curricula – or they themselves have taught or still teach in the university, particularly in connection with illustrating how creative thought can enhance reflective thought. As some of these writers have also experienced being in exile, whether imposed or self-imposed, one finds an added bonus in charting their experiences with writing from the margins in relation to epistemic matters. It is my contention that these writers are interested in epistemology and creative knowledge by definition. Once they are on new territory they are forced not only to figure out but also devise and navigate through strategies of survival, which means that their writings are informed by some of the energies released by these tensions. Some are into beauty, some are into truth, and some into dismantling them both, but only with view to reconstructing what goes into the process of thinking about such generally perceived universal concepts.

For instance, as with Beckett, the good news about beauty is that it forces one to keep silent. In the face of beauty, one neither blesses nor curses one's existence. Beckett himself couldn't make up his mind about which way to go, so he repeatedly stated he wasn't going anywhere while nevertheless going. Beckett's ambivalence, famously captured in the phrase: "I can't go on. I'll go on" is thus an expression of the ultimate acknowledgment that in the face of beauty one does nothing and says nothing. For Beckett, this nothingness induces a state of crisis and despair, which is necessary for the thinking act and its formulation as epistemic writing *par excellence.* Real despair is connected with impotence. The impotence to go beyond, or behind the text, and throw oneself at all that which has the potential to unfold itself unto one as beautiful. It is in this sense that beauty can be said to be a form of hierophantic manifestation. As such, it is also linked to the idea of consecration. From consecration to consumption there's only one step. Religious leaders and mass media know all about it already, and writers such as Codrescu have already charted the subtle relation of collaborative and adversarial icon work to the spiritual and intellectual state of the US today. When thinking about symmetries we thus pose the perennial question: How to 'think' knowledge, and can my writing about it produce more knowledge?

In my analyses of the mentioned writers I intend to not only use but also perform comparative approaches to creative writing across disciplines in an entangled discussion of suggested differences: transatlantic differences (the American tradition vs. the European) – for instance, look at generic aspects of literary concepts, such as the fragment, the aphorism, the epitaph – and visual writing, cyborg writing, poetry as philosophy and philosophy as poetic scholarship. I am particularly interested in devising epistemic rules for such performative acts that combine an autobiographical mode with formal philosophy and poetry.

This study aims at being systematic to the extent that it addresses in a sustained manner, albeit not always explicitly, the question of method in academic creative writing. But where the corpus of the chosen texts to look at is concerned, the approach to my selection is motivated by a set of criteria that follows both a factual and a creative line of thought:

1. Dealing with fact, it can be argued that the authors discussed here share the following precepts about creativity that produces knowledge:

All academic creative writing is instructive. All academic creative writing creates a space for the reader to inhabit and to consequently coproduce the heuristics of the text.

2. Dealing with assumption, we can argue that the authors discussed here share an explicit disgust for systems. These writers' feelings about having their thoughts contained by culture invites any one reader to partake in their creative rebellion. So,

what we are dealing with here is in fact a paradox, namely, the dilemma of writers who want to engage with academic creative writing, yet by being neither academic nor creative about it, but rather instructive in some way. A way in which instruction can occur, in fact, outside of set methodical approaches. It is often therefore that such writers place a demand on critics that THEY be creative, and that *they* take license with what they want to do over and above what is expected of them to do – here, often to comply with standard academic writing. To put it bluntly, the critics are invited to consider all the texts under scrutiny as bogus and play along.

The primary assumption here is that academic creative writing works by suggestion rather than by demonstration. As a critic, suggesting, rather than demonstrating that, for instance, what links Gertrude Stein with Wittgenstein is an interest in (corner) stones, is more powerful than the situation when the critic, via cultural and literary history demonstrates that this is the case, only so that his reader might want to exclaim the following: 'so what if the Steins want to talk about stones? And what is the relevance of this to anything at all anyway?'

What I am trying to say is that although my choice of writers, on this second level, may seem random, there is a system at work even when piloting through such seemingly incongruous diversity. As creativity rules the game, allowing for texts to speak their own mind in dialogue and juxtaposition enhances none other than the venerable tradition that goes all the way back to Socrates, namely, the tradition that rests on the notion that one learns more through inquiry, rather than merely through selection or through forcing a motivation for selection.

But why these writers and not others, one might still want to know. Indeed, ultimately it can be argued that all writing produces knowledge, but how much of it is the effect of information, how much of certainty, and how much of having a system?

The writers I have chosen to look at seem to answer this question by formulating what I can see unambiguously at work as being an epistemic theory of creative writing. They all seem to be pointing to a simple strategy: in the face of having or not having a system for writing, a theory of nothingness is proposed in relation to the futility of writing, while simultaneously engaging the situation of the 'and yet'. What keeps them going is this scenario, in which we can imagine them say the following: 'we write but we don't really believe in words; we teach but we don't really believe in masters; we are creative but we don't really believe in inspiration; and yet'.

When Beckett says: "I can't go on, I'll go on," he retorts to 'and yet.' Beckett is a master of the use of the 'and yet.' For Beckett, what ensures continuity between having a system and eradicating it at the same time, or between writing and denouncing writing, is the constant deployment of the 'and yet' in the immanence of thought in non-thought and vice versa. This sounds complicated? It isn't, for this stands at the very core of an aesthetic project that takes seriously the task of being heuristic and instructive in an allusive kind of way. I'm quite convinced that for Beckett and the rest here, creativity is clarity.

It is not through explanation that things become clear, but rather, through making distinctions and then standing against them too. For the writers mentioned here, creativity is not something that one writes about, only to muddle things up, but something that one experiences beyond words. So, one can only write about things as they happen in between worlds, the world of rational thinking and the world of creative myth.

The strong suggestion here is that the place between worlds is the only place that a serious epistemic writer can inhabit. This is the only place that can always veto the 'and so it is' of the general academic discourse on creative writing. In the place between logos and mythos the smart writer will declare to everyone's exasperation: 'and yet,' every time a verdict on the state of things is passed. Ask Beckett.

It is thus my main contention that through the simple use of the 'and yet' – through seeing it as an instance of poesis in the position mediating between all relations – the writers I look at produce knowledge that allows for both creativity and method (perhaps even as non-method) to emerge side by side and be in constant dialogue with each other. This dialogue can also be seen as a powerful source for inquiry, and one can almost hear what the selected writers here demand of their own text: 'speak to me first.'

I shall argue that what all the writers discussed here do, which is remarkable, is to dare ask their own texts to speak to them. And interestingly enough, the more these writers distance themselves from immanent or religious thought, the more such a demand: 'speak to me first,' appeals to them on the level of what can be deemed mystical, dealing with the prophetic voice of the text. Things can be certain from an oracular, predictive point of view, but not so certain where the interpretation of what is heard is concerned. Here, I want to argue that the writers I chose as practitioners of academic creative writing also have this in common: they are all mystics. They all place a constant tension between having their texts instruct: 'follow me' and having their texts suggest: 'but meanwhile walk ahead.'

We can begin to get a sense of how the interplay between the creative and the academic impetus occurs. At the level of form, we have slogan-like formulations operated by temporal modifiers such as 'and yet' and 'meanwhile.' At the level of content, the creative teaching is supported by a constant question: 'why bother with such small details, minimal phrases, an obsessive insistence on nothing, nothing being passed on (and yet)?' In other words, if we stick to such micro-level analysis, we could say that what enables a following from the leading position is precisely the enunciation of the 'and yet.' The performative 'and yet' is thus a most powerful tool that eradicates not only any system but also the most negatively powerful ones, such as the ones associated with the cynic's lot which dictate that whatever action is taken – 'should I write or should I not, meanwhile, I do it anyway, as it will mean nothing.' The 'whatever' of the situation is thus superseded by the 'and yet.' In this sense all the writers I look at here are radical or can be said to be writers of the extravagant. They are capable of finding a middle ground for formulating their theories of epistemology of creative writing outside of employing a systematic method.

Proceed to nothing – Precede from nothing

Can nothing be knowledge? And if it can, what shape does it assume in relation to creativity and style? More than a matter of course, and rather more as a matter of style, some modern and postmodern texts claim to be about nothing. The assumption is that literary imagination, when taking issue with the 'nothing that is' in relation to what kind of message or knowledge such nothingness nonetheless construes, proposes, and transmits, relies on a presupposed poetics of form as a stylized liminality. If thought not in terms of negative value, such as when 'nothing' is conceptualized against the background of there being something, the idea of 'nothing' opens up a liminal space where it can be considered a pure abstract, yet only through a stylistic manoeuvre.

When 'nothing' is represented, it is often represented through stylistic devices, such as gaps, ellipsis, blank pages, or silence in the text. 'Nothing' thus leaves a trace, as it is itself traced by sight (on site). In other words, when 'nothing' is not thought of in terms of structural and binary relations, it can only be conceived of in terms of convergence towards the horizon of boundlessness. In formal philosophy, methodology and convergence equals knowledge. In literature, methodology and convergence can easily equal or rather prefigure knowledge as 'nothing.' As Franco Moretti put it: "near the border, figurality goes up" (Moretti, 1998: 45).

As a preamble to the following analyses, I want to explore the following axioms: 1) in theory, there is nothing more elegant than 'nothing'; and 2) in style, academic creative writing begins not in the chiasmic relation of 'nothing' to style or nothing in style and style in nothing, but more in a relation of stripping: stripping style of theory. My central question here will revolve around what happens when form is stripped away by the power of nothing, and where that leaves the epistemic knowledge that is contingent on creativity.

The philosophical problem of nothingness in its relation to the existing world of which we are part has not been investigated in any serious terms until Leibniz. Leibniz's paper, "On the Ultimate Origination of Things" from 1697, in which he questions not the wonder of the world's existence but the fact that there is a world to begin with, opened the space for analytical thinking that later inspired philosophers such as Wittgenstein. Wittgenstein's now famous formulation regarding which element is the more mysterious in the conflation of the world with the modalities in which the world is perceived: "Not *how* the world is, is the mystical, but *that* it is" (Wittgenstein, 1922: 107), opens further the space in which nothingness can be considered not only in its opposition to something, or in categorical terms that designate a void, but as a dimension. I call this dimension the style of existence.

Obviously the idea of nothing has pervaded literature and science alike and we have countless considerations of nothing, from Shakespeare – who was interested in how something can come out of nothing – to Sartre, whose *Being and Nothingness* investigates the paradoxes of nihilism and the origins of negation, as this statement suggests: "The Being by which Nothingness is a Being such that in its Being, the Nothingness of its Being is in question" (Sartre, 1998: 23). If for Sartre, to annihilate, or 'the nothing that is,' is defined as that by which consciousness exists, for Shakespeare, the designation of an empty space, of which men of religion and philosophy at the time were suspicious, goes hand in hand with the formulation of paradoxes through puns and word plays. One need only think of the playful passage in *The Winter's Tale*:

> Is this nothing?
> Why, then the world, and all that's in't, is nothing [...]
> My wife is nothing, nor nothing have these nothings,
> If this be nothing.
> (Shakespeare, 2009: 15)

What these examples show is a double concern: first, how to make sense of nothing in relation to knowledge, and second, how to formulate a poetics of space in which nothingness is part of a creative act. One can make the inference that, if 'nothing' is to be expressed, then, it can only be so by virtue of a reduction. But then the question is: how can 'nothing' be more reduced than it is already by and in itself? If 'nothing' is to *be*, to exist, then it can only be so by virtue of its being reduced to stylistic representation. 'Nothing' thus begins nothing and ends nothing. (And here I lose my trail on how to use the citation marks around nothing, as any consideration of nothing, parenthetically speaking, invites the thinker to consider following the logic of sense, rather than the logic of reason.) And yet. Taken as a frame of representation, 'nothing' can sanction the degree to which a text can be said to suggest movement, energy, or what the creative impulse consists of. The clear link to style here is in the question: is this text about nothing interesting? 'Nothing' thus undergoes an aesthetic evaluation.

In his popular science book, *The Book of Nothing,* John Barrow quotes Tim Joseph's article, "Unified Field Theory" (April 6, 1978, New York Times), which confers agency to nothing thus parodying the function that 'nothing' has, both in relation to style and theory, insofar as both style and theory, when they profess interestingness do so by emphasizing how creation is possible out of nothing:

In the beginning there was Aristotle,
And objects at rest tended to remain at rest,
And objects in motion tended to come to rest,
And soon everything was at rest,
And God saw that it was boring.
(Barrow, 2001: 292)

What is an epistemology of creative writing? And what is an epistemic creative writer? Taken against the background of the realization that there is no such thing as artistic originality, personality, or singularity, knowledge about the well of creativity is more about the realization that a writer, if not original, is good enough. But good enough for what? In his seminal collection of essays about modernist English and American poets, *The Strength of Poetry*, James Fenton begins with anecdotal considerations of how renaissance artists contributed to the understanding of how creative genius, while professing to start out of nothing, hence the epithet of genius, was mainly the result of strings of information being entangled and shared (Fenton, 2001: 1-5).

Although Fenton does not state it explicitly it in his account of how paranoid Michelangelo was, keeping a secret and burning upon his nearing end all of his notes and sketches of fear that someone might steal his ideas, and how Leonardo Da Vinci couldn't care less about being credited or not for his work, what becomes clear is that when several geniuses could not co-exist, when one was good and the other only good enough, an intersticial place was marked as a void. Fenton's argument is that in the void there is always the possibility of inhabiting different places, and this plurality is what becomes the ultimate marker of how 'the nothing that is' can then be valued. If Da Vinci was a genius in Rome but not as good as Michelangelo, in Florence he was better than good enough. Meanwhile he was just creating.

What this example illustrates is that in any consideration of how to formulate an epistemology of creativity one must take into one's calculations all the devils one lives next to. This gives rise to considering first and foremost how nothingness reduces to a seemingly empty head, as it were. Thus a first axiom in this relation that a writer must formulate must be this one: *(1) My writing begins with the turning of my head.* That all writing is context-situated and context-based is no news, but that all writing must be more than the sum of causal relations that one can predict is better than merely good enough.

In his essay from *The Metaphysician in the Dark*, on Fenton's own work as a poet as well as a critic, such as he appears in *The Strength of Poetry*, contemporary poet and Pulitzer prize winner, Charles Simic, formulates six answers that all attempt to say something about who the real author of a poem is. Each is an example of different schools of theory which show how genius is always tagged not only to the question of nothing but also to that of the extent to which nothing can be stylized according to context. Here's Simic's list:

1. The poet and no one else writes the poem.
2. The unconscious of the poet writes the poem.
3. All of past poetry writes the poem.
4. Language itself writes the poem.
5. Some higher power, angelic or demonic, writes the poem.
6. The spirit of the time writes the poem.

    (Simic, 2003: 125)

Here, while one is tempted to add: '7. Nothing writes the poem,' one is also forced to consider the materiality of nothing and anticipate some criticisms: what would the New Critics say? The psychoanalysts? The Marxists? The structuralists? The post-structuralists? The cultural theorists? And so on. 'Nothing' must thus be calculated but only in relation to non-predictability. This is what Simic has to say about the way in which a lyrical poem resists interpretation, suggesting that it is perhaps precisely 'nothing' as style which "won't reveal to us the secret of how it came about or how it seduces the reader" (126). He follows up on his argument by way of quoting Fenton:

> There must be such a thing as causality, we assume; but we cannot expect to understand its workings. In the writing of poetry we may say that the thing we predict will not happen. If we can predict it, it is not poetry. We have to surprise ourselves. We have to outpace our colder calculations (Fenton in Simic, 126).

And then Simic concludes with this telling fragment:

> This is the crux of the problem. If there's no clear relationship between cause and effect – goodbye theory. And if there's no theory how is the intellect going to revenge itself against the imagination by locking it up in some conceptual cage? It is worth emphasizing that the poet is not in control of his poems. He is like someone who imagines he is driving from New York to Boston only to find himself in Tuscaloosa, Alabama. The point being, we cannot turn to our imagination and say, give me an original description of what the moon looks like tonight because I need it for the poem I'm writing. An image like Rimbaud's famous "Madame X installed a piano in the Alps" literally pops out of nowhere. Our intellect wants to understand how poetry works, but it has no

ability to cough up a single poetic image worth making a fuss about (126).

What Simic does here that is interesting is point to the reduction of nowhere to elsewhere. In this sense, it is always the elsewhere that constitutes the stylistic device of the nowhere, or nothing. In other words, the possibility of 'elsewhere' undermines the impossibility of nothing there to be articulated.

Thus we come to formulating another axiom: *(2) Keep it simple. Write nothing.* Now, as with any axiom, we might ask: why start here? Why trust, even provisionally, this starting point? In mathematics we might appeal to beauty, power, or 'fit' with what has become before. In literature, we need to think about texts. Perhaps texts such as Samuel Beckett's that combine an awareness of the fact that in order for 'nothing' to take place it needs first of all to be stylized, even if only by quotation marks. In Beckett, 'nothing' is both a matter of style and a matter of theory. One of the most powerful suggestions of how 'nothing' depends on stylizing the minimal in one's betrayal of language, the body, and breath, is found in the exchange in *Endgame*, when one of the characters, Hamm, says to the other, Clov, by way of summing up the meaning of life: "it's better than nothing," to which Clov replies: "Better than nothing? Is it possible?" (Beckett, 1986: 121).

Let us begin our journey in search of an epistemology of creative academic writing by way of assessing what IS, what is possible and what is probable in the kind of writing that formulates knowledge in the acknowledgement of the 'nothing that is,' the 'everything that is,' the 'meanwhile in between,' the 'preferred undisclosed,' and the 'chances are.' Think of this book as a game of catch. The rule of the method is this: it takes a liar to catch a philosopher; a poet to catch an epistemologist; and a monk to catch a cynic. And of course, it takes a ghost to catch a machine, a cemetery to catch epitaphs, and a text to catch epigraphs. And while apes catch knowledge, rituals catch magic, and inspiration catches writing, it takes a creative writer to catch a scholar.

The structure

The first two chapters after this introduction (2 and 3) have two modernists in sight, plus a 'postmodern modernist': Samuel Beckett, Raymond Federman, and Gertrude Stein. Here my aim is to catch these authors as they frame writing; Beckett from the inside – 'there is nothing,' he claims – Stein from the outside – 'there is everything,' she claims, especially with love as an economy, and Federman from the middle – 'the interstice is the thing,' he claims. Meanwhile, here comes a state of grace, when the reader of epistemic writing needs to take a breath and make a leap of faith. For how are we to determine what's in between nothing and everything? How can we mobilize the abundance of signs around us? What can a writer write about, really? Everything he knows, as Hemingway once suggested? Research that can be embellished on creatively, or flourishing that one then calls research? What is an epistemic creative writer? And how can she write without a method?

Jacques Lacan, in tandem with Frank O'Hara, serves us as an interlude in chapter 4, and since he was into syllogisms, I allowed myself here to also check with a few mathematicians on what the status of creative invention is in the context of inspiration and knowledge acquisition for the epistemic creative writer. Douglas Hofstadter and Brian Rotman enlighten us on recursive structures in writing and how we go from the n-th level to the more specific ghost in the machine through embodiment. What exactly is it that the epistemic creative writer embodies? A straight message devoid of (number) symbolism? How does he pass it on, if that is the case? This chapter addresses the significance of considering the relation of memory to image and how it lodges onto writing.

Chapter 5 is about preference in Herman Melville and disembodiment in Kathy Acker. The question here is about how the epistemic creative writer can wire herself to the crossing of thresholds: academic writer or just writer? Or maybe both. Or neither. Nietzsche gets tagged at the very end here with a suggestion that love is all it takes. Love of writing. Throw some eternity into it, and you're set to go. The epistemic creative writer begins to exhale after the long breath initiated by Beckett. But it takes the gushing of some blood first in order to understand what is at stake in the penning of scholarship in the blood-ink of creativity.

David Markson makes an entrance in chapter 6 to talk about death, and Andrei Codrescu, accompanied by a few Beat poets and New York School poets, intones about nonconformism in writing. Dying is pretty conventional. Hence, a discussion about reconsidering genre and how to categorize epistemic creative writing is called for.

The book ends with a take on axiomatic thinking in which the epistemic creative writer ponders about the art of brevity. Chapter 7 is intended to be the short version of *In Cite: Epistemologies of Creative Writing*, and a performance of inciting to reclaiming Beckett as a dead man: Say nothing. Write nothing. Keep quiet. I allow myself here to also offer a small contribution to the world of creative writing in the form of a few prose poems that honor some of the writers mentioned in this book. So I don't keep quiet.

In other words, although this book is intended to say something about the significance of silence in creative writing and how that gets translated into an epistemic discourse, the plan is to claim that an epistemic creative writer always writes against the background of the unvoiced. The last chapter here is an attempt to demonstrate that, even if in a rather non-traditional fashion.

Chapter 7 is thus intended as a short piece that counters my verbose engaging with what, at the end of the day, may still seem a body of unrelated writers. But, from a pedagogical point of view, I actually want this chapter to be regarded as a perfomance of what I imagine the task of the academic creative writer is, namely to develop a potential that unifies the scholarly with the creative practice precisely in the dismantling of the myth that there is ever such unity anywhere in either. The 33 phrases that begin in the infinitive mode à la 'to create something under the sign of knowing first,' to… (do something, be something, think something, know something), offer a pragmatic suggestion to the impossible task of bringing interminable teaching to a knowing halt. So, in a sense, this IS a book about silence. I suggest this much in the series of prose poems that come after my 'axiomatic' formulations. These poems, that also end this book, come from two volumes of prose poetry that I've published over the span of some 5 years.[1] They all deal

---

1   See *Eight Senses Plus Two* (2009) and *The Logician* (2010). The prose poems engage with a number of notable philosophers, literary critics, and novelists who all engage with critical discourse.

with how a creative writer enters the space of another writer and asks questions. Just as Markson exclaims in one of his novels, "Wittgenstein, it is you who is creating all this confusion?" in my poems I try to address the ways in which we can live with the confusion. Perhaps even find value in it. Take it to a place where we can declare: confusion = knowledge.

All this being the case then, I warn the reader expecting a treatise on epistemology or a history of creative writing that this is a book about neither.[2] Nor is this a book about pedagogy in the classroom, or stories about teaching writing in college. This is a book about a few good men and women who thought that epistemic writing is about following this axiom: It takes silence to catch the rhetorical noise and a guillotine to decapitate the clichés.

---

2 To some extent I have covered the ground of creative writing in the academia in my book on the poet Lynn Emanuel, *Pulverizing Portraits: Lynn Emanuel's Poetry of Becoming*, (2010), where I look at some of the history of creative writing and its institutionalization in the context of the university. I refer the reader interested in my take on the pedagogy of writing to this work.

2

NO-SITE CRITI-CITE
BECKETT AND FEDERMAN

> *The sun shone, having no alternative, on the nothing new.*
> – Beckett, *Murphy*

In most of Beckett's texts, we have a conscious movement from breaking up the linguistic idiom by reducing it to enunciations that rely on stylizing 'nothing' to texts which clearly are intended to convey a theory of nothingness, among other things by letting breath take over. The breath thus usurps not only the language which is made to fail on purpose, but it also transcends the decaying body. In one of the last pieces written by Beckett in 1983, *Worstward Ho!*, published under the tile, *Nohow On, Worstward Ho*, we find a final variation of Beckett's obsession with how to go on when one cannot, in an elaborate stylization of the 'and yet.'

In one of the beginning passages, the speaker, devoid of agency, manages not only to establish, but also control the symmetry between style and theory, between saying it in words and the radical eradication even of the attempt to reach an empty space with words, as is the case in the end.

> Whose words? Ask in vain. Or not in vain if say no knowing. No saying. No words for him whose words. Him? One. No words for one whose words. One? It. No words for it whose words. Better worse so (Beckett, 1983: 19).

According to Dirk Van Hulle, what Beckett does in *Worstward Ho!* is to "attempt to reach the worst possible condition, which proves to be an asymptotic journey: like the infinitesimal attempt to reach 'nothing' with words, the worst cannot be attained with words" (Van Hulle, 2004). Between the beginning of the piece, with its clear demand: "On. Say on." and the final words: "said nohow on," Beckett circles around such concepts as the "unlessenable least" (32), an "unworsenable worst" (33), a "meremost minimum" (9) that is "better than nothing" (27), because it is "a little better worse than nothing so" (23).

This can be said to constitute Beckett's final actual performance of his earlier work entitled *Texts for Nothing* (1955). Although critics have identified the workings of negativity in all of Beckett's works either as necessary manifestations of an a-theological thought which aims at disclosing an inner authenticity (Arnaould, 1996), others have also noted the countermovement in negativity, such as when negativity is negated by its own negative dynamics (Wolosky, 1991). Shira Wolosky notes that:

> The *Texts for Nothing* concede – indeed insist – that language immediately plunges the self into multiplicity and exteriority. But the *Texts* no less question whether this need compromise the self – indeed, whether outside of this linguistic multiplicity there is any self at all (Wolosky, 1991: 226).

Here I am tempted to say that what Beckett does that can be considered a project close to formulating an epistemology of creative writing is ask and answer precisely this question "Whose words? Ask in vain." For Beckett the very condition of an inner interiority which is in constant tension with the desire for authenticity that relies on an outer form for expression is all about affirming the instance of the 'and yet' as the first and "meremost minimum" of knowledge. For Beckett, one begins to know not when one acknowledges that one knows nothing, but when one acknowledges that 'the nothing that is,' in theory, is not a way of pushing "negation to its limit" (Conor, 1992: 89), but a way of approximating the 'and yet.'

The remarkable event that begins *Texts for Nothing* – one that we find in the lamentation of not being able to go on that a disembodied voice in the text sounds and heralds in the first line: "Suddenly, no, at last, long last, I couldn't anymore, I couldn't go on." (Beckett, 1967: 75) – finds resonance precisely in the 'and yet,' as thinking, beyond the materiality of the exterior sound, conjures other bodies into play. The next line thus indicates a search for strategies to cope not only with the meaning of not being altogether there, physically, but also the meaning of the meaning of such significance about void, or nothingness, that only an exterior body can enact and make manifest. Thus there must be someone. "Someone said, You can't stay here. And I couldn't stay there and I couldn't go on" (75). Going from a subjective first person narrative, the voice then shifts to a third person narrative as soon as the thinking of chance is produced, as if echoing the perennial, albeit romantic, question: what are the odds of finding someone completely symmetrical with one self? At this point the voice is not only compliant with itself but also suggests that implicit in its argument is the idea that such questions can only be answered by epistemologists who are better at betting than at producing theories about knowledge. Thus enters Vincent, the voice's accompanying partner, who, through his physical presence, manages not only to undo the lamentation about the limitation of life and language, but also perform it in reverse. "I can't go on" thus transforms into "and yet," and the ground for a symmetrical relation is thus laid in this line: "We envy each other, I envy him, he envies me" (87). And yet again, as the reader reads on, she understands that there is more to the relation between voice and appearance, as this following passage, which begins with the desire not only to see the other come but also explain the effects of his coming, indicates:

> To see the remains of Vincent arriving in sheets of rain, with the brave involuntary swagger of the old tar, his head swathed in a bloody clout and a glitter in his eye, was for the acute observer an example of what man is capable of, in pursuit of his pleasure. With one hand he sustained his sternum, with the heel of the other his spinal column, as if tempted to break into a hornpipe, no, that's all memories, last shifts older than the flood. See what's happening here, where there's no one, where nothing happens, get something to happen here, then put an end to it, have silence, get into silence, or another sound, a sound of other voices than those of life and death, of lives and deaths everyone's but mine, get into my story in order to get out of it (89).

"Right," we exclaim. Or is it "write?" Or don't write? And if one doesn't (write or write oneself out of the story), then what? If Beckett doesn't get the reader to think about writing, then he certainly gets the reader to contemplate the possibility of the 'and yet', as in, 'and yet, what if even nothing can yield something? (with a little bit of skill, *nothing* can in fact be arranged as Watt also suggested). Hence, perhaps, "write nothing," or rather, the demand that one write nothing must be seen in the Beckettian scheme as the ultimate manifestation of the 'and yet.'

In creative writing, being faced with the nothing of the white page, is being faced with the question of when the 'and yet' begins to style the writer's thinking. How can we see this, and why is this so, one might ask? Here I would venture to suggest that it is because of our Babylonian existence; what any agent speaks is never his or her tongue, but always another's. A quick view of some of the titles to the latest essays on Beckett disclose how much critics theorize, for instance, on Beckett's modernism, his theories on writing – of relevance for cultural studies – his theology, structuralism or even post-structuralism, by way of stylizing Beckett's own discourse. Here I like Steven Connor's "Absolute Rubbish," Frank Kermode's "Miserable Splendour," and Jean-Luc Nancy's "The Unsacrificeable."

What these titles suggest is that in Beckett, contradictions are always raised to the status of sublime logics of insufficient knowledge and reason. What Beckett operates with is deploying the metaphysics of ontology into epistemic knowledge. While the first is seen as an instance of abstract transcendence of finitude, especially that of the body facing nothingness, or falling into nothingness, the latter is construed as a concrete manifestation of figuring out how finitude works when finitude is not thought of in terms of its opposite, namely the infinite, but in terms of a constant possibility to go on as a process of undermining the impossibility to go on. Beckett formulates this quite clearly in his work *Molloy*, one of his works that articulates the best his credo regarding the relation between creative writing and epistemology:

> To know nothing is nothing, not to want to know anything likewise, but to be beyond knowing anything, to know you are beyond knowing anything, that is when peace enters in, to the soul of the incurious seeker. It is then the true division begins, of twenty-two by seven for example, and the pages fill with the true ciphers at last (Beckett, 1958: 64).

From this we can extrapolate another axiom, following the line of axioms started in the introduction: *The only way in which you can achieve nothing is if nothing is self-imposed.* Beckett's protagonists – insofar as they can be said to go from the representation and figuration of life and death – to the extent that one can say it, or put it into words – to the abstract manifestation of life and death – to the extent that one can acknowledge an impasse as words fail to represent such states – can be said to be recalcitrant when it comes to the question of weighing figuration, as in figuring out, wanting to know how one is, against uncountable states, those states which do not lend themselves to being known by numbers, as it were, such as the very act of dying may be.

There is something refractory about dying which Beckett identifies as a sort of nothing that is good enough where adequate knowledge about it is concerned. Quite literally, one reduces one's ideas of playing with the cards one is dealt through life to an endgame that involves an attempt at counting: what one did in the past, what one does now, what one will do in the future, and so on. In a passage that accounts for the daily bodily functions, literally counting how many times one farts in a day,

Molloy exclaims: "Extraordinary how mathematics help you to know yourself" (30).

Thus we go from negativity, from formulating suggestions that *nothing* is never good, but only good enough in relation to its own radical absoluteness, to its polarization towards astonishment. For Beckett, 'the nothing that is,' insofar as it relies on a conditional, as he proposes in this statement, "For the only way one can speak of nothing is to speak of it as though it were something" (Beckett, 1953: 77), becomes a matter of an artifice raised to the power of two. What you say, or don't want to say is what you say, or don't want to say, twice over. This is the cipher that fills the pages of composition. Thus says Beckett further on in a seminal fragment that sums up the notion of what I suggest an epistemology of creative writing may be:

> Not to want to say, not to know what you want to say, not to be able to say what you think you want to say, and never to stop saying, or hardly ever, that is the thing to keep in mind, even in the heat of composition (Beckett, 1958: 28).

In theory things get hot. In theory, you take a deep breath. Perhaps just before you put it stylishly though: Westward, Ho! Unword Ho!

My breath in brackets

In one of his numerous essays, writings, and 'critificitional' remarks on Beckett, Raymond Federman, one of the best practitioners of postmodern writing that is heavily influenced by Beckett, has this to say, on being asked to link the question of readability and unreadability to the existential aspect of avant-garde writing:

> Imagine then how lost, how confused, how desperate some unprepared readers must feel when reading a text where nothing happens twice, as in some of Samuel Beckett's novels or plays, or where the language moves in a nonsensical direction and therefore means-not (Federman, 1993: 71).

Even without any knowledge of Beckett, the reader of this paragraph, presupposing that the reader is an informed reader who appreciates language-games, is bound to be out of breath by the time she reaches to the idea that some texts "mean-not." For what does it mean to say that a text "means-not?" That it is devoid of signification? That it is non-sensical, or that it has no direction, temporal or spatial? What interests me in this gap that is created between the experience of reading a text which resists us at the level of signification and the context in which such a text leaves us breathless is its connection to how epistemological relevance of various notions of creative writing as a practice in the context of inquiry, of attribution, of assessment, and so on is established.

Authors such as Beckett are notorious for their minimal take on how to assess readability against the background of inquiry. Various contexts for understanding a text are thus played against each other to the point that a reader is forced to ask herself questions pertaining to what exactly she attributes to the text which, insofar as it is deemed unreadable, resisting interpretation, thus demands the reader's contribution. It is my contention that when reading Beckett, both the reader's contribution and attribution consist of a phatic relation often manifested or expressed through interjections and exclamations. "Ahhhh, what does he mean, this Beckett?" must thus be the first reaction formulated as a question posed as to the significance of the text. This question is often also fraught with frustration and deployed in an instant of breath. A long, rather than deep, breath.

As to the length of breath in writing, Beckett uses several strategies through which to convey it. Most often this consists of an insertion of the word "pause" between the lines. Particularly his work *How It Is* from 1964 uses this form. This is a novel in fragments about a narrator who wanders about without any knowledge of either where he came from, where he goes and why he does what he does. On his peregrination, he meets other characters, who can be said to be the figment of his imagination. The whole text revolves around the idea that voices befall one in the dark, and that is when one has to start imagining. For instance the narrator's relationship with Pim is rendered without cause, yet as some effects of this relationship are anticipated, they take place only as a means of experiencing the other, as the other reveals himself to the narrator in a bracketed form. Here this form takes the shape of various ways of breathing which occur either between the fragments, which are not always complete, and nor are they connected, or within the fragments themselves.

When within fragments, stylistically it is noteworthy to see that bracketed breathing, as it were, is almost always linked to forms of affirmation or negation. But there is never any conclusiveness as to which enunciation wins and when, the yes or the no. This suggests that language itself is on a pilgrimage track, but not towards an end where purification awaits but towards incorporating what remains forever dark and impenetrable.

One can think of the breath in brackets as the voice of contamination. As Beckett makes use of the dialogue form, even when it appears as monologic speech, he explores what it means to write without a purpose, against the background of contaminating speech which instructs more powerfully than its purified counter-form, namely silence. When breath is contained within narrative, what it does is teach particularly about the value of impenetrability. The silent walls of the brackets get penetrated by the articulation of affirmation and negation, or the 'yes' and the 'no' of what one can or cannot know. Quite literally, breath, if thought of in terms of form, can be said to be the only thing that penetrates the void, as what takes place between the brackets can also be emptiness. It is for this reason that in *How It Is*, the process of figuring out how you don't know that you know things, even in the dark, about yourself and the other, is rendered as an endless process of conjecturing which is mirrored in the acts of the narrator whose imagination is completely dependent on what he can guess the other one is thinking. Here's a passage that illustrates not only how breathing links the 'how it is' state of thoughts, imagination, actions, and gestures, but also how it prompts the inquiry into, assessment of, and attribution to 'what it is' that one is thinking about:

> if he talks to himself no thinks no believes in God yes every day no wishes to die yes but doesn't expect to no he expects to stay where he is yes flat as a cowclap on his belly yes in the mud yes without motion yes without thought yes eternally yes
>
> if he is sure of what he says no he can't affirm anything no he may have forgotten many things no certain little things yes the little

there was yes such as having crawled a little yes eaten little yes thought a little murmured a little for himself alone yes heard a human voice no he wouldn't have forgotten that no brushed against a brother before me no he wouldn't have forgotten that no

if he wants me to leave him yes in peace yes without me there is peace yes was peace yes every day no if he thinks I'll leave him no I'll stay where I am yes glued to him yes tormenting him yes eternally yes

but he can't affirm anything no deny anything no things may have been different yes his life here pause YOUR LIFE HERE good and deep in the furrows howls thump face in the mud nose mouth howls good he wins he can't (Beckett, 1964: 84-85).

A more concrete example of the breath in brackets would be to think of the common real-life situation in which before we say to someone, 'can I ask you a question' we always, always take a deep breath. This breath marks the gravity of the subject matter by an inflection of the act of inhaling if the situation of 'can I ask you a question' is aimed at disclosing something serious. The deeper the breath, the more there is a sense that something more ominous than pleasant will be revealed. And in Beckett, the ominous is always hovering above one's head, as the characters are marked in their obsessive reflectiveness by a distinct feeling that they cannot be cured of thinking. For Beckett, the incurable character never has any existential quandaries, but rather is more interested in the extent to which he can possess his own thoughts. For Beckett the question 'to be or not to be' is always suspended in the question 'to have or not to have'.

Thus, the subject in Beckett struggles with resisting passing on any information that he might possess of fear that he may not really possess any at all. And yet, insofar as this fear gets to be communicated because of the compulsion to think and hear oneself think aloud, some epistemic rules are devised and follow closely this question: how can I know things, and more importantly, how can I know the other, who participates in my discovery of things? At some point in *How It Is,* the narrator turns Pim on his belly, and presses his face in the mud, almost suffocating him, only so that he can speculate on Pim's reaction, which is not one of thinking but one of bodily response. One senses here that what Beckett is interested in is to see how having one's wits about oneself can be a matter solely of instinctual impulse rather than reasoning. The narrator wants to see whether Pim can breathe through his consciousness in the impenetrable mud. Of course the two are the same, though the narrator is the one who drives the action forward while also making recourse to the materiality of things and their absence. Throughout the narrative, a sack is carried around, lost and found again, and pondered on in metaphysical ways. So he says:

> in the dark the mud my head against his my side glued to his my right arm around his shoulders his cries have ceased we lie thus a good moment they are good moments

> how long thus without motion or sound of any kind were it but of breath vast a vast stretch of time under my arm now and then a deeper breath heaves him slowly up leaves him at last and sets him slowly down others would say a sigh

> thus our life in common we begin it thus I do not say it is not said as others at the end of theirs clinging almost to each other I never saw any it seems never any such but even beasts observe each other I saw some once it seems and they observing each other let him understand who has a wish to I have none

> almost clinging that's too strong as always he can't repel me it's like my sack when I had it still this providential flesh I'll never let it go call that constancy if you wish
>
> when I had it still but I have it still it's in my mouth no it's not there anymore I don't have it anymore I am right I was right (47).

Things in the mud get muddled, and yet it is clear that what emerges here is a concern with having it, the sack, the knowledge, the breath. Without the sack the sense of entitlement diminishes, without knowledge, the sense of meaninglessness diminishes, but without breath, the curtain goes down. And as they say, one cannot have that. The show must go on. Which it does in this text, because this is precisely *how it is*.

Given Beckett's liminal writing, indeed nothing ever seems to be repeated twice, but nothing does happen twice. A Beckett text literally seems to take the Heraclitean injunction to its core: if we do step twice into the same river, it is the river of our range of flowing breath that we step into. A paradox is experienced when one observes that in spite of reading sparse and economical language, one is exhausted. In Beckett, one climbs the Everest of writing as an event, rather than as a heap of words, put there to stumble on. The thinner the air gets, the heavier the breath. Here, one can contend that Beckett is interested in how language is used when at limit, and what the effect of eradicating syntax and grammar may be for the reader who reads for the elegant formulation or an axiom.

There is a lot performance in Beckett of precisely the value of evaluating such discourse which relies on timing: when to say what rather than what to say when. When the reader is out of breath, because of the cadences in the text, the Beckettian pause marked by either inhaling or exhaling often takes the form of a thematic phrasal full stop. "No matter," says Beckett all the time, almost as a counter to his other well known phrase: "I can't go on I'll go on." Between such bathetic and defeatist lines, if Beckett invites his reader to enter his linguistic universe and play the language games that he invents through the use of either minimal or embellished on situations, he does so because he wants to test the reader's ability to stretch the elastic of her imagination.

Beckett seems to anticipate two consequences here in terms of reader response: if the elastic breaks, what will the reader value: the process of stretching itself or the pieces from the broken line? About his dramatic work, *Breath*, Beckett states that it is "a dramatic comma" (Federman, 1976), thus a performance of the void that is imaginary graphed. In writing, however, the breath remains precisely a physical sense more so than a physical performance, whether imagined or not. The breath in writing is rather more of a conceptual performance. Unlike on stage, where one can see and follow an actor's actions, and perhaps also breathe down his or her neck, especially if one sits in close proximity to the scene, in writing, breath is experienced as a different kind of excitement. Insofar as writing as rendered in words is meant for reading not for seeing, it thus appeals mainly to the eyes as they are linked to the sense of internal hearing rather than external seeing. In contrast, breath rendered in writing through blanks, ellipses, gaps, or more interestingly, through the institution of a quick series of alternating affirmations and negations, exasperates the reader, who, thus breathless because of the indecision about which direction to go – the only option is to go linearly, but the text defies it – wants to yell at Beckett: what do you want from me?

In the short stories *Ill Seen Ill Said* and *First Love* Beckett explores the relation between breath, air, smell and the geography of the word. This relation suggests that writing which is haunted by the timing of breath takes the form of an epistemic creative act at the point when breath imposes a state of crisis which locks both the writer and consequently the reader into the language of the text. The relevant question to pose here is one that links writing to epistemologies of creativity: what do we learn from breathing with Beckett, and can such an act be used formally in the formulation of axioms of epistemologies of creative writing?

In *Ill Seen Ill Said*, the protagonist, an old woman, spends her last days in a cottage surveyed by twelve mysterious watchers. Several times during the narrative – which is about the woman's walking between zones marked by stones around the cabin – she is reported to drop dead. The watchers are always with her, behind her, beside her, or beyond her field of vision. She senses their presence, or rather, although not mentioned in the text, their breathing, as they watch and walk beside her silently. They never say anything. The woman's time is also marked as seasonal. "Winter in her winter haunts she wanders," (50) says Beckett, and the ensuing lines freeze the reader's own breath by the time she reads that the woman drops dead again. What is it that resurrects her, one would like to ask?

Insofar as Beckett's language both mirrors and performs what it narrates, in this case the focus thus goes from gazing to breathing in brackets. Says Beckett: "the eye breathes again but not for long." As the woman keeps reappearing after dying, her breath is thus contained or bracketed within her own and the others' field of vision. The eye controls the breath.

We are between seeing and tracing the knowledge that the breath gathers between emotion and the words. The gut senses, the eyes see, and the breath knows it first, when falling in love occurs, or when dying and disaster arrive. The breath also registers presence and absence. It is thus a barometer of form. Though formless itself, the breath suspends or initiates reasoning. For Beckett, the fragment is the best form that captures the performance of the breath as it passes though various modes of registering and manifestation, from fear to awe of the sublime. The fragment is Beckett's corner of the eye. As such it can take everything sideways, both the face and the trace. Says Beckett, exploring the omen in the nomen in the last passage of *Ill Seen Ill Said*:

> Absence supreme good and yet. Illumination then go again and on return no more trace. On earth's face. Of what was never. And if by mishap some left then go again. For good again. So on. Till no more trace. On earth's face. Instead of always the same place. Slaving away forever in the same place. At this and that trace. And what if the eye could not? No more tear itself away from the remains of trace. Of what was never. Quick say it suddenly can and farewell say say farewell. If only to the face. Of her tenacious trace (77).

In the short story *First Love* (1973, composed in 1945) Beckett's protagonist, a man in love with a prostitute, flees the scene of facing love as it announces itself in the form of a concrete trace. As Lulu, the supreme first love, is in the midst of delivering what she claim is hers and the protagonist's baby, her lover, breathless, takes off while carrying with him the baby's cries. These sounds remain with him as an emblem of his first love, which, as he puts it, brings the worst out in man. There is a fine symmetry at work in this story, between the cemetery, where the father is buried and with whose description the narrative commences, and the breathing for nothing, as it were, while scribbling on dirt the name of the beloved.

The question that presses on the narrator's mind is the extent to which he can decide whether what he experiences can be called love at all, and if so, what kind of love. A primary relation is here established: ashes turns to ashes and so does love, here mixed with a sense of the last breath. Thus we go from earthly considerations of a soul ghosting through the air, on the first page, to cosmic considerations of what name to give love that borders on mythological construction on the last page. So says Beckett:

> Personally, I have no bone to pick with graveyards, I take the air there willingly, perhaps more willingly than elsewhere, when take the air I must. The smell of corpses, distinctly perceptible under those of grass and humus mingled, I do not find unpleasant, a trifle on the sweet side perhaps, a trifle heady, but how infinitely preferable to what the living emit, their feet, teeth, armpits, arses, sticky foreskins and frustrated ovules. And when my father's remains join in, however modestly, I can almost shed a tear (61).

And then a few pages later:

> Love brings out the worst in man and no error. But what kind of love was this, exactly? Love-passion? Somehow I think not. That's the priapic one, is it not? Or is this a different variety? There are so many, are there not? Or equally if not more delicious, are they not? Platonic love, for example, there's another just occurs to me. It's disinterested. Perhaps I loved her with a platonic love? But somehow I think not. Would I have been tracing her name in old cowshit if my love had been pure and disinterested? And with my

devil's finger into the bargain which I then sucked. My thoughts were all of Lulu and if that doesn't give you some idea nothing will (69-70).

Here we have musings on the materiality of death and love as they are inscribed on or within the earth, at the moment of their transcendence. Insofar as the tension is between a form of platonic conception vs. realistic perception, breath as articulation is rendered by Beckett as a form of style *par excellence.* Here, the repeated rhetorical questions about the varieties of love in the love passage, 'is it not,' 'are there not,' 'are they not?' can be seen as instances of a desire to eradicate the skepticism about the meaning of life when all goes down the drain, or, rather, down the whole, which initiates the story. Quite literally, and from a performative point of view, when one asks, 'is it not?', about something that one clearly wants confirmation of, the exhaling moment in the last breath before the question mark, as it were, has hope tagged to it. One hopes to have one's knowledge or suspicion confirmed. It is precisely this hope that renders breath itself in a bracket, and it is in the end left up to the eye or the gaze to respond affirmatively.

When Beckett writes for the breath he writes for the astonished eye. He goes for the writing that astounds, not the truth. The only truth he believes in is the one he can catch in the astonished eye. There is enough knowledge in it to confirm his certitudes as there is enough mystery in it to keep him in a state of marvel if he lived forever. Beckett brackets himself in this sense as a theologian of the marvellous. It is also in this sense that one can say that he moves, through an exploration of how breath breathes knowledge, towards the writing that 'means-not.'

What Beckett does in his resistance to create a clear methodology of the politics, theology, or poetics of writing is to try to fix, albeit in vain, what philosophers refer to as the misfortune of writing. In his book of essays, *The Flesh of Words* (2004), Jacques Rancière has this to say about good writing that cannot escape being oracular and presenting itself as if in waiting for the reader or some other writer to complete the voice, as it were, or the breath of the truth that is only suggested but never fully articulated in the text: "No living word is enough to remedy the disorder of writing. The remedy for the misfortune of writing is another writing, a writing below or beyond words, that opposes their talk as well as their silence with another mode of inscription or circulation" (Rancière, 2004: 106).

Referring to a conversation between Phaedrus and Socrates, in which Phaedrus accuses Socrates of not verifying his Egyptian sources, Rancière makes the point that when Socrates responded in turn by accusing the young generation of being too methodical about that which lends itself to a reading from the soul rather than the source, he was suggesting that if oracular writing is true, and if it manifests itself through the wind or the breath, then it needs no verification once it is recognized as true. This baffled Phaedrus, as he could sense that the process of recognition itself must then rely on a logic of place rather than of narrative. We can now return to the question raised at the start of this chapter: what does it mean to say that a text means-not? Says Rancière:

> It is another idea of truth and of writing that is contrasted here with the restless wandering of silent-talkative words. A writing that is less than the written, a pure trajectory of breath – of spirit – communicated as the immediate respiration of truth.

But "good" writing can also be writing that is more than what is written on papyrus, parchment, or paper. But is inscribed in the very texture of things as an actual modification of the perceptual world (106).

For Beckett the system of writing seen from the soul's perspective, and one which follows the trajectory of breath, is given in the last line in the *First Love* story. This line is not only symptomatic, but also emblematic of the kind of writing which situates itself between the two necessary breathing moments that indicate the wandering of words from the 'either' to the 'or' of the situation of 'there it is' that is recognized as such and as truthful. Ahhh, "either you love [hhha] or you don't."

Beckett is not interested in reason. His writings suggest this: if you strip creativity of reason, what you've got on your hands is connection; cosmic connection and tautology. In this sense, Beckett's epistemic adventure is not about the trouble with the the fact that there can be no new writing under the sun, but with the fact that the sun doesn't care about writing. The sun moons writing, and the lesson that we learn is one of circularity. Beckett allows us all to breathe into the O, the void, and while doing so create our own analogies. The sun is round, the moon is round, the earth used to be flat but then was found round, and a fragment of writing is linear unless we begin again. Begin in the unbeginning, post-constructing the lessons we teach.

Enters Raymond Federman.

The logic of critifiction

As already mentioned, one of the best practitioners of post-modern writing that not only draws on Beckett but also redefines Beckett is the celebrated author Raymond Federman. His credo has always been the idea that "to create fiction is, in fact, a way to abolish reality, and especially to abolish the notion that reality is truth" (Federman 1981a: 8). Given this premise, Federman believes that "history is bankrupt" and thus unable to account for notions of identity formations within a cultural realm. Whereas history can be seen as an enforced actuality of certain events, for Federman history is interlinked with potentiality. The agent operating in the past or present is thus seen primarily as the embodiment of things to come, rather than the sum of his or her actions. This obviously has implications for the way in which the self is represented.

Here I want to discuss the idea of narrating identity within a framework where fiction is faked in order to represent what is unrepresentable. From this we can then extrapolate some notions as to what we can say about the identity of the epistemic creative writer. Who is he? A writer of fiction, of academic fiction, an academically fictitious writer, a preacher of knowledge, a non-methodist, a cynic who likes to research, an nihilist existentialist floating in space, a non-conformist logician who likes to weave myths, a lover of games, of quotes, of nothing?

As one of my primary claims is that the epistemic creative writer conflates theories of knowledge with the creative act of denouncing claims to knowledge so that the text may write itself in the vein of instruction but without following a method, looking at how authors probe the void within themselves discloses a poetics of living according to the logic of an inner script. This script is drafted by a creative authority that the epistemic writer taps into by making recourse to exploring the territory of how one knows that one knows without knowing it (more on this in Chapter 4). The epistemic creative writer is thus an intuitive epistemologist who finds support for his axioms in the fusion of his experiences with the nothing that is. The epistemic creative writer writes in this very gap of experiencing writing in the void, and he always begins with what Federman calls "the paradoxical pursuit of non-knowledge" (Federman, 1993: 9).

It begins with death in the family

As most of Federman's fiction takes its point of departure in one single event, his escape from the concentration camps on the day when his whole family was sent to Auschwitz, it deals with the physical circumstance that made it possible for him to survive. He was pushed into a closet by his mother, where he remained for three days. The closet has since functioned for Federman as a space in which fiction itself is made the circumstance of reality. What kind of knowledge does the writing out of the closet entail then, especially when this writing is very much based on the thoughts occurring in the closet?

To mediate between the inside and the outside of the metaphor of enclosure and its literal representation, Federman coined a useful term: critifiction. Critifiction expresses the conflagration of fictional and critical discourse with view to showing that an agent writing autobiographically is neither existentially determined by his thoughts, nor ontologically determined by his acts. An agent's history is thus bound to remain in a suspended state. But while there is conflagration of terms, there is also separation, insofar as what the concept of critifiction suggests is an easy shift between states expressed by the co-existence of contradictory states, such as, both/and – criticism and fiction – and neither/nor – neither criticism, nor fiction.

Here, I want to look at Federman's poetics of creative writing that relies on the combination of epistemic knowledge with fictional writing through critifiction, epistemic logic being the motor for the production of meaning in the image of fiction as sense and commonsense. The commonsensical aspect in Federman's fiction is tightly interlinked with his desire to not only represent but also overcome the trauma of having lost all of his family in the concentration camps. This traumatic experience becomes for Federman more real the more fictitiously he renders it. It is my contention that what is achieved in this kind of writing whose aim is to instruct – as most Holocaust writing does – while however abolishing the methodical approach to the notion of how to go about it – is a form of mercy. I venture to suggest that what Federman actually calls for in all of his writings, and even more so in the writing in which he exposes his poetics of writing, is an invocation akin to a religious ceremony. The cry, "Lord, have mercy on our souls" is translated in Federman into a specific theology of textual mercy.

Already from the outset, in his seminal work, *Critifiction* (1993) – a collection of essays on the state of literature, history of ideas and new fiction, both experimental but also quite commonsensical in its testing of limits which exceed the rational – Federman queers the possibility of expressing any thoughts, especially as he claims that it is impossible to ever locate the origins of thoughts. Rather, what one does in writing is appropriate. And this can be seen already in the first epigraph to the first essay, "Fiction Today and the Pursuit of Non-Knowledge" where Federman's favorite author, Beckett, and on whom he wrote repeatedly, gets the honor of setting the tone for the entire volume. *Critifiction* is not a conventional collection of essays on writing and the fictions of others, but engages playfully with Federman's own works. In other words, it appropriates Federman as well. Thus, this is a work which is both literary criticism in its approach to the question of what literature is and what it can do today, and a monograph.

The examples used to illustrate what I call epistemic creative writing come mainly from Federman's novels. A double voice permeates the work, as Federman writes on Federman. The irony is that insofar as he does an excellent job as a critic, he renders the work of any critic after him redundant. What is however suggested in a very subtle and fascinating way, is precisely this idea, which one finds as if formulated in Federman's voice behind the text: 'yes, I've said all there is to say about Federman, and in an intelligent manner too, but I have mercy on you people, the rest of the critical lot. You can write fragments on Federman.'

As far as I'm concerned, I like the notion that it is not so much the totalizing and synthesizing thought about an author that is interesting, but the fact that one can say better and more engaging things about an author in a fragmentary way, and because the author has bestowed mercy on the critic, beginning with himself, in this case Federman on Federman. But here is Beckett in the first epigraph, which seems to suggest a parallel take on the point I'm trying to make here:

> Reality, whether approached imaginatively, or empirically remains a surface, hermetic. Imagination, applied to what is absent, is exercised in a vacuum and cannot tolerate the limits of the real (Beckett, epigraph in Federman, 1993: 1).

For Federman this is the crux of all matter: how to write in the face of the unrepresentable, yet, unlike in Beckett, where the 'unrepresentable' roams in an unrealized state, in Federman, it has already happened. Thus we have here a contradiction in terms between the representation of the impossible, which by virtue of definition implies the eradication of time, and the time within which the impossible did take place and is consequently subject to any interpretation. So we begin to feel the pressure and say it with Federman: Lord, have mercy!

Referring to the fictions of Italo Calvino and Beckett, which Federman categorizes within the genre of the New Fiction in which particularly reality and spatiality are freed of all contradiction and constraints, says Federman:

> The impossible becomes possible in the New Fiction because language escapes analytical logic. It is a language which accepts and even indulges in its contradictions; a language that plays with repetitions, permutations, neologisms, puns; a language that dislocates conventional syntax while designing a new typography, and in so doing renders the world even more unintelligible.
>
> How, then, can the contemporary writer be engagé – socially and politically committed – since to be engagé, in the old Sartrean sense, there must be an intelligible and recognizable world, a world of stable and accepted values? (14)

The logic of critifiction is thus here meant to cover the space of the impossibility to say things not because events didn't happen, or because they happened but you don't like what happened, but because everything can be said about possible or impossible things twice over, or many times over. And if repetition happens, it happens with added emphasis. Creating variations on the same theme is in fact what Federman does throughout all of his writings, and even his work *Critifiction* is informed by performing repetition. As with Robert Pinget, whom Federman quotes: "What is said is never said since one can always say it differently" (14).

Should one then, perhaps, just shut up? Beckett was convinced that that was it. Yet Federman thinks that the value of a good story resides precisely in its being told again and again. Here one could say that Federman does not only take Beckett's indecision to his heart: "I can't go on, I'll go on," but performs it in all its glorious contradiction. In a passage from the essay called "Federman on Federman: Lie or Die" from *Critifiction* he returns again to his closet experience and retells unabashedly how there may be some ambiguity as to how the whole affair of escaping through the roof, and such details as to the placing on the roof of the shit that the protagonist took while locked in the closet, really unfolded. Says Federman here on recounting what he already said in his book *The Voice in the Closet,* thus questioning not only the function of repetition in fiction, but also implicitly the desire to fixate memory in language at the moment when fiction is anchored in autobiography.

> No, there is no way to know if I was locked in a closet when I was a little boy, if the moon tiptoed across the roof that night, if I stumbled on the steps while going down the staircase, if the doors opened to stare at my nakedness, if a bird really flew into my head, and so on. And what about the filthy package of excrement left on the roof? Who can believe that? It was dark that night. No one saw the boy. There were no witnesses. And if there were some, by now they must either be lost or dead, or have forgotten the whole sordid affair.

And so, Federman has perhaps been lying about this life, or else he has been inventing for himself an experience so that he could write it. Or even better, Federman has borrowed that experience from someone else, and has attributed it to himself. Writers often do that, borrow stories from others. After all, Federman has openly stated, on several occasions, that all writers are pla[y]giarizers (99).

From a psychoanalytical point of view, it is clear that what Federman recounts here, corresponds exactly to the picture of his experience as it happened, and that all the details concerning the escape are a perfect mirror of the actual event. But insofar as he does not want to admit it directly, the story remains in the realm of the unrepresentable. Thus it is the ineffable in the question: 'did it happen, or did it not?' that keeps ambiguity in check. The fact also that Federman questions reliability while insisting that the reader had better believe him – after all, he has been saying all these things on several occasions – testifies to a desire to activate what otherwise can be seen as mute speech. As if following Wittgenstein's injunction in his *Tractatus*: "whereof one cannot speak, thereof one must be silent" – a formula which echoes Federman's own methods of investigating the relation of truth to fiction – in this meta-critifictional text Federman captures the desire to let everything perspire against the background of the unspeakable. As he contends, not only is the function of repeating the story to ensure that he himself gets to be convinced of its accuracy, but also to suggest that repetition has a global implication. The more the story gets to be told, the more trivial it appears. And in its banal manifestation it thus has the potential to become anybody and everybody's story. In other words, coping with the trauma of surviving is for Federman a question of disseminating the unspeakable and the unrepresentable in a form that testifies to the idea that no matter how hard one tries to keep silent on certain things, things come back to haunt you.

But there is a difference in experiencing the haunting: as a personal experience or as a shared one. And this is where Federman shines brilliantly as a psychoanalyst himself, insofar as he suggests that the more the personal experience is rendered potentially as that of everyone else's, and thus enters public circulation and collective memory, the more it will serve as a cure for the traumatized agent. So we must all be haunted if Federman is to be saved. 'Lord, have mercy,' once more.

What interests Federman here is the position of the subject vis-à-vis the moment of enunciating a traumatic event in a way which has the eradication of logic as a primary discursive motor, or rather in a way that allows for telling the story from a perspective of both/and, which does not have the reconstitution of the subject as a whole as its primary goal. The whole notion of fiction being there to purport some truth horrifies Federman, and he criticizes all nineteenth century novels, yet that fiction creates knowledge in the moment of reading is not something that he denies. Truth is thus in the telling not in the told, and while reading, the reader may also tell himself a story that is different from what is actually on the page. Here, Federman goes against established psychoanalytic theories, and has this to say, which is of relevance for the way in which we may understand what is at stake in his poetics of epistemic writing:

> Psychoanalysis uses oedipal reduction and substitution to have the patient believe that he is going to speak in his own name, but it is a trap. He will never speak his own personal words, he will

never be allowed to speak his own original words. He will only repeat the words put in his mouth. Therefore, he may speak of wolves, cry like a wolf, act like a wolf, but the psychiatrist thinks dogs, and answers DADDY, and the patient repeats DADDY, and believes he has gotten rid of the wolf in him. As long as this imposture works, it is called a neurosis, but if the patient cracks, if he refuses to say the words put in his mouth, then it is called a psychosis. At the very moment when the patient is convinced that he is speaking his own name the conditions of the enunciation are removed (59).

This passage, from the essay "Imagination as Plagiarism" discloses that epistemic knowledge, or the knowledge that an agent accumulates through speaking, and then through formulating in writing what has left the agent speechless, is a type of knowledge that is not derived from descriptive or expository language alone, à la, 'and then I dreamt of a wolf, or, 'and then I took a shit in the closet.' Epistemic knowledge derives from what the agent is able to formulate in the gaps, in the fragments of memory, and in the kind of discourse that is above all contradictory, and hence silencing. In this sense it is not for nothing that Aristotle concluded that it's not a good idea for a subject to contradict himself, as he will be no more than a plant, or a lifeless object. Yet, in analysis, the agent must allow for the idea that everything speaks, including inanimate things.

In his short essay, "Two Forms of Mute Speech," from *The Aesthetic Unconscious*, Jacques Rancière has this to say:

The silent revolution that we have called aesthetic opens the space in which an idea of thought and a corresponding idea of writing can be elaborated. This idea of thought rests upon a fundamental affirmation: there is thought that does not think, thought at work not only in the foreign element of non-thought but in the very form of non-thought. Conversely there is non-thought that inhabits thought and gives it a power all its own. This non-thought is not simply a form of absence of thought, it is an efficacious presence of its opposite. From whichever side we approach the equation, the identity of thought and non-thought is the source of a distinctive power [...] In opposition to this living speech that provided the representative order with its norm, writing is the mode of speech that keeps silent at the same time, that both knows and does not know what is saying. But there are two major figures of this contradictory mode, corresponding to the two opposite forms of the relation between thought and non-thought [...] Mute writing in the first sense is the speech borne by mute things themselves. It is the capability of signification that is inscribed upon their very body, summarized by the "everything speaks" of Novalis, the poet-mineralogist. Everything is trace, vestige or fossil. Every sensible form, beginning from the stone or the shell, tells a story. In their striations and ridges they all bear the traces of their history and the mark of their destination [...] The second form of mute speech is likewise at work here [the work of logos and pathos in literature, CE]. In place of the hieroglyph inscribed on the body and subject to deciphering we encounter speech as soliloquy, speaking to no one and saying nothing but the impersonal and unconscious conditions of speech itself" (Rancière, 2010: 31-39).

Federman's *Critifiction* can be seen through Rancière's take on the significance of Freud's theories today, and within this context we can advance the argument that both Rancière and Federman can be said to elaborate either implicitly (Rancière) or explicitly (Federman) on Wittgenstein's statement: "Whereof one cannot speak, thereof one must be silent" (Wittgenstein, 2009: 27).

Federman is preoccupied with Wittgenstein's *Tractatus* as it manages to make anti-metaphysical propositions, but which, in Federman's view, also stand as modes of rationalizing language (Federman, 1993: 13). Where does the limit go in the limitless? The premise for Wittgenstein's formulation that has baffled philosophers ever since is, in my opinion, precisely this one: "everything speaks." Only in this light can we understand what Wittgenstein means when he also says that all his writing is meaningless. It is meaningless in the sense that it always relies on a form of mercy, being at the mercy of interpreters. So, it comes down to an interpreter's ability to match both the thought and non-thought in Wittgenstein, the "everything speaks" already, if Rancière's "power" is to be enforced.

For Federman, the idea of powerful writing in the face of "everything speaks" becomes central, and one can identify some subtle implications in the relation between powerful and merciful discourse, for, insofar as one has the power to raise himself above meaningless discourse, one also has the power to descend to the lowest level of signification when signification is precisely least signifying. This means that one goes down on one's knees, and instead of stretching an arm, saying, 'here's a writing tool that will get you out of the gutter, use my hand' – one says instead, 'I have mercy. I give you not writing, but the mute speech of my presence.' This descent is the cost of power. Power over the silence that signifies nothing and everything at the same time. Power over the unrepresentable. With this power comes the obligation to answer the ethical call: 'do not remain silent.' Why? Because mercy must be shown when total surrender has been proven.

This is crucial for Federman, for the whole idea with inventing composites of his own persona – which are played out as variations on his own name: Federman, Namredef, Moinous, Featherman, Hombre della Pluma, Penman, and so on – is so show that one type can surrender to another, and by surrendering save the other. Mercy must thus be shown to all, oneself and the other, both forms of mute speech, the 'everything speaks' and the silent story of 'I'm here.'

What Federman does that is significant in *Critifiction* is to show the reader that there is always an unambiguous position that the author can assume vis-à-vis what he wants to preach, even when he contradicts himself. By always saying: 'I'm here, I've managed to stay here,' he says that there is hope. Hope for assuming an identity. In other words, the story comes first, for Federman, and he insists that the only reason why he can enunciate 'I'm here' is because he makes himself one with the story that is told by himself or by the fictional characters that he invents as extended variations of and on the story.

The more the story of survival gets to be repeated, the more it is appropriated by everyone. In this appropriation, while the story becomes a universal story, it also becomes more proper than the initial proper, it becomes in fact critifiction. And Federman is good at marking these transitions: from the unique to the general and from the personal to the political. The story as critifiction is thus capitalized even in its typographical manifestation. The story becomes the *nom proper* of both language and imagination. Says Federman:

> [E]verything is fiction because everything always begins with language, everything is language. The great silence within us must be decoded into words in order to be and to mean [...] Whether

we think of language as a blessing or as a curse, we cannot escape it. But we must accept the fact that it is both a means of communication and an obstacle to communication, or as Samuel Beckett once put it: "Language is what gets us where we want to go and prevents us from getting there" (89).

Yet again, 'Lord, have mercy,' we all want to say, insofar as what we are left with is the blessing or the curse of never being able to rid ourselves of the continuity of the STORY. The story never reaches a final destination and that is why we need language to express our speechlessness about unending relations. Conversely, the consequence of breaking the silence, of not being merciful enough with being precise about the position of the crucial enunciation of 'I'm here,' is that one ends up creating confusion. It is therefore not incidental that Federman's last words in *Critifiction* are those of Beckett. Thus in the language of appropriation:

> Here all is clear… No all is not clear… but the discourse must go on… so one invents obscurities… RHETORIC (133).

As these lines are emphasized in block letters with the word "RHETORIC" leading the final way in a capitalized form too, one is led to conclude that, perhaps, if an epistemology of creative writing is formulated here, then it begins with a moment of waiting. Waiting for oneself to make up one's mind as to what STORY one wants to tell and why. Meanwhile, let us hear what Gertrude Stein has to say about it. She likes to begin.

3

MYSTICAL SITE
A STONE FOR STEIN

> *A circle is a necessity. Otherwise you would see no one.*
> – Gertrude Stein, *A Circular Play*

Critics claim that there's no connection between Gertrude Stein and mysticism, but the passages they quote to support this claim show exactly the opposite. While it may be that Stein was no Zen master, her writing discloses something about the psychology of creativity. For Stein, the creation of an 'other' world through writing has not only a symbolic significance but also a metaphysical one – an idea also explored by her professor at Radcliffe, William James, in his work, *The Varieties of Religious Experience* (1902). Stein's compositions can be said to resemble old shamanic and mystical practices of creating out of ritualistic words and visions an 'other' physical reality. My claim is that by enlarging the horizon of the word, one turns writing not only into a tool for higher expression, but also into a gate that opens towards a higher form of consciousness. Here, whereas Beckett explored the void through nothingness, Gertrude Stein takes it to a place where nothingness can sit on a throne.

The notion that words have a horizon has been explored by European authors whose sensibility tapped right into that of the exiled Americans. Edmond Jabès, an Algerian immigrant in France, seems to pay direct tribute to not only Gertrude Stein, but also to the two brothers who influenced her, William and Henry James, and who, with their insistence on the unlimited potential of experience, have opened the way towards formulations which aim at saying something about the mystery in the obvious. Thus, when Jabès proclaims that "only what touches us closely, preoccupies us. We prepare in solitude to face it," (Jabès, 1996: 65) he shows, as William James did, the same concern with how the immense sensibility of experience can reduce to incompletion.

In Gertrude Stein, the idea that the obvious can be captured in a discourse about nothing can be taken on two levels: one which rejects mysticism, especially at the contextual level, and one which adopts it, especially at the conceptual level. In her early essay from 1957, "The Quality of Gertrude Stein's Creativity" Allegra Stewart argues that Stein's 'mysticism' must be taken not at face-value, but as a form of joyous rapture. In a significant passage she says:

> No matter what her subject matter was – and paradoxically, as she became more playful, she wrote more and more frequently about "saints and singing"– she was never solemn or conventionally religious. She had wit and a love of the comic, and since her object was only to be present both to her writing and to her reader, she gives the impression of childlike intentness, as though she were concentrating upon each movement in an absorbing game (Stewart, 1957: 502).

While Stewart rightly asserts that 'play' is at the heart of Stein's writing, she is not so willing to associate play with any form of transcendental experience. She sees Stein's repeated phrase about the importance of "doing nothing" – both in writing and otherwise – as a case of taking part in the creation of a momentary pleasure without an aim. "She sings a song that we all can sing" writes Stewart, and then continues, "in those moments when we really live consciously in the actual present and affirm life as an end in itself. In singing this song, one is "doing nothing" in exactly the way the saints are "doing nothing" when they pray or sing or perform their ritual tasks" (502).

Here I want to reject the notion that what Stein is doing is merely stripping her discourse of rhetoric for the sake of creating objectivity, and argue instead that in spite even of her own claims, Stein was neither a mere realist, nor a positivist, or an economist of the word. It is my contention that there's more to Stein's writing than what is implicitly assumed in arguments that tend to dissociate her psychology of mystery from her psychology of materiality. Here, says Stewart, following Stein from her *Everybody's Autobiography,* and avoiding addressing the possibility that what Stein defines as mysticism may be more than the metamorphosis of religious experience, or a transformation into some kind of non-mystical morality:

> To Gertrude Stein, the human mind was mysterious, but she was not mystical about it. She had 'an intellectual passion for exactitude in the description of inner and outer reality,' and neither had nor sought mystical experience. She defined mysticism as a kind of metamorphosis: 'if you believe in anything deeply enough it turns into something else and so money turns into not money. That is what mysticism is' [...] Thus she seems to deny nearly ev-

erything that we ordinarily call religion-mystical and nonmystical alike (497).

In a more contemporary setting, one can point to a more solid conviction about Stein's mysticism in the wonderful and equally solid statue of Gertrude as a Buddha made by sculptor Jo Davidson. Explaining what inspired his art, Davidson makes the comment that it was Stein's poem "Stanzas in Meditation" that did it. For Davidson, this long poem is the epitome of Stein's experimenting with Buddhist philosophy. "Stanzas in Meditation" opens with these lines:

> I caught a bird which made a ball
> And they thought better of it.
> But it is all of which they taught
> That they were in a hurry yet
> In a kind of a way they meant it best
> That they should change in and on account
> But they must not stare when they manage
> Whatever they are occasionally liable to do
> It is often easy to pursue them once in a while
> And in a way there is no repose
> They like it as well as they ever did
> But it is very often just by the time
> That they are able to separate
> In which case in effect they could
> Not only be very often present perfectly
> In each way whichever they chose.

It ends with these lines:

> Why am I if I am uncertain reasons may inclose.
> Remain remain propose repose chose.

> I call carelessly that the door is open
> Which if they may refuse to open
> No one can rush to close.
> Let them be mine therefor.
> Everybody knows that I chose.
> Therefor if therefore before I close.
> I will therefore offer therefore I offer this.
> Which if I refuse to miss may be miss is mine.
> I will be well welcome when I come.
> Because I am coming.
> Certainly I come having come.
> > These stanzas are done.

Even without any knowledge of Oriental religion, one might consider as key phrases the lines emphasizing doors opening towards something higher than words can express. According to poet Karren LaLonde Alenier, author of *The Steiny Road to Operadom: The Making of American Operas,* there is a connection between Gertrude Stein's imagery and the world of magic and imagination described in the *Diamond Sutra* that highlights the power nature has to disclose the magic in matter. LaLonde Alenier speculates on the possibility that Gertrude Stein might have seen the scroll of this ancient text when it was brought to the public attention by Sir Marc Aurel Stein. The gentleman bought the Diamond Sutra from a Chinese monk in 1907, and then had it placed at the British Museum where it has been on display ever since. Thus she comments on this possible connection:

> While Stein does not believe or say that the world is an illusion, she does acknowledge in this work and much of her other work that living in the time that is known as now, is difficult to do. Her

Harvard professor William James said the present is a tiny window that exists between the past and the future. Gertrude's goal was to widen 'now' through her 'ing' verbs to keep things moving. What Gertrude Stein's "Stanzas in Meditation" has in common with The Diamond Sutra are the following: lots of images from the natural world, constant duality that plays back and forth (think yin yang), and what Judy Grahn in Really Reading Gertrude Stein calls the principal of rhythm ("everything flows, out and in, in measured motion" p. 263). While Buddha was trying to detach his disciples from dependence on the exterior world which may or may not exist, Gertrude Stein was trying to bring new life into the English language, which had been worn out from ordinary use [...] "Stanzas in Meditation" could be chanted just like The Diamond Sutra with a similar musical and harmonious effect. In fact, composer Sarah Kirkland Snider has set passages of 'Stanzas'" (Alenier, 2009).

This idea of chanting words with the double view of emptying the mind and making the word a specific medium or channel for revelations comes close to the method of writing that preoccupies Stein. My favorite quote here is her line that: "Generally speaking, anybody is more interesting doing nothing than doing something," (Stein, 2004: 112) which discloses that if Stein was not into Zen Buddhism then she was definitely still a Zen Buddhist, as the idea of doing nothing and being anybody by declaring herself to be nobody lies at the very paradox of Zen.

Furthermore, what is always striking in all of Stein's works is her acute consciousness about the problem with presenting a discourse discursively, yet without betraying either the presentation or the explanation. This fundamental distinction also lies at the heart of Zen. On this, following philosopher Suzanne Langer, who was interested in formal composition and the creative potential, says Zen teacher Robert Aitken in his book *The Gateless Barrier*:

> The presentational mode of communication is very important in Zen Buddhist teaching. This mode can be clarified by Susanne Langer's landmark book on symbolic logic called Philosophy in a New Key. She distinguishes between two kinds of language: 'Presentational' and 'Discursive.' The presentational might be in words, but it might also be a laugh, a cry, a blow, or any other kind of communicative action. It is poetical and nonexplanatory - the expression of Zen. The discursive, by contrast, is prosaic and explanatory [...] The discursive has a place in a Zen discourse like this one, but it tends to dilute direct teaching (Aitken, 1991: 48-49).

It is my contention that when critics miss the mystical connection in Stein's work, they end up assessing as a work of a failed psychologist what could otherwise easily be identified as a Zen practice. For instance in a review from 1936 Michael Gold writes that Stein is "a literary idiot," whose work represents "an example of the most extreme subjectivism of the contemporary artist." Then he goes on to suggest that "the monotonous gibberings of paranoiacs" belong "in the private wards of asylums." While he grants that something is going on in Stein's head, claiming that "the woman's not insane, but possessed of a strong, clear, shrewd mind. She was an excellent medical student, a brilliant psychologist, and in her more "popular" writings one sees evidence of wit and some wisdom" he still wants to conclude adamantly that Stein's off-beat works "read like the literature of the students of padded cells in Matteawan" (Gold, 1936).

Unlike Gold, who uses the example of what he calls Steinian nonsense in these lines: "I see the moon and the moon sees me.

God bless the moon and God bless me and this you see remember me. In this way one fifth of the bananas were bought," I see such an utterance as example of what may well serve us as a koan, waiting there to be interpreted, yet not in any discursive way that follows logical argumentation, but rather in a way that awaits experiencing a revelation. Whereas Gold obviously chooses to focus on bananas, the Zen master would probably stick to the moon. One is after all not insane oneself. Better to acknowledge the power of lunacy than go bananas. Here, the most striking, yet heuristic, quality of Stein's works is to be found in her position. While structurally she might stand between dualities, on the intuitional level – the one beyond rationality – she goes with the same type of enlightenment found in this zen illumination: "What does one do before enlightenment? Chop wood and carry water. What does one do after enlightenment? Chop wood and carry water." Repetition is the word, and it has little to do with what we 'make' of it. But, and this is what finally interests me here, regarding this project, namely to say something about the epistemic creative writer. If the 'before' and 'after' mirror in the Zen philosophy, what happens during Zen is worth considering. For here we have a state of awareness that dictates how to perceive water and how to perceive wood. During Zen water is a stream from heaven and wood the spirit of wisdom.

Stein's writing, while offering the same old same in the margins of writing that get to mirror each other, in between she has no qualms about saying what she loves. Though love, for Stein, is circumscribed by a specific economy. I will get back to this shortly in a more ample analysis. Meanwhile, seen within the historical context and the zeitgeist at the time, statements such as Gold's are not as aberrant and merely vitriolic as they seem. For, the prevalent notions around the turn of the century and well into the '30s regarding mysticism were indeed tensioned. The more established psychologists at the time, who viewed the creative potential as the result of a blend consisting of mixing anxiety with a phenomenological reaction to a physically felt problem arising from over-intellectualizing everything, identified mysticism unambiguously with the manifestation of hysteria. Freud, for instance, associated visions with repressed sexuality throughout all of his works. His colleague, Joseph Breuer, even described St. Theresa as "the patron saint of hysteria," and that in spite of his seeing her basically as "a woman of genius" (Breuer, 1895), in Mazzoni, 1996: 42). William James, while more benevolent in his considerations of saintliness and meditation, saw them in the context of a purely subjective experience. As mediumistic visions, they heralded that these experiences were not to be trusted.

In their work, *Gertrude Stein: The Language that Rises* (2008), Ulla Dydo and William Rice make clear the connection between the discrepancy in juxtaposing subjective vision with its objective realization and Stein's knowledge of these notions at least as far as her discussion of saints and hysterics in the context of real artists is concerned (Dydo and Rice, 2008: 181-182). Here, although the argument is also that Stein directly engaged with close readings of some of the texts of women mystics, particularly St. Teresa, what is unacknowledged is the possibility that Stein was uneasy about the readiness of psychologists to deem 'men who know things' as visionary and geniuses, and dismiss 'women who know things' as unlucky. Even now, alas, the tendency to see visionary women as any good tilts towards pitying them for missing out on things, such as having children and being good mothers. Dydo and Rice demonstrate, however, that Stein pondered carefully on St. Teresa's call for the need for enclosure – no domestic life – something which a religious devotee must experience by way of detachment, and its relation to the disciplined artist who gets ideas precisely at the point when she instructs herself not to get any. They thus intuit that Stein was anxious about the relation of sex to creativity and that she might have groped with the basic assumption that perhaps, indeed, as a saint, you can't both fuck and have your soul in heaven.

On this, one would like to hear more about the implication of what St. Teresa knew for Stein's writings, also as it relates to religions other than the Christian. For, it seems to be the case that while Stein may not have bothered too much about Oriental philosophy, her general idea of just sitting and doing nothing discloses an interesting correspondence between her take on the visual elements in writing (as in her use of Cubism, for instance) and the visionary aspect of writing, which holds the prophetic voice in high regard. There is thus a close alignment of nothingness with the everything-ness of the expression. In other words, for Stein, what is important is to register the nuances in the experience of a vision as opposed to its visual representation through symbols.

How to go about it without saying anything, and yet disclosing a whole lot of facets in the flaws of both, the creative yet controlled aspect of writing, and man as subjective medium, was something that Stein saw as the most powerful and efficient method of describing objectively. And yet again, for her, describing objectively clearly had a mystical element in it, and she insisted on letting subjectivity rule the sentence. The challenge was how to go whole-heartedly all-in and headlong, so that ultimately what would be achieved is an opening of the heart through which writing could flow with such energy that it would make consciousness redundant.

Throughout her works the repetition of words such as 'there there' and 'here here' are thus clearly meant as mantra words intended to burst out even of the medium of language itself into pure emotion, bypassing the hierarchy of the commanding head always being on top and at the top of everything. Stein could intuit that if the highest creative aim is to reach a state beyond consciousness, then, the last thing that one needed as an artist was precisely a head. For what is there to do with a head when you are beyond creating forms? Create law and order for formlessness? Hardly. Stein saw such cultural constraints as utterly boring and devoid of free flow. Seen in this context her often quoted line, that "It is awfully important to know what is and what is not your business" (Stein, 1935: 13), acquires a specifically mystical ring to it, as it implicitly alludes to the existence of an other world, namely a world whose very condition for existence lies precisely not in the business of questioning its physical reality, but in the business of not being in any business. Again, doing nothing, seems indeed to be the secret. Thus what Stein is suggesting is that there IS a mystical world. And it is this mystical world that makes a writer a creative epistemologist.

We find more concrete evidence of this in her lecture "Composition as Explanation," which gathers her most insightful ideas about creative academic writing, or the writing which dares to dream itself as a system of thought. This piece also discloses her anxiety about being presentational in a discursive way without betraying the task of the first person singular. As she puts it: "I am not I any longer when I write" (111).

Critics often interpret such statements to be the manifestation of a desire to get rid of explanation in writing (Dydo, 1993: 493), but by a stretch of the imagination, we could also take this to mean that what Stein desires is not a substitution of the 'I' with the potential 'many' who can identify with the I, but an evolved consciousness. "Composition as Explanation" is intended to say something about the writer's predicament of being stuck in time, caught in the prison of words. This lecture, then, charts Stein's difficulty with what she calls a 'groping' with what she was trying to do in her early works, groping with the imprecision of the expression. After the repeated phrase that "Everything is the same except composition and time" (Stein in Dydo, 1993: 497), one that identifies time as the main factor coming in the way of how an evolved consciousness might be experienced, Stein goes on to suggest that the way towards achieving a state beyond ambivalence is through getting a sense of what goes into the mix between word and wonder. Here she demonstrates that through creating a pattern for the writing of nothing, she breaks the pattern of writing everything, or anything at all.

As there is even now a consensus in the art-world that the best art is the result of struggle, the result of "groping" with the tension between dualistic states, one must give Stein credit for her suspicion that this is so indeed. We can thus appreciate her prophetic vision which suggests that mystery lies not in formalizing formlessness but in leaving it alone, and experiencing it as a preparation for a differentiation that never comes. This can be considered close to the Zen idea that raw energy need not always be divided. Says Stein:

> Now the few who make writing the way that it is made and it is to be remarked that the most decided of them are those that are prepared by preparing, are prepared just as the world around them is prepared and is preparing to do it this way and so if you do not mind I will again tell you how it happens. Naturally one does not know how it happened until it is well over beginning happening (Stein, 1935: 498).

If we look at Stein's insistence on preparation, we could make the inference that she is in fact worried that neither the world nor the writer are prepared enough. And for what exactly, one might as well ask, if that were to be the case? Stein seems to be in no doubt. One must be prepared for that which, through good equilibrium, might take us over to the other level, to the experience of a mystical revelation. By imagining ourselves in such a space, the idea is that we might, then, also be able to conclude on what we're preparing to experience without knowing, and without explanation. We can see on the lines a few pages later:

> And so one now finds oneself interesting oneself in an equilibration, that of course means words as well as things and distribution as well as between themselves between the words and themselves and the things and themselves, a distribution as distribution. This makes what follows what follows and now there is every reason why there should be an arrangement made. Distribution is interesting and equilibration is interesting when a continuous present and a beginning again and again and using everything and everything alike and everything naturally simply different has been done (501-502).

Here, Stein does not explain what arrangement there needs to be done after what follows, but it is clear that it is left up to the sensitive reader to make the inference that what she is talking about is her desire to name the absolute. And one can even speculate to what extent the words of William James in his chapter on "Mysticism" from his work, *Varieties of Religious Experience*, reverberate right through Stein on Stein, through impenetrable stones which desire themselves dissolved. Says James:

> Whoso calls the Absolute anything in particular, or says that it is *this*, seems implicitly to shut it off from being *that* - it is as if he lessened it. So we deny the "this," negating the negation which it seems to us to imply, in the interests of the higher affirmative attitude by which we are possessed (James, 2008: 305).

If Gertrude Stein was not a mystic, then she was certainly at the horizon. In the following I want to pursue an investigation into the formal property of Stein's writing, and thus attempt to answer a few questions: What makes Gertrude Stein an epistemic creative writer? What is the significance of breaking sentences apart for her way of conceptualizing the notion of the fragment as an important moment in epistemic creative writing? And how does love factor into all this? "Identity always worries me and memory and eternity," (EA, 97) she claims, and one gets the impression that she shares the exact same concern with how to love as Federman did when confronted with the possibility that if identity is personality and thus nothing other than an empty mask, then love of the other, writing, the world, and creativity is also nothing. Perhaps creative epistemics begins with this consideration, namely, that love is leaving it be.

Economies of love

One of Gertrude Stein's main preoccupations has been to investigate various positions of enunciation available to the agent who, while desiring to establish herself as an innovative writer also has to submit to rules of conventions. Here, quite literally, a good look in the mirror marks the beginning of realizing under which conditions the statement, 'I love what I see,' or rather, more radically, 'I love myself,' can also be a statement that may have an emancipating character on a larger scale than the individual. For what exactly are the implications of saying that one writes for oneself and strangers, as Stein has repeatedly insisted? What is the premise for such uttering? That one is not a stranger oneself, and therefore what one can place in the space between oneself and the others may be interesting to consider, or that one is very much a stranger, first to oneself, and then the others? Does one then write to understand oneself or the others? Or does one write with view to instructing oneself as one sees oneself in the third person?

Given the highly original autobiographical works that Gertrude Stein wrote, namely, *The Autobiography of Alice B. Toklas*, and *Everybody's Autobiography*, one could imagine Stein standing in front of a mirror rather than at her desk, and saying: 'This is Gertrude Stein. She loves herself.' Addressing herself in the third person, yet also using the second person direct speech, as if embodying the mirror at its moment of answering back and saying, 'are you talking to me?' Stein suggests that there is an interesting interplay between personae engaged in learning about each other, especially when each is aware of the possibility of tampering with the position of pronouns. The 'you' here indicates more a 'she', the one in the mirror rather than the 'I' of the enunciation, which suggests that some flexible identification mechanisms are activated beyond the field of immediate vision.

The sense of selfhood is reduced to an economy of shifting pronoun signifiers and we find Stein triangulating between 'I', 'you', and 'she'. Identifying with herself as she appears in the mirror, a second body, yet one which is addressed in a third person narrative, Stein performs what has always been the main aim in all of her writings: to be as precise as possible in her descriptions of what she knows, and in how she got to know what she knows. As she puts it herself:

> Gertrude Stein, in her work, had always been possessed by the intellectual passion for exactitude in the description of inner and outer reality. She has produced a simplification by this concentration, and as a result the destruction of associational emotion in poetry and prose. She knows that beauty, music, decoration, the result of emotion should never be the cause, even events should not be the cause of emotion nor should they be the material of poetry and prose. Nor should emotion itself be the cause of poetry or prose. They should consist of an exact reproduction of either an outer or inner reality.
>
> It was this conception of exactitude that made the close understanding between Gertrude Stein and Juan Gris.
>
> Juan Gris also conceived exactitude but in him exactitude had a mythical basis. As a mystic it was necessary for him to be exact. In Gertrude Stein the necessity was intellectual, a pure passion for exactitude. It is because of this that her work has often been compared to that of mathematicians and by a certain french critic to the work of Bach (Stein, 2001: 228).

What is noteworthy here is the passage from the subject, when the subject subjectivizes her own desires to be recognized, to the object, or the act in which the subject becomes the desired object, in this case Gertrude herself desiring to own the self independent of pronoun fixation and positionality. This is Gertrude Stein, the writer with no self – the 'auto' in 'autobiography' has been lent to Alice – going from an indistinct selfhood to graphing the bios of distinctive individuals, nominalized and endowed with concrete attributes. Thus we have embodiments through the fictionalization of the subject as an object in the mirror of the intellectual, the philosopher, the mathematician, and the musician.

Here, although I want to look at economies of love in Gertrude Stein more in terms of exchange currency, I find what psychoanalysts have to say about love as a form of neurosis that links currency with identification relevant to consider. Particularly the Lacanian concept of a spontaneous 'passage to the act' can reveal what is at stake in the writing of an autobiography from which the self is excluded, or talked about in the third person, and whose narrative force is driven by a special form of epistemic logic that goes against the idea of spontaneous writing, thus favouring more calculation and cold rhetoric. One pertinent question to ask here, to begin with, is this: Can one stage a *passage à l'acte?* Can one plan it or arrange it or organize it?

Lacan's dissecting of the Freudian notion of *agieren*, acting out, to also include, beside a call for attention as a defence against anxiety, what Lacan calls a "passage to the act," is interesting to consider, especially since Lacan never talked about this notion as being anything other than spontaneous. There are times, Lacan contends in *Seminar X* on anxiety, when, because of strong desire for an object which the subject sees as unattainable, the subject may experience a moment of total identification with the object. This brings about a sense of falling, an inverse kind of *afhebung* often manifested in some violent act that is unmotivated and devoid of message to anyone. It can take the form of slapping someone on her face, saying something really stupid, or more drastically, throwing oneself in front of a train. As the subject becomes object, the subject exits the scene. Some passages in Stein's *Autobiography* suggest the possibility that the passage to the act can be consciously premeditated, and that it can use the third person narrative form as a vehicle for manifestation. What is manifested in the conflation of the first and third person narrative is both a concrete type of knowledge of what one is doing, but also knowledge that stems from channels that do not necessarily operate with factual evidence. Such knowledge is often disseminated in oracular statements such as these: 'something tells me,' 'my gut feeling tells me,' or 'a bell rings in my head.' What the 'I' knows is not always the same as what the 'she' knows, yet the interplay between the kinds of information each signals to the other is what enables the subject to consciously identify with a desired object and then also consciously engage in an act that has the potential to reveal the 'I' in the 'she' and vice versa. What is at stake is the extent to which the 'I' of the narrative can account for the sum of experiencing the other to the other's full potential. The implication of such an act has to do with distinguishing between modes of perception that are both external and internal to one's own field of experience. Says Stein in *The Autobiography of Alice B. Toklas*:

I may say that only three times in my life have I met a genius and each time a bell within me rang and I was not mistaken, and I may say in each case it was before there was any general recognition of the quality of genius in them. The three geniuses of whom I wish to speak are Gertrude Stein, Pablo Picasso, and Alfred Whitehead (Stein, 2001: 9).

What happens here is a cross between what can be perceived as a liminal statement on self-love as an economy of enunciation and its unfolding against the background of another economy, namely an economy of geography. Gertrude Stein as "Gertrude Stein" takes herself out of "here" and places herself over "there." Gertrude knows the genius of herself but she cannot localize it within the space of enunciation that reflects a first person's perspective, one that is already part of a dominant discourse with fixed hierarchies: man is a genius and woman is merely aspiring. For a woman, where is this 'there', then? In the slapping of all men so that the subject can cross over to consciously enact the object, arguably that of embracing one's womanhood in Stein's case. 'I am', Gertrude suggests, 'the premium genius' when I become "Gertrude Stein," the desired object – here, genius or not – and the one talked about in the third person, and one that is also aligned perfectly with men. The subject in general as a recognized genius resists localization which brings about a desire to escape fantasmatic narratives about geniuses into the real space of 'there is' or 'it's there' precisely as this space is devoid, or rather it is desired to be devoid, of any symbolization, whether contingent on gender difference or not. If you are a genius, then you are a genius, and that's all there is to it. If anything, it is funny, as Gertrude says:

> It is funny this business being a genius. Everything is funny.
>
> And identity is funny being yourself is funny as you are never yourself to yourself except as you remember yourself and then of course you do not believe yourself. That is really the trouble with an autobiography you do not of course you do not really believe yourself why should you, you know so well so very well that it is not yourself, it could not be yourself because you cannot remember right and if you do remember right it does not sound right and of course it does not sound right because it is not right. You are of course never yourself (53).

Gertrude, the writer of the autobiography becomes an object of her own desire to be herself even in the face of knowing that you are never yourself. Gertrude desires to desire herself desiring. Thus, geographically speaking, an economy of love can be expressed at the limit of the point of convergence between first and third person narrating voices, when the border of figurality dissolves both the structure of 'there is' or 'it's there' and 'there is not', you are 'it' or you are not (a genius, or yourself). What is suggested is that there is a whole different country between the enunciating 'I' and the receiving 'other,' which allows for a premeditated crisscrossing of 'there is' with 'there is not'. It is as if Gertrude says that when something 'is there' beyond the opposite of what may be expressed in words through 'but there is also'– a new situation, a new stage, or a new act – the only position that makes sense in acknowledging the significance of topos and one which accounts for the function of a premeditated *passage à l'acte* is the one which relies on repetition. One of Gertrude's favorite phrases in her writing is namely the reminder to her reader: "As I was saying…" In this sense it can be contended that in its relation to the passage to the act, the economy of love can be described as an act of losing one's head to own the words (or the love of another).

In his influential book, *A Lover's Discourse*, Roland Barthes sets out to deconstruct the figures of speech which mark the language of lovers. As he deconstructs love by pointing to the tension in the universality of feeling vs. individual expression, he demonstrates not only that love is a solitary experience but that it is also the result of learned behavior. Barthes's implicit claim is that one knows what love is because one has read nineteenth century novels. In other words, if the experience of love happens, it does so on the basis of an economy: one appropriates other 'love' texts which are then transformed into an exchange currency. Thus what makes love creative, and ultimately a potentially unique experience, is its expenditure, not transcendental power.

Gertrude Stein shows a similar concern with writing which makes manifest contradictory types of love in connection with writing that is both autobiographical yet also written by everybody. Related to love as a construct as against the love of self as a more unconscious construct – but one that nonetheless gets to be clearly enunciated via various channels of expression, such as mirrors, or shifting pronouns that can also be argued follow an 'unconscious' constructing pattern – I'm interested in exploring Stein's statement, namely that she writes for herself and strangers, and look at other axioms of self-idolatry that she formulates with the purpose of creating a poetics of creative epistemology.

One of the effects of writing about herself in the third person is in Stein a question of how to approximate tenderness in relation to the self. There is an incredibly soft tone in her formulations, and although fairly formal, given that Stein almost always refers to her full name, the way in which the sound pattern is constructed in what precedes and follows the naming of her name, convinces us of the idea that the very definition of love relies on saying that it is linked to the degree of the concern one can show towards the other. Stein is very careful with placing very strategically a certain intonation within this concern whenever she pronounces her name. This suggests both a highly conscious construction of her persona in the image of the genius who supersedes all, and yet also a persona who submits to the control of the loving master, the one who sets things in motion and who dictates ultimately what the genius "Gertrude Stein" needs to say or show she is like. In other words, the genius is only so much in control, and without the guiding voice of a meta-discursive power she cannot pass as one who consciously knows how to love herself, nor can she know what the implication of such love might be, as one would expect a genius to know. There is thus already an economy of love at work according to whose rules the constructed genius operates within.

Borrowing the voice of Alice B. Toklas, Stein explains the motives behind writing her autobiography the way she did, by entitling it conventionally *The Autobiography of Alice B. Toklas*, when the work clearly is neither about Alice, nor written by Alice. Furthermore, the fact that she gives details as to the alternative title she wanted the book to have, apart from the conventional frame, testifies to the idea that when the love of self is traded for the words of others – the book is in fact a collection of gossipy recollections about the lives of artists and writers who frequented Stein's household – this love can assume exactly the size and shape that one is capable of imagining. We have an example of this in a beginning passage that deals with Stein's fascination, not so much with the ones who came to see her, because they themselves already had fairly high thoughts of themselves which Stein didn't think was so interesting, but with their wives, the observant standbys, the real potential geniuses who were capable of both listening and talking a the same time:

> Before I decided to write this book my twenty-five years with Gertrude Stein, I had often said that I would write, the wives of geniuses I have sat with. I have sat with so many. I have sat with wives who were not wives, of geniuses who were real geniuses. I have sat with real wives of geniuses who were not real geniuses. I have sat with wives of geniuses, of near geniuses, of would be geniuses, in short I have sat very often and very long with many wives and wives of many geniuses (18).

What emerges here is yet another strong suggestion that one way in which one can determine what an economy of love consists of is by looking at the difference between connection and correspondence. As previously pointed out in Toklas's observation, while sitting in the proximity of a genius, she never got it wrong because the bells were ringing in her head. This clearly indicates a relation of connection that is not based on reasoning; bells were ringing. Conversely, however, insofar as what the bells were announcing was an indication of the degree of genius on the scale of genius typology, one that ranges from first class genius, real genius, almost genius, aspiring or would be genius, what we are dealing with is a relation of correspondence. Such juxtapositions are crucial in Stein, and they enhance very clearly the position of enunciation of the subject vi-à-vis what the subject approximates in relation to herself. The closer to the truth, the better.

Such desire for precision makes Stein's voice as channelled through Toklas all the more credible and convincing, and if love emerges as an element that supersedes both reason and emotion, then it does so through trust. Stein trusts Toklas, as it were, to make sure that the message she purports is not one of information about the whereabouts of the geniuses encountered, but the fact that she reached a state of knowing herself by trusting Stein in turn to make sure to pass on to her what she knows. Such complete circularity between voice and medium, or voice and filter, enforces the significance of what may lie behind the tautological statement: I know what I know. And if I know what I know, then I can just as well stick to it. Insofar as trust circumscribes the type of knowledge that is not always the result of reasonable certitude, it thus renders the love of self in relation to the love of others economical. In other words, when you trust yourself because you know what you know, what you distinguish between is the number of tautologies that are formulated against the background of either connection or correspondence. Thus Toklas speaks from a position of knowing when she implicitly passes judgement on the meaning of sitting and listening with the marginal class, the wives, in this case. She shares the predicament of these wives. She, as Gertrude Stein, however, as Stein speaks through her, is a corresponding number: the number two corresponding to the prime in the genius typology, or if not a genius with attributes, then a genius nonetheless, a genius who is in attendance to the first class genius, that of Stein herself.

The genius in Stein thus has a particularly special status, and shows precisely what is at stake in the go between construction and self-perception that has love as a primary mechanism. As she also puts it later in *Everybody's Autobiography*, a work that now expands to including not only the third person as filtered through the first person perspective, but also everybody's perspective: "It takes a lot of time to be a genius, you have to sit around so much doing nothing, really doing nothing" (Stein, 2004: 70). What kind of knowledge such an axiom elicits is here related to how all-inclusiveness can be reduced to an economy of generality. The tensions inherent in such a concept that combines an element of generality with an economy are eradicated at the moment when knowledge, or the injunction to know thyself – the first rule that a genius must obey – relates to love, or the injunction to love thy neighbor – which is the second rule that a genius must obey if she is also wise. Thus we read a central passage in *Everybody's Autobiography*, which is offered as a meta-comment on the significance of knowing precisely what one is, in addition to what one knows in general. Says Stein:

> In writing *The Making of Americans* I said I write for myself and strangers and then later now I know these strangers, are they still strangers, well anyway that too does not really bother me, the only thing that really bothers me is that the earth now is all covered over with people and that knowing anybody is not of any particular importance because anybody can know anybody (82).

What enables Stein to make such a statement, which at first eye glance can be considered the statement of a cynic, rather than that of a lover of all, is the fact that, for Stein, combination and correspondence, which the genius must be able to profess simultaneously through listening and talking at the same time, or at least know the distinction between them, is a matter primarily of imagination. The only way in which anybody can know anybody is if one can imagine it. Says Stein on the function of imagination: "One has to remember that about imagination. That is when the world gets dull when everybody does not know what they can or they cannot imagine" (72). Her example prior to this conclusion relates very much to the significance of what we can imagine intuitively, and how if we get it wrong, or are unable to imagine it, renders our world of connection irrelevant or useless. Recounting how she was once given a question that would test her level of viciousness in relation to people she didn't really know, Stein answered by making the following inference:

> Would I if I could by pressing a button would I kill five thousand Chinamen if I could save my brother from anything. Well I was very fond of my brother and I could completely imagine his suffering and I replied that five thousand Chinamen were something I could not imagine and so it was not interesting (72).

Stein thus makes a relation between the experience of everyday life and the fact that when it comes to counting, people are very bad at it. Especially large numbers cannot be imagined, which obviously in her example has consequences for her decision. The love of her brother remains locked within the economy of imagination. The inference is thus one of failing to imagine that which exceeds the scope of one's daily routines: yes, I could save my brother, but insofar as I can't relate to this massive crowd of strangers, I will not. The fact that it could be interesting to imagine how to do away with five thousand Chinamen is rendered as uninteresting, which is Stein's way of warning against the danger of not being able to imagine anything at all.

In *The Making of Americans* we have some descriptions that border the neutral formulation which takes care of saying something about what the function of the genius is, among other things to let himself be open to interpretation. In *The Autobiography of Alice B. Toklas,* precisely because self-perception is filtered through another's voice, even when it is one's own, the concerns with oneself that one shows lends the general definition of the genius which one recognizes oneself as such a more nuanced form. However, insofar as the economy of love is dependent on a medium of expression that allows for negotiations even beyond settlement, love itself becomes subject to contamination. That the flow of thought from master through pupil, from the first class genius through the regular genius does not go undisturbed by the dimension, space, and time of this other through which love passes, can be seen particularly in texts that are marked by phrases such as "as I was saying," and "the thing that bothers me." Gertrude Stein is always ready for a passage to the act, yet unlike in Lacanian psychoanalysis, in Stein's writing it unfolds ever so slowly and it is utterly controlled and premeditated. To give an example, when Stein goes about describing the philosopher and social Darwinist Herbert Spencer as a genius, she allows him to speak through her, yet it is still her words that Spencer uses, thus becoming in the end a species himself, a type of a being who has just managed to baffle Stein with his behavior and beliefs, and whom she catalogues all according to how he enters a loving rather than a living relation. Thus, it is not life that interests Stein, but love, and she would like to know whether love can be a thing that is capable of transcending its own construct. Stein wants love to be immanent on the outside, as it were.

The following passage illustrates how a concrete description of a person can turn into a precise formulation of a generic, or even transgeneric "bottom nature" that fits all:

> This made this one baffling. This made this one puzzling for this one had profound impression by beauty and this was complete and poignant and quick in him and he had the rationalizing mind acting on each piece of impression and shutting him off from getting deep and poignant and complete impressions from things before him and he was so puzzling, he had opportunism so strongly in him that each time he was open to a new relation with anything in life or a man or a woman he acted in this way toward them and also he had created for himself a whole rationalized scheme of living of beauty and goodness and fairness to every one because that was the way to make the living that would be successful and beautiful, to him. Always to himself he was always open to feeling beauty and goodness and nobility in living, always to himself he had made a scheme of complete living in luxury and success and winning admiration, always to himself he could completely understand everything with his mind which was to himself a great thing in him, never was he ever knowing that his running himself by his mind which was making always for him his theory of beauty and goodness and luxury was closing him to impressions of beauty and luxury and learning. This he never knew in him (Stein, 1995: 368).

What is remarkable in this passage is Stein's tone which indicates a progression of the degree to which she knows precisely what she knows but does not tell to begin with. First we have Spencer described as a ruthless man, then we have a justification of his ruthlessness in the suggestion that anyone interested in beauty must be OK at bottom, and finally there's a lamentation of the fact that although there is interest in beauty on Spencer's part, beauty teaches him nothing unless it is filtered through an opening towards others who, consciously or not, can reveal it to him in him. And what interests Gertrude is this: how to be the one who can teach Spencer to know himself. As she is bothered by Spencer's way of being, she is on a track to enlightening the man, but she is only interested in doing that to the extent that in the end she gets to conclude that what she can formulate can fit all.

Here one can gauge that the subtle lesson that Gertrude wants to pass on to Spencer, in saying that what she can say about him after all that individual thinking that goes into evaluating him, is that we are not all individuals, but that we all submit to individual rules that make us think that we are. And yet, in spite of such subtlety, one gets the impression that what Gertrude really wants is to actually shout at the man who thinks that we are all individuals: 'fallacious thinking, my man,' Gertrude would thus yell if she could, which would be precisely the kind of message that would baffle Spencer in turn and that would run counter to his Darwinist belief in the power of the individual. So says Stein, befittingly, then, and following the bell inside her ringing:

> This one then was baffling, there was complete contradiction in him and yet he was all of one kind of being, this one then was baffling and for a long time this one was not a whole one to me and then I understood the meaning in him, he had it in him all the qualities of this kind of being [...]

> This is very clear to me know. Now I am not any longer puzzling about this one. This is not very clear yet in my telling. This will be clearer when I have told of the loving being in this one.

> There are many ways of having loving feeling, this one that I am now describing had loving feeling in every kind of way [...]
>
> Those having this kind of being have as I was saying much nervous being that is not energy in them as attacking being, as loving, though it is very much like repressed active being, or repressed loving being, but it is not that in them. This so far is clear to me [...]
>
> Generally then in this kind of them although there is much loving being in them it does not express itself in loving any particular one until some particular one having very strongly being in them enormously stimulating these makes the loving being in them active to loving that one (368-369).

What such discourse discloses here is a complete entanglement of self-love with the love of another, yet as it is revealed, what each comes to know of the other, or other things, such as beauty, is completely dependent on transmutations of the concrete and precise information that one has available of the other and that one exchanges for the more imprecise and indescribable gut feeling of the other, the bells ringing, and the tautology of knowing what you know beyond justification. What Stein leaves open in her investigations of economies of love is the question of the extent to which love can be taught. Thus if there is any beauty in it, it must be in the performing of that question and anticipating the response: If I can teach you love, what will you say and do? And here one can sense Stein's anxiety as far as an acknowledgement from the other is concerned, one that she expects to hear: will one confess to having learnt anything at all? And what would such a confession entail? As being certain of what the other will say is, however, not an option, Stein suspends her speculation in economizing the fact. If there is anything she will know for sure is what SHE would say, if she posed this question to herself, if she confessed to herself. Thus she says in a highly intimate and vulnerable tone in *Lectures in America:*

> One must never confess to oneself that one loves oneself. The secret of this confession is the life principle of the one true and eternal love. The first kiss in this understanding is the principle of philosophy - the origin of a new world - the beginning of absolute chronology - the completion of an infinitely growing bond with the self. Who would not like a philosophy whose germ is a first kiss? (Stein, 1985: 58-59).

The economy of love is thus captured here as a lesson in epistemology. What one learns is that creativity begins with a knowledge about how you move, how you gesture, and how you act. These moves, however, have to follow the imagination. One has to imagine what kissing philosophy must be like. One has to be able to imagine how saying 'I love myself' can enter a signifying and parallel relation to saying 'I kiss my philosophy goodbye.' Insofar as knowing the other fully is bound to remain an impenetrable act, what one is left with is knowing what philosophy feels like in relation to factual knowledge that resists transcending. And yet, while epistemic creative knowledge is just contact with the facts, what is obvious about the love of words that one forces unto others, including oneself, is that this very obviousness constitutes a mystery that leaves only one opening, namely towards being grateful for having experiencing thought itself, the thought of self and that of the other.

After her typologies and autobiographies of love and self, Gertrude Stein went on to write *A Novel of Thank You.* Perhaps *thank you* is the only word that can, in the end, describe best, not only the economy of love, but also its epistemic structures in relation to creativity and imagination. Thank you.

The epi-fragment: Bachelard and Barthes turning over Steinian stones

We have seen how the dialectics of the negative works in Beckett, where what is emphasized is a form of transgressive parody in which philosophy formulates an epistemology of creative writing almost in the guise of a fool's lament over the decay of history and morals. Beckett was largely inspired by Nietzsche and his idea that any creative impetus should begin in the valorization of the idea of nothingness both as a start, middle, and end point of any creative process and act. The lesson that is given the epistemic creative writer is that he must alter critical thinking not behind, but besides the insignificant and irreligious double of such concepts as 'method.' If Nietzsche, in his *Genealogy of Morals*, is a philosopher in the business of playfully appropriating the critique of reason, hijacking the *gene* in *logos*, then one can advance the idea that he can't (and perhaps we can read that as Kant) circumvent his methods without blowing himself away, wasting his writing, becoming a cantor instead of a reasonable glyph'er inscribing his methodical mark within the space of morality. Beckett follows suit, and modernists such Gertrude Stein, have managed to show how paying attention to the sounding of trumpets announcing the collapse of universals that have teleological aims – one is born, one lives, one dies – sharpens the sensual pens.

Writing nothing, as it were, formulates itself in Gertrude Stein, for instance, as a moment of insight that combines the awareness of the futility of writing with the genius that dictates that writing in circles, as it were, is the only way to navigate among the shored up ruins of dynamited knowledge precepts. A befitting slogan that would characterize what is at stake in Stein must be this one: salute the fragment as you go round and round.

The fragment can be said to be one of the few genres that establishes itself as a poetics from the start. The fragment comes as a whole package, as it were, insofar as what forms this poetics is precisely a question of where it begins. However, insofar as the fragment may begin in the middle or at the end of a text, its beginning forces the critic to become a master of suspicion. The first impulse is to see the fragment as a detachment from a whole, a residue or a remnant. As such, the fragment may be thought of as an ending rather than beginning; a vintage vestige which may mark the end of an era. On second thought, the fact that the fragment begins here or there, has more to do with a poetics of topos than totality. This can be formulated thus: the fragment begins in separation but ends in a wholesome space. To perceive the fragment as separation, yet imagine it as a whole, are two activities as antithetical as presence and absence.

Here I want to perform the task of the suspicious critic and propose that the poetics of the fragment – that which marks a beginning against the grain of beginnings – is a space of roundness in which the fragment is imagined as an interruption that unites Aristotelian poetic devices such as beginnings, middles, and ends in a movement of circularity. Insofar as the process of detachment indicates mobility rather than stability, being suspicious of the place the fragment comes to occupy – if it ever settles in any stable beginnings, middles, and endings – marks a space of roundness rather than linearity. In the round space of the fragment the suspicious critic does not enter a world of answers but a world of potentialities and processes.

The potential world in which the fragment enjoys the freedom of circularity, the freedom of being found round, and stumbled upon, is a world which stands in an antithetical relation to the world of totalities. What enables us to imagine the fragment itself as a round entity is the fact that the almost-text of the fragment, its potential to actualize a text of origin – never gets to be actualized, as originality itself is without origin. Remnants, then, become supplements, in the Derridean sense, which go all the way around linearity. The function of the poetics of the fragment as a topos of roundness is thus to undo linearity in the very process in which linearity attempts to stabilize, according to itself, actual positions for remnants and residues. The fragment's relation to its totality, if there ever is one, is that of roundness in which separation is imagined as an orbiting process of *unbeginning*. Here I want to relate what is at stake in Gertrude Stein's writings to what Gaston Bachelard called "the essential mobility of concepts."

Bachelard's work with its emphasis on the poetics of space, developed in a book from 1953 with the same title, represents a seminal moment in contemporary criticism that combines notions of linearity with those of roundness. In Bachelard's phenomenological world, in which the materiality of words can only be perceived, apprehended, and heightened through making recourse to experiencing roundness in various degrees, what makes concepts mobile – for instance, concepts that describe stages of development in the human cultural consciousness – is not a "deductive or an additive pattern" (Gaudin in Bachelard, 1971: xxxiv), but one that emphasizes movement and progress.

Bachelard's philosophy is thus also a philosophy of suspicion, only, unlike other masters of suspicion such as Freud, Marx, and Nietzsche, his thought on suspicion is informed by potentialities rather than actualizations; roundness rather than linearity. His statement as to what he would like to create in his philosophy emphasizes potentiality at its most round point, (if roundness has a rising point, which I think it does when it indicates a potential): "I should like to develop a philosophy that has no point of departure" (xxxiv). What we find in this line is a fine example of a fragment that begins in a moment of *unbeginning*. Insofar as philosophy never takes off, yet articulates an experience of the undecidable, it creates a space that gives Bachelard room for his claim that "being is round" (Bachelard, 1958: 234). This round being, or the phenomenology of being, according to Bachelard, establishes itself in its roundness while at the same time developing roundness (240). Insofar as being thus becomes becoming, and becoming becomes being, the dialectical relationship between being and becoming is mediated in the round space of the philosophy that has no point of departure.

The relevance of Bachelard's discourse here is in establishing the extent to which we can argue that the writing which never seems to take off creates knowledge not of an empty space that it keeps running into, but of a space that has a distinctive shape in it, one that awaits sighting. If Beckett has breath in sight, Gertrude Stein is all about inhaling and exhaling. Her 'reporting' on what happens when you breathe words that others can learn to write with articulates clearly what the repetitious, circular, incantatory, and round writing relies on, namely an erotic structure. The main insight here is that without such roundness there would be no experience of either writing or reading. "Repetition itself creates bliss," writes Roland Barthes in *The Pleasures of the Text* (Barthes, 1975: 41), and at least where authors such as Gertrude Stein is concerned we get the picture when we read such passages as hers below:

> I love it, I tell it. I love it, I live it and I tell it. Always I will tell it. They live it and I see it and I hear it and I feel it. They live it and I see it and I hear it and I feel it and I love it (Stein, 1995: 305).

Briefly put, Barthes, who started out as a prominent structuralist, but then went on to endorsing post-structuralist ideas, has been identified by others as a critic who insisted on practicing the creative method. As Johnathan Culler observes, Barthes embodies both the academic and the creative writer. This comes to expression already in Barthes's first book, *Le Degré Zéro de l'Écriture* (1953) in which he demonstrates what it means to be the critic *par excellence* of literary history without a method. According to Culler, Barthes "criticizes literary historians for having a historical method but neglecting the historical nature of their object of study. Here we seem to have just the opposite problem: Barthes emphasizes the historical character of his object – writing, or the literary function – but lacks a historical method" (Culler, 2002: 21). What characterizes Barthes's writing is thus a form of circularity. Through this form he advocates for the kind of writing that produces knowledge about the degree of writing that starts at zero – and if we stretch it, it looks like zero too. His famous 'autobiography', *Roland Barthes par Roland Barthes* (1975), is a piece of critical fictitious writing about the complexity of writing and the self inscribed as writing. In a seminal passage, he explains the function of writing that comes, if not in degrees, then in fragments, maxims, aphorisms, in the short approach to things, one that can be said to constitute what we might understand by epistemic creative writing:

> An aphoristic tone hangs about this book (*we, one, always*). Now the maxim is complicitous with an essentialist notion of human nature; it is linked to classical ideology: it is the most arrogant (often the stupidest) of the forms of language. Why then not reject it? The reason is as always, emotive: I write maxims (or I sketch their movement) *in order to reassure myself*: when some disturbance arises, I attenuate it by confiding myself to a fixity which exceeds my powers: 'Actually it's always like that': and the maxim is born. The maxim is a sort of *sentence-name*, and to name is to pacify. Moreover, this too is a maxim: it attenuates my fear of seeking extravagance by writing maxims (Barthes, 1977: 181).

Beckett's breath has reached Barthes's ear. Meanwhile Gertrude Stein begins again. In the following I want to further illustrate how Stein addresses three important stages in the poetics of the fragment as a moment of epistemic creative writing, which relates to the *unbeginning* of writing, roundness, and material potentiality. She continues the modernist impetus of authors such as Beckett pointing to the workings of the imagology of the sign – the zero itself, the O, can be thought of in terms of imagology – as represented through the creation of identifications rather than identities, process rather than method.

I feel it

Nowhere is the question of *unbeginning* addressed more masterfully and more poetically than in Gertrude Stein's *The Making of the Americans* (1925), this mastodon of a book that fills almost 1000 pages. Given the book's thematic structure – which presumes to tell the story of every American that has ever lived – the fact that the narrator never gets past beginning suggests that the many pages in fact form a rather large literary fragment. After setting the tone by informing the reader that "we all begin well," Gertrude Stein makes recourse to at least 24 instances of beginnings in her long narrative. What throws Stein's discourse into the space of *unbeginning* is not so much the obsessive repetition of telling us that now she will begin, again, but the fact that prior to the beginning proper, the beginning of each instance of beginning is cast first as a description; "a little description," to be more precise. The beginning of narrative thus stumbles over the beginning of description that is set aside from the narrative voice by constituting itself as the materiality of repetition. The lines that follow form a specific rhythm and cadence, thus relying on a sound pattern. This pattern indicates that while beginnings only seemingly exist in genres that have to do with memoirs or family sagas, as in Stein's case, they are in fact bound to an experience and articulation of the undecidable.

What makes *The Making of Americans* a perfect example of a moment of *unbeginning* and thus a fragment as a round space is the fact that the articulation of the undecidable gets the work stuck in what Bachelard calls "a philosophy of the cosmic imagination" which looks for centers of cosmic dimension. As Bachelard further puts it: "Seized in its center and brevity, the mere designation of this roundness is astonishingly complete" (258). Whatever roundness Bachelard talks about here is translated by Gertrude Stein into relations of being to becoming via suggesting that what is at stake in epistemic writing is an attempt to recover the unknown, or lost, or not yet found element always at the horizon of knowledge. I quote here one moment of *unbeginning* that circumscribes the roundness of the fragment which, on the one hand, undoes the notion of brevity, and hence closure (the little, or short descriptions) and, on the other hand, engages on a path of identification with time rather than space (Stein makes the point here that for a story to work, one must first frame it in time and only then give it space):

> Now again to begin. The relation of learning and thinking to being, of feeling to realising is a complicated question. There will now be very little talking of such way of being. As I was saying some have it in them to have slowly resisting as their natural way of being can have learning and thinking come quickly enough in them. This is then not bottom being in them. It is bottom being in some of such of them. This is very clear now in my knowing. Now to begin again with it as telling (Stein, 1995: 299).

Insofar as it never becomes clear as to what or whom Stein is talking about, in spite of her claim to clarity for what she says, we can assume that the function of deixis in this text is to point not so much to signification but to the process that has signifiers float around. The text begins by never taking off, and thus constitutes itself as a floating negation of beginnings. Stein produces a poetics of subversion by challenging the excluded middle and end of *The Making of Americans*. The beings that Stein intends to describe by orbiting them circularly and thus undoing their individual narrative in a space that unbegins become cosmic beings, in Bachelard's sense. They become potentials of signifying repetitions; they become an iconosphere, which is to say that they function in a total image-world whose distinctiveness at any given time is given by an interlinked series of signifying objects present in it. Anthony Johnson develops Jan Bialostocki's first elaboration of the term iconosphere, and points to the distinction between the psychological or internal world of images that we conjure in our heads and the material and exterior world of images that are conjured by the iconosphere. According to Johnson:

> [T]he iconosphere connotes [...] a mapped world of possibilities from a particular period which has been realized in material form: whether it be in paper, parchment, wood, silk, canvas, clay, stone, plastic, film, or even digitized and encrypted in binary code. Shored up against the irrecoverable horizons of knowledge which were available to past minds, the iconosphere of a period consists of the traces that have survived, in whatever form, from individuals of that passing world (Johnson, 2005: 52-53).

What is interesting about Johnson's idea of the iconosphere is that the iconosphere relies and depends on agency. For example the mapping of the material signifying objects in writing, such as words in a specific order, punctuation, tone, and imagery, enters in a relation where it is the world of possibilities that determines the mapping of the various identifications we make in relation to what we read. Thus we do not pass judgment on the material identity of particular objects as we see them in themselves, but rather turn towards their immaterial reification. When Gertrude Stein proclaims that now she will begin, she means to say that now she will *imagine* a beginning as a possibility for the potential materialization of a story. This suggests that in the iconosphere a text is always in a state of *unbeginning* from whence it coerces both the writer and the reader to construct notions out of the available elements. These notions are fragments of the iconosphere and as such they emulate the round form of this total image world. Stein's genius consists of her realizing that the fragment that begins in the *unbeginning* must occupy a round space. Thus, the point in Stein's narrative of *unbeginning* is to suggest that the understanding of such dimensions as the iconosphere can only take place in the fragment as a round space. Stein does not see her beings as something other than beings, and this is what makes her work a material network of operations within the iconosphere. As established earlier, Stein is a Zen master where such relations of acknowledging what *is* are concerned. The following lines illustrate:

> [...] Always from the beginning there was to me all living as repeating. This is now a description of loving repeating as a being (Stein, 1995: 294).

> [...] To begin again then with some description of the meaning of loving repeating being when it is strongly in a man or in a woman, when it is in them their way of understanding everything in living and there are very many always living of such being. This is now again a beginning of a little description of it in one (297).

> [...] In the beginning then, in remembering, repeating was strongly in the feeling of one, in the feeling of many, in the feeling of most of them who have it to have strongly in them their earthly feeling of being part of the solid dirt around them. This is one kind of being. This is mostly of one kind of being, of slow-minded

resisting fighting being. This is now a little description of one (298).

[...] There are so many ways of beginning this description, and now once more to make a beginning (300).

[...] Sometime there will be written a long history of such a beginning (302).

What Stein does here is capture the iconosphere of a world that signifies through repetition its passing us by. The making of Americans in the image of iconospheric beings marks a potentiality that confers the fragment the status of *unbeginner*. This is to say that an *unbeginner* fragment that *unbegins* itself in a work is beyond interpretation. Taken as such, we can make the inference that if something were to mark the iconosphere unambiguously, then that would have to be precisely such a fragment: a fragment which must never be interpreted, only repeated.

This is the very working of the iconosphere: its signifying objects are repeated objects that begin in an unidentified time and end in an identified *unbeginning*. Here the value of Gertrude Stein not making sense is her roundness, insofar as the objects and beings she refers to are caught in "the essential mobility of concepts," to use again Bachelard's apt phrasing. As the objects in an iconosphere cannot stand still, their movement is bound to create noise, traces, and clashes. What we identify, then, is the process through which things acquire a nature, not the identity of things in themselves. Stein's message seems to be that *what goes a/round comes a/round*, which means that in the space of the *unbeginning* time and space concepts are beyond interpretation. (A)round Gertrude Stein, then, I begin again, which is to say, or she would say, I unbegin.

I see it

> A writer must always try to have a philosophy and he should also have a psychology and a philology and many other things. Without a philosophy and a psychology and all these various other things he is not really worthy of being called a writer. I agree with Kant and Schopenhauer and Plato and Spinoza and that is quite enough to be called a philosophy. But then of course a philosophy is not the same thing as a style (Stein in Prokosch, 1983).

The construction of the modernist fragment follows two directions. There are writers who emphasize totality in their juxtapositions of pieces of texts, and others who break that totality by juxtaposing fragments that are incompatible. In the first case the fragment which may yet be complete in its elaboration closes itself around a certain meaning that the fragment as such proposes. In the second case, incompatibility elicits an openness which grounds meaning, not in the text, but in the wide space where the search itself for meaning becomes meaningful. Put more clearly, these two approaches to the fragment answer two different questions: whereas in the first case the question is *what is the meaning of the fragment?*, the second case deals with *what is the meaning of having the fragment mean anything?*. Ultimately this is what distinguishes between writing a fragment and writing fragmentarily.

Among the modernists who theorize the difference between writing a fragment and fragmented writing is the novelist Alain Robbe-Grillet. Claiming affinity with writers for whom the fragment works, on the one hand as a "contingent", or "antitranscendent" text, such as Sartre's *La Nausée*, and on the other hand as a "transcendent" text, such as the novels of Balzac, Robbe-Grillet points first to the aesthetic quality of incompatible fragments. He says in an interview with Tom Bishop: "The shock of seeing them together creates a kind of opening onto potential meaning" (in Kritzman, 1981: 294). In other words, the modernist fragment is first and foremost a construction of a text that has a calculated structure and an unpredictable content.

As already demonstrated, Gertrude Stein employs the method which renders the fragment an "opening onto potential meaning" in order to distinguish between genres: long and short texts, the fragment and the aphorism. Potentiality in fact characterizes the calculations inherent in a surrealist text which posits meaning as a latent potential extracted from the will to incompatibility. Insofar as potential is latent, it is also able to make manifest the will for repetition and resoluteness. For Stein, the act of defining the genre to which their writing subscribes is an act of engaging with what is potential in writing. For writers such as Stein, potential writing is an actualization of a style that unfolds what is always uncertain in an idea. Her writing expresses an attempt at finding a language that is able to accommodate the fragment and at the same time be appropriate to the fragment. For Stein, the act of defining the genre to which her writing subscribes is an act of engaging with what is potential in writing. I argue that Stein's concern with style engages in a similar project on potentiality as Giorgio Agamben does, using repetition as the prime device for the construction of a fragment which is not a fragment, but style in the making, and an aphorism which is not an aphorism, but style in the breaking.

Giorgio Agamben's collection of essays in the book *Potentialities* (1999) represents his systematic work over twenty years on potentiality and actuality, possibility and reality. Although my concern is not with these categories in the light that Agamben sheds on them, which begins with distinctions between Aristotle's *dynamis* and *energeia*, and between Plato's *thing* and the *thing itself*, the idea that the act of defining can also exist in a state of potentiality is something that I argue applies to the way some modernists construe the fragment. For modernists such as Stein the fragment constitutes a matter of style insofar as the act of defining the fragment shows itself not to concern itself with itself. Whereas for Stein style is expressed by the notion of the "unnecessary" in the act of defining: "Therefore a masterpiece has essentially not to be necessary" (Stein 1975: xiii), for Beckett, defining finds expression in the abstractness of "simple" formulations. Anything distinct has no future. So far, for Beckett and Stein writing is situated outside the domain where definitions enforce the certainty of their ideas. Both writers are engaged in a project of illustrating how ideas (that is, the "uncertain" ones, if they are to be progressive) can be articulated in a form appropriate to their uncertainty. It is in this sense that we can say that Stein uses repetition as the motor behind epistemic writing in which genres are merely functions of specific styles.

Agamben's examinations in *Potentialities* orbit around the problem of names for which there is no definition as they form the foundation of speech. In his essay on Derrida, "Pardes," Agamben tackles what he calls the "White Knight's theorem" based on a Lewis Carroll proposition in *Through the Looking Glass*: "the name of the name is not a name." Here Agamben says:

It is worth noting that this "White Knight's theorem" lies at the basis both of Wittgenstein's thesis according to which "we cannot express through language what expresses *itself* in language" and Milner's linguistic axiom, "the linguistic term has no proper name." In each case, what is essential is that if I want to say an *intentio*, to name the name I will no longer be able to distinguish between word and thing, concept and object, the term and its reference (Agamben, 1999: 213).

It is my contention that, as far as modernist writing is concerned, "naming the name" has to pass through different potential states in which what is actualized is the incompatible. My concern here is with examining to what extent repetition can be said to inform and be employed in epistemic creative writing as a potential to create knowledge only then to dismiss it. Here I have deliberately chosen not to look at representative modernist texts that merely exhibit repetition through a fragmentary form, but texts that engage with defining, where defining is a representation of its own potential.

One of the chief characteristics of epistemic writing is also a concern with how to define things without being too pedantic. Consequently, Stein, while using repetition as a means to both show and represent an *intentio* in its potential to repeat itself, also leaves room to suggest that the fragment's *intentio* shows itself as a resolute proposition on potentiality as such. Indirectly she is, however, concerned with *intentio secunda* which orbits around the questions: what does it mean to signify an *intentio*, what does it mean to signify fragmented writing or fragmentary writing, what does it mean for the fragment to be in a potential state of the fragmentary, and what exactly is the function of repetition for epistemic creative writing?

The interesting aspect of the modernist fragment lies not in its dealing with the difference between the fragment and the fragmentary but in the way this difference opens up a potentiality whose markers – redundancy, repetition, and resoluteness – attempt to show whether discussing any difference is worth the while.

Unlike other modernists, Stein shows a concern with the *idea* of a difference between the fragment and the fragmentary, which she then analyzes, scrutinizes, and dismisses with grand style. The modernist fragment, I argue, is a fragmentary representation of the image in the mirror of difference and definition. The modernist writer is a self-proclaimed literature philosopher. The epistemic writer thus tells herself: I can feel it in my gut that I am an epistemologist. Even if what I hear (from others) may be a different opinion.

I hear it

As mentioned earlier, Gertrude Stein experiments with language and clarity in her book, *How to Write* (written between 1927-1931). The work is a masterpiece of theorizing on style without defining it. Here, Stein's main contention is that writing can be heard through a certain style, a style that waits for the writer to discover on the horizon of knowledge 'how to' write. That is, if style appears as nothing other than a theory insofar as it can be defined, then making use of it, once defined, style itself proves unnecessary in that relation. Hence, Stein's emphasis is not on style as such, but on the meaning of what makes style necessary. Any investigation into the necessity of style becomes an inquiry into the nature of the repetitive potential that writing exhibits independently of the writer's calculations. Says Stein:

> Clarity is of no importance because nobody listens and nobody knows what you mean no matter what you mean, nor how clearly you mean what you mean. But if you have vitality enough of knowing enough of what you mean, somebody and sometime and sometimes a great many will have to realize that you know what you mean and so they will agree that you mean what you know, what you know you mean which is as near as anybody can come to understanding anyone (Stein, 1975: xxv).

Stein's working premise stems from her desire to make writing reflect itself in a repetitive potential. Repetition, in Stein – which situates itself in the difference between a fragment and writing fragmentarily – displays a potential which consists of endowing the text with a conceptual independence that is able to distinguish between different acts: thinking and naming, action and thought. Etymologically, the word "repetition" consists of two acts: "re" (again) and "petitio" (request, or seeking). Here one could make an inference and say that repetition is about "looking twice." The potential for understanding is registered in what one re-sees, or re-registers, in the writing that opposes words to form. For Stein, standing in close proximity to understanding is an elaboration of the fragment which is there – proper to its own improper being – and whose singular presence mediates between action and thought. "It is very difficult to think twice" (27) she says, thus emphasizing the idea that first there is writing which is contained by thought, and then there is writing which is contained by writing.

For Stein, proximity to understanding means working through nonsense in a very commonsensical way. The aim is not that one understand everything. Quite the contrary. "I ask you," she says, "What is knowledge. Of course knowledge is what you know is what you do know" (Stein, 1967: 60). That is to say, one knows already that knowledge begins with a question and ends with a question. One ends up in the enlightened state of not understanding. This is the wisdom of modernism: when one knows what one knows, one does not repeat the knowing, but the potential to know. The epistemic creative writer writes that down.

The epistemic creative writer knows how to combine the intention in creative writing with the knowledge of how to formulate a good question. As Stein puts it: "the question does not come before there is a quotation" (162). First there is the connection and then there is the connection's potential to repeat and be repeated. The effect of repetition is not only indexical, pointing to what comes first and what comes next, but also performative. Questions have styles. They are great or they are small, and they can prompt thinking. In other words, as with Stein, "the great question is can you think a sentence" (1975: 35), can you hear it?

If you can see it, you can be it

One is tempted to ask: can you think a fragment? And why is the fragment good for our understanding of what is at stake in creative epistemic writing? Can one think of a reason why we have fragments which are complete, fragments which are incomplete, 'full' texts which are fragmented – intentionally or unintentionally – fragments that define a context of proximity, fragments that enclose a whole text (the intertextual fragment), fragments that precede other fragments (pretexting fragments)? The list could continue. These fragments are conventionally associated with a period's notion of completion: if the fragment is not defined as a ruin or a constructed ruin, most studies on the fragment settle with calling the fragment Romantic or Ancient, depending on the period in focus.[1]

These fragments almost completely rely on form in the sense that what is manifested at the formal level is, one could say, a potentiality of circumstance. But there is more to the fragment if one shifts the focus from the form/content dichotomy to function. Here I want to argue that repetition is a function of the fragment, and that it maintains the tension between form and content as "sameness," yet without making "sameness" unnecessary. Insofar as the fragment is a marker of sameness, it cannot at the same time be potential. The fragment is thus repetitive. The fragment *is* as it never gets beyond the state of potentially *becoming*.

The fragment as a "paradigm of textuality," to use David Couzens Hoy's denomination, forms a genre which determines its subject according to the way the fragment is finally presented. Here, says Hoy of the various ways fragments are presented

---

[1] Most studies on the fragment provide definitions on the fragment from an intentional point of view. Issues such as the fragment's function, performativity, and agency are not dealt with to the same extent as labelling the fragment according to period or genre. See Marjorie Levinson, *The Romantic Fragment Poem – A Critique of a Form*, (Chapel Hill: University of North Carolina Press, 1986); Thomas McFarland, *Romanticism and the Forms of Ruin – Wordsworth, Coleridge, and Modalities of Fragmentation*, (Princeton: Princeton University Press, 1981); Elisabeth Wanning Harries, *The Unfinished Manner – Essays on the Fragment in the later Eighteen Century*, (Charlottesville and London: University Press of Virginia, 1994). As a counter to this line of thought, see my work: *The Fragment: Towards a History and Poetics of a Performative Genre* (2004).

by their writers as independent of the framework that fragments form on their own:

> If we take Nietzsche's style seriously, and particularly the fragmentary character of his writing as we have it (both because Nietzsche intended some of it to be that way and because he could not complete the projects of the last years), we may want to consider as the paradigm of textuality not the Book, a metaphysical construct, but the fragment (Hoy, 1981: 172).

Hoy, however, engages on the same path as other critics, for whom the difference between the fragment and the fragmentary gives itself as a moment of coercion[2]. My suggestion is that coercion, or other forms of deliberating on this difference can be replaced by potentiality. The difference could thus be seen in another equation where it would be precisely a kind of *intentio secunda* of representation, or "looking twice."

Asserting redundancy – Stein's idea of the unnecessary – opens up the space for repetition as a potential for the text that goes against its grain. The text becomes a fragmentary fragment, or a modernist aphorism. The fragment brought on a collision course with itself is necessarily governed by imagination. Imagination here means style, and as such is able to govern the aphoristic fragment's framework. The fragment that is called fragmentary involves the question of the fragment's literariness which cannot be activated without the reader's hermeneutic engagement. That is to say, whatever the fragment enunciates enters into relation with both, what makes the parameter for that enunciation, and the way the reader engages with it.

---

2 See Paisley Livingston, *Counting Fragments, and Frenhofer's Paradox*, Institut for Filosofi, Skriftserie, no. 17, ed. Steen Wackerhausen (Aarhus: Aarhus University, 1998).

When Agamben talks of the mediaeval interest in distinguishing between *intentio prima*, which designates an object, and *intentio secunda*, which designates a string of signs signifying the *intentio prima*, another sign, he claims that when signs signify signs they cannot designate an *intentio* as such, but an *intentum* (Agamben, 1999: 213). Insofar as we can talk of the fragment's parameter as *intentum*, the fragment escapes what a writer chooses to call it. Escaping nomination, as it were, makes the fragment place itself outside the question of the difference between the fragment and the fragmentary. What the "paradigm of textuality" then opens up to is the creation of a text with no name other than a predicative qualification. As a predicate without a subject, the fragment's name is 'intriguing.' It falls under aesthetic evaluations and involves a degree of subjectivity.

To give an example, how does one read the repetition in Gertrude Stein's: "A rose is a rose is a rose"? Is the "rose" named or nominated in any of the three instances it appears? Is the resistance to the text replaced with an identification of a double discourse that breaks apart into fragments? Is Stein's text part of a fragment in which the idea of a rose is being represented, or is it a nonsense metaphor of which we can only make sense by virtue of its intertext? Leo Stein – Gertrude Stein's brother who never quite understood his sister's style—is on the verge of theorizing the situation when he remarks: "When Jesus said, 'Verily, verily,' the second verily added much to the expression. But if he said, 'Verily, verily, verily, verily, verily, verily, verily, verily,' it wouldn't have been so good" (in Watson, 1991: 49). Redundancy and repetition, while the same, yet different, involve the same degree of style that cannot be measured. What *adds to the expression* is neither too much, nor too little, but exactly as much as is needed – one knows what one knows, and that becomes a repetitive framework for the organization of the space of the text.

The logic of knowing what one knows relies, of course, on a tautological structure. But this is the very point in Stein, namely to draw attention to the arrogance of knowledge when it makes claims to be enlightening even when it is not. In other words, the subtler implication of this critique of knowledge involves the suggestion that when knowledge enter a circuitous system, it ceases to be knowledge and becomes information. Thus we have in Stein a very developed sense of how to value information in the writing process. For Stein, the question that begs an answer is precisely this one: what does it take to make writing experimental, yet also able to capture the cultural *geist* that inspires the experimental element in it? In this sense, we can say that when writing that produces knowledge is more informational rather than knowledgeable, then it relies on a structure of an economical style. 'Keep it simple and go round,' seems to work and it does the job.

The interesting aspect of this kind of simple repetition is its mnemonic quality. Stein points to the general tendency to remember anything that *goes round*, that is circular. A grammatical rule, for example, becomes less of a rule and more of a piece of memory when it is engaged in a roundabout way. Says Stein: "what is grammar when they make it round and round. As round as they are called" [...] "Grammar in continuity" [...] "A grammar of appointment. Disunion. Double-doubling" (Stein, 1975: 57-63). It is clear that the third "rose" adds something to the first, banal statement "a rose is a rose," but since it is the same, it functions as a double and thus marks a division. We can say that the repetition "is a rose," posits the first statement as ambiguous, and is therefore significant. Of course, to say that Gertrude Stein's discourse in general is ambiguous is to say the least. However, I would claim that the lack of connectives does not minimize the significance of internal structural themes – from a stylistic point of view one might argue that significance cannot be attached to something that is missing – but rather enforces the idea that the theme is a manifestation of what is precisely unnecessary. The "rose" discourse can only be addressed imperatively and aphoristically. This insight is also offered obliquely by Nicola Goode Shaughnessy in an analysis of Stein's play *Doctor Faustus Lights the Lights*:

> The main female presence in Doctor Faustus is similarly a projection of Stein, a divided self as her two pairs of names indicate: Marguerite Ida and Helena Annabel. Paradoxically both singular and plural, her (their?) names are themselves subject to dispute: Faustus stresses that 'her name is Marguerite Ida and Helena Annabel' (p. 209), but contradicts himself in dialogue with the dog: 'She will not says Dr Faustus, never, never, never, will her name be Mary Ida and Helena Annabel' (p. 210). Stein foregrounds and interrogates the practice of naming through a form of double double-take, in that the conjunction 'and' which links the names is made central, emphasizing the arbitrary and constructed nature of naming itself as a signifying practice (Shaughnessy, 1994: 173).

Put differently, what one remembers well is the meta-dimension of the phrase. The ability to connect things in a text via memory is for Stein a way of putting into practice what is essential about repetition in order to show what the text's literary potential *means* to signify. This is to say that repetition becomes a *piece* of language that necessarily has the same value and comments on the banal first-order reality that is manifested in the statement that everybody recognizes. Here it should also be emphasized that insofar as repetition itself is arbitrary, it cannot designate a signifying practice as such. The way Stein uses repetition is precisely as a potential, which is, of course, what makes her modernism interesting. The fact that sometimes she does go seven times around goes to show that one knows what one knows. Through this method she demonstrates what Barthes wanted to achieve too: doing literary history without a method and thus be an epistemic creative writer.

Gertrude Stein's modernist fragment that displays a repetitive potential consists of insuring the text with a conceptual independence that is able to distinguish between thinking and naming. Distinguishing between the fragment and the fragmentary becomes a secondary framework to the dynamics of the modernist fragment as a paradigmatic catalogue for naming and thinking. That is to say, the modernist fragment is not characterized solely by the dynamics that develops the fragmentary either in the direction of completeness or incompleteness. Nor is it characterized by the dynamics of the fragment that exhibits either detachment or appropriation, but by a dynamic potential to repeat in a fragment what is contained in the vocabulary of thinking. What characterizes the modernist fragment is its potential to become the unnecessary masterpiece. Working through style as a substitute for the premises that might make ground for a masterpiece is a move away from thinking and an approach to considering banality: so, you want to write?

Repetitive style for Gertrude Stein is the essence of her aphorisms. She challenges these aphorisms at their formal level insofar as verbs rather than nouns drive the aphorisms. When she asks: "what is the difference between a sentence and words?" her immediate answer relates to the impressionistic effect of sentences on words:

> A sentence has been ample [...]
>
> What is the difference between a sentence and a sewn. Pictures are important if they have been followed. Thank you for following. What is the difference between a sentence and a picture. A sentence sends it most about. Most is more than most. Most and best. A sentence is very mainly leave known.
>
> How can a sentence have their hope. This makes it turn around. Leave a sentence in mainly (Stein, 1975: 118-119).

Turning it and us around is what makes Gertrude Stein's modernist fragment an aphoristic performance of, say, Valéry in Blanchot's mirror. But what the mirror reflects back is also the epistemic author at work, as she creatively disposes of what knowledge proposes: namely, that there be insight before claim, and vision before understanding.

> (Valéry said sometime ago that one of the errors of philosophy is to limit itself to *words* and neglect *sentences*: "O philosophers, what should be elucidated is not words... but sentences.") But this does not resolve anything either. The privilege accorded the verb, which reduces the noun to the status of an action that has simply been congealed, leads – even if it impedes the Cratylist option, and makes etymological creation more difficult—to the same, scarcely modified problems: sentences, series of sentences, sentences being born and fading away in one language or in a plurality of languages. As soon as we write we carry these problems around with us, thinking without thinking about them (Blanchot, 1995: 96).

4

GRACE IN SIGHT
LACAN, O'HARA, HOFSTADTER, ROTMAN

Inasmuch as grace is a certain accidental quality, it does not act upon the soul efficiently, but formally, as whiteness makes a surface white.
– Thomas Aquinas, *Summa Theologiae*

If we agree that we can define the epistemic creative writer as the writer who proposes a program but stays away from method, then we can argue that the space between 'the nothing that is' and 'the everything that is' is a space of grace. For Beckett, the epistemic creative writer must work with the breath. Your words must breathe air. What you think is not nearly as important as what you breathe. If your writing breathes words, then your language is a game of grace. Between the randomly falling letters on the whiteness of the page, letters which can go on to form words, there is breathing. Beckett's extraordinary insight is that for words to have power they must acknowledge the space of grace where letters are just letters and writing is nothing. In contrast, for Stein words must acknowledge everything. But this acknowledgement is a negation of all relations. 'Now I write a history of everyone,' she claims while filling page after page with nothing. What is happening? Although this book here is neither a literary history nor a treatise on knowledge in any traditional sense, I want to propose that what is happening in between literary history and epistemology is a valorization of the space of grace. And let grace be understood here as an accidental insight, a space one stumbles upon and where one first loses one's breath only to find it again a moment later. Let us see what happens between nothing and everything and let us see to what extent the unconscious in language can rule a convention. In the following I want to look at a few language theorists, epistemologists, poets who like to count, and mathematicians who say grace when called to sing a praise to inspiration.

The quietude of knowledge

One of Jacques Lacan's most famous statements is that the unconscious is structured like a language. In Lacanian philosophy uncovering the structure of the unconscious through identifying desire as the main vehicle for the constitution of the subject is a project which has the acquisition of knowledge about the self as primary. But while self-knowledge can be thought of as always being finite and limited in relation to self-perception, the process of acquiring knowledge can be thought of as being infinite and unlimited. This being the case, one can infer that if the unconscious has any structure at all, then it is not one which lends itself easily to any limiting hermeneutic imposition. This is due to the fact that, as Lacan also suggested, where signs are concerned, we always mobilize many more of them than we know. Thus what we learn about ourselves rests on what we remember that we don't know that we already know. Taking her cue from Lacan who also stated that the unconscious is "knowledge that can't tolerate one's knowing that one knows" (*Seminar,* 19 February, 1974, unpublished), Shoshana Felman makes the interesting assumption that the unconscious must be some kind of *"unmeant knowledge"* (Felman, 77). Knowledge thought in these terms is thus mediated not only by memory but also by the signs that we mobilize through the body as a means of transport, including thoughts. More specifically, says Felman:

> For knowledge to be spoken, linguistically articulated, it would constitutively have to be supported by the ignorance carried by language, the ignorance of the *excess of signs* that of necessity its language, its articulation – "mobilizes". Thus human knowledge is by definition that which is *untotalizable*, that which rules out any possibility of totalizing what it knows, or of eradicating its own ignorance" (78).

The reason why Lacan was attracted to the methods of reading literature, and the methods of devising specific reading protocols, is because literature, as a form which allows creativity to stream through words which one can arrange structurally, is the form *par excellence* that allows for unconscious forces to surface in a constrained manner. Literature allows for unmeant knowledge to be realized in a manner that combines in equal measure restrained form and unrestrained content. Felman further makes this point clear in her discussion of literature's relation to psychoanalysis and how this relation is mediated by an interminable form of instruction. The mechanism of the vehicle for such mediation is this one: one thinks – metaphysical thoughts or pragmatic ones – and then one teaches. What lies at the core of Felman's argument is the idea that psychoanalytic learning is not something that one finishes with, "acquires" and then "possesses" once and for all. It takes place gradually, it may also happen all of a sudden, and it never ends. Psychoanalytic knowledge in general and psychoanalytic knowledge as it is mediated by literary forms in particular is something that is the result of active work. Knowledge itself, as Felman has it and following Lacan, must be *put to work* in order to generate itself; it must be exercised (Felman, 1987: 81). In terms of relations that cut across disciplines, while literature is the product of thinking to the same extent that philosophy is, it also enjoys a special status, which philosophy doesn't. Says Felman again:

> From a philosophical perspective knowledge is mastery – that which is mastery of its own meaning. Unlike Hegelian philosophy, which believes it knows all that there is to know; unlike Socratic (or contemporary post-Nietzschean) philosophy, which believes it knows it does not know – literature, for its part, knows it knows but does not know the meaning of its knowledge – does not know what it knows (Felman, 1982: 41).

Insofar as Lacanian psychoanalysis can be said to be informed by the desire to be scientifically rigorous, and developing of solutions that rest on the idea that truth can be uncovered and arrived at, it is interesting to observe that when it comes to the relation between psychoanalysis and creativity, what is most intriguing is the idea that creativity stands in an asymmetrical relation to the *whatness* of knowledge, or the meaning of knowledge. In other words, knowledge remains silent on the way in which the mobilized signifiers of language, the symbolic meanings of referents are articulated and arranged. Lacan tried to deal with what I like to call the quietude of knowledge by making recourse to formal approaches to language. And here I don't have structuralist ideas in mind but formal philosophy. For instance, it is now common knowledge that Lacan read everything that the philosopher and epistemologist Jaakko Hintikka wrote. Particularly Hintikka's theory of epistemic knowledge has proved influential. What Lacan takes on board from Hintikka's logic is the idea of recursive structures, repetition, and quotation, all of which can also be said to be elements that literature puts to work, which knowledge exercises actively. According to Hintikka's main argument throughout his entire oeuvre language is based on game-theoretical semantics which can be understood if an interrogative approach to inquiry is exercised. What attracts Lacan to Hintikka is the fact that Hintikka extends the Socratic notion of knowledge acquisition via questioning by introducing the notion of partitioning. In one of his latest works, *Socratic Epistemology,* a collection of new and revised essays that go all the way back to the 60s, Hintikka asserts the following:

> In order to use my knowledge, I must know which possibilities it rules out. In other words, any one scenario must therefore be either incompatible or compatible with what I know, for I am either entitled or not entitled to disregard it. Thus the totality of incompatible scenarios determines what I know and what I do not know, and vice versa. In principle, all that there is to the logic of knowledge is this dichotomy between epistemically impossible and epistemically possible scenarios (Hintikka, 2007: 12).

What for Hintikka is a process of partitioning knowledge according to an agent's attitude which is either compatible or incompatible to the worlds and scenarios within which an agent operates, for Lacan, this type of partitioning which relativizes knowledge to a unified whole is a mode of resisting. Perhaps, here, the best example of the way in which knowledge can also happen when it runs counter to and is not the result of inquiry, thus being deployed in other acquisition strategies, is the saying: 'no pain, no gain.'

According to Lacan knowledge penetrates when it most resists articulation. Agents resist knowledge in silence. Teachers resist knowing that not all students can learn; students resist knowing that they can learn. Yet neither party says a thing as this acknowledgment would ruin the unified image each has of himself. This is Lacan's major point: that knowledge is resisted at all times because it has the potential to destroy the illusion of wholeness. Against this background, the sense that knowledge is transformative is also the sense that knowledge is perverse: it forces the agent to *remember*, as it were, that he or she is already forever split, fragmented, and ruined to pieces. By the same token, it is also for this reason that we assume that literature is transformative, precisely because it opens a door towards self-understanding. This door, however, is never left wide-open, but ajar. One enters it with difficulty, by getting squeezed, quite literally, both physically and mentally.

The paradox of literature is that it combines an awareness of the activity of reading – as an activity which has the recreation and understanding of the meaning of the text as its main scope – with the unconscious sense that arriving at a final truth or interpretation is impossible. This unconscious sense, by virtue of its being both a sense and unconscious manifests itself as a form of quietude, or silence. Thus, if one learns anything, it is through silence that one learns. Words disclose this silence, but only by way of activating memory. Often what is provoked by remembrance, which counters an agent's resistance to knowledge, is guilt, anger, denial, and a "passion for ignorance."[1] Frank O'Hara's poem, "In Memory of my Feelings," which I'll discuss shortly, is an example.

But first, what does it mean to say that knowledge is the Janus-face of silence? That it has two faces? A knowledge that "does not know itself," and a knowledge that "does know itself?" For Lacan, what puts things in motion is the knowledge that does not know itself insofar as it is directly linked to the working of *jouissance*. This has been considered before by scholars such as Felman who is particularly interested in the pedagogical aspect of the relation of knowledge to creativity. Here the claim is that what sustains ambivalence, the double face of knowledge, is the fact that knowledge shapes itself according to an agent's attitude in context. Again, with Hintikka, it is the sum of incompatible scenarios that determine the look of knowledge, or rather the mask of knowledge: what I know and what I don't know. An even better illustration of this is Lacan's statement on how our knowledge of things, or things themselves, acquire the status of knowledge or things as such, by giving an example taken from the world of formal and pure mathematics and an analogy to the myth of the origin of numbers. Says Lacan:

> I propose that you consider the real numerical genesis of two. It is necessary that this two constitute the first integer which is not yet born as a number before the two appears. You have made this

---

[1] See also Alice Pitt, Judith Robertson, and Sharon Todd (1998): "Psychoanalytic Encounters: Putting Pedagogy on the Couch," a special issue of the *Journal of Curriculum Theorizing*.

possible because the *two* is here to grant existence to the first *one*: put *two* in the place of *one*, and consequently in the place of *two* you see *three* appear. What we have here is something which I can call the *mark*. You already have something which is marked or something which is not marked. It is with the first mark that we have the status of the thing (Lacan, 1972: 191).

What Lacan points out in his essay, whose long title I write here in full as I like it, "Of Structure as an Inmixing of an Otherness Prerequisite to any Subject Whatever," is the idea that in order for things to get a status they need to enter a process of repetition. It is through repetition that things and knowledge alike enter a dissemination process which is both circular and infinite. We've had ample examples of this in our analyses of Gertrude Stein's epistemic dynamics. As repetition enables the constitution of the subject – as the subject is forever mirrored in the imaginary – the subject, in turn, enables things to perpetuate themselves, and thus create new possibilities for other imaginary worlds and scenarios.

Psychoanalytical analysis discloses under what conditions knowledge of things and the self in relation to things and events is interminable. Says Lacan further on, consolidating this point: "The first repetition is the only one necessary to explain the genesis of the number, and only one repetition is necessary to constitute the status of the subject" (191). The subject is thus one, and two, and three, through repetition, addition and subtraction, and substitution. The fact that *two* can replace *one* to allow for *three* to appear is an act of continuous reflection and self-reflection akin to a state of being surreal. What is put to work here is the idea that while knowledge that "does not know itself" is nonetheless the creative motor, the fact that it goes somewhere through self-generation makes it acquire its status of having another side, that of "knowing itself."

Jouissance as the work that works is consequently interminably entangled with an analysis of the place of reality against whose background the very idea of infinity is not only grasped but can also unfold. In an essay on surrealism, Ana Balakian made this pertinent observation that: "The infinite is the plane of reality in which combinations that we might call absurd in the normal order of things, or logically impossible are accepted as possible" (Balakian, 1959: 11). In other words, all one needs to do, if and when one is ambivalent about knowledge, both wanting it and resisting it, is count.

Through the grace of combination

In his poetry the New York poet Frank O'Hara is known for counting event after event and detail after detail, with an insistence that recalls the same mechanism of the interrogative approach to inquiry and one which combines desire with reality, as if repeating the Lacanian mantra: "knowledge insists when it most resists." O'Hara thematizes some of Lacan's concerns with knowledge as linguistically articulated against the background of the excess of signs. I now turn to looking particularly at the poem "In Memory of My Feelings" and advance the claim that what the body remembers to remember is that excessive signs have an intentional quietude in them even in the face of loudly articulated knowledge which is yet bound to fall outside totalizing systems of thought and desire. O'Hara's epistemic take on writing is through assessing how much listening is part of a writing act. The epistemic creative writer listens first and then remembers what to write.

Yet critical opinions are divided as to what "In Memory of My Feelings" is about. Marjorie Perloff claims it is about "the fragmentation and the reintegration of the inner-self," while Lytle Shaw insists on the opposite, namely that the poem is about a collective self. I go with this latter argument and Shaw's statement that the poem is about "the larger social concern of how subjects imagine themselves as parts of collectivities within a given moment and historically" (Shaw, 2006: 82). Here Shaw emphasizes the experimental milieu of the surrealists that was of particular influence for O'Hara. Culturally, the only way in which one could account for one's dreams as a set of impossibilities that could be accepted as possible was if one was part of a collectivity that believed in the shared knowledge as the type of knowledge which precisely "does not know itself".

If we are to unpack the implications of Lacan's notions, then we would have to assert that what makes O'Hara's poem worth considering from an epistemic logic point of view is its commonsensical approach to the idea of occasion. One writes about special events in the lives of people one knows. One learns how others incorporate the idea that some knowledge is always consecrated through performative acts – one is that which one performs what others perform – while other knowledge is the result of not knowing itself, the result of an individual creative impetus generated by pure pleasure. On this, what Lacan and O'Hara have in common is the same kind of logic which can be called epistemic, that is, reasoning about knowledge. As the assumption is that one learns quite literally from a well or pool of information one has at hand, the thought that fascinates here is the fact that there may be some knowledge which one acquires via meta-reasoning. O'Hara identifies this meta-level as a form of quietude, and so does Lacan, but what for O'Hara is the site of occasioned creativity that ends in devising strategies for affirming one's agency – I do (marry you), I am (gay) – for Lacan is the site of interminable becoming by negation: I don't (know anything), I'm not (that which I pretend to be). In this regard, if one is to make any sense of what the reasoning about knowledge as that which exceeds knowledge itself entails – for what does it mean to suggest that one is not deterred by endlessness in thinking about infinite becoming? – one must make recourse to the idea of masquerade (an idea that queer theorists such as Judith Butler have borrowed from Lacan). Epistemic knowledge is thus thinking about the logic of empty masks, the belief in the nothing that is, and the performance of quietude.

O'Hara's poem begins with these lines:

My quietness has a man in it, he is transparent
and he carries me quietly, like a gondola, through the streets.
He has several likenesses, like stars and years, like numerals.

My quietness has a number of naked selves,
so many pistols I have borrowed to protect myselves
from creatures who too readily recognize my weapons
and have murder in their heart! (O'Hara, 1995: 252)

The poem entangles transparencies with a number of mythical totem-like figures; from vipers and serpents to the head of the Medusa, from "the dead hunting, and the alive ahunted", from numbering the deaths of relatives to the lives of the multiple selves of the poet speaker. What perspires through such transparencies is the idea that the logic of the knowledge that "does not know itself" is the logic of what O'Hara calls an "algebraic position" in a set that includes the self as a relational self. This position is also the position one assumes in killing off the family so that the symbolic order of things can go back to a real state. In Lacan, it is virtually impossible to return to the Real, the state of pure instinct and pleasure, once one learns the constitutive meaning of negation. In the symbolic realm, we all do like our fathers, we all act according to injunctions that have the "no" into focus. How can one be creative, then? This is a question that both poets and epistemologists alike should keep asking, as this question is also the most dynamic in the relation of inquiry to knowledge acquisition. O'Hara seems to think that he can be creative by activating his sense of numbering, or as he puts it, his "sentimental longing for number." Thus he counts:

>   My 10   my 19,
> my 9,   and the several years. My
> 12 years since they all died, philosophically speaking.
> And now the coolness of the mind
> like a shuttered suite in the Hotel Grand
> where mail arrives at my incognito
>   whose facade
> has been slipping into the Grand Canal for centuries;
> rockets slay over the *sposalizio*,
>   fleeing into night
> from their Chinese memories, and it is a celebration
> the trying desperately to count them as they die.
> But who will stay to be these numbers?
> When all the lights are dead? (254)

Between the listed numbers, O'Hara takes a breath in quietude. There is space on the page between these numbers as if to suggest that one can think about it without the thinking, without the thinking that goes into it, without the thinking about that which puts things to work. This is the space of *jouissance,* or the logic of sense. How one goes from the logic of sense to the logic of knowledge is something that preoccupies O'Hara. I like the suggestion that it is perhaps through grace that one undergoes that journey which is also meant to establish some sort of symmetry between sense and nonsense. Says O'Hara, performing his own dedication of this poem to his friend, the painter Grace Hardigan, whom he also thinks of as one of his other selves:

                        Grace
To be born and live as variously as possible. The conception
of the mask barely suggests the sordid identification.
I am a Hittite in love with a horse. I don't know what blood's
in me I feel like an african prince I am a girl walking downstairs
in a red pleated dress with heels I am a champion taking a fall
I am a jockey with a sprained ass-hole I am the light mist
                            in which a face appears
and it is another face of blonde I am a baboon eating a banana
I am dictator looking at his wife I am a doctor eating a child
and the child's mother smiling I am chinaman climbing a mountain
I am child smelling his father's underwear I am an Indian
sleeping on a scalp
                  and my pony is stamping in the birches,
and I've just caught sight of the *Nina,* the *Pinta* and the *Santa Maria.*
                  What land is this so free? (256)

The poet speaker here learns by watching, and by asking questions. The masks don't answer back, as masks only provide means of identification, not means of intelligence. And yet, their powerful presence is felt as a form of articulated grace. Gazes take turns and thus we read lines which clearly are meant to indicate assessment. How is the other? What can I learn from the other? How can I know the other? Says O'Hara:

> And now it is the serpent's turn.
> I am not quite you, but almost, the opposite of visionary.
> You are coiled around the central figure,
>   the heart
> that bubbles with red ghosts, since to move is to love
> and the scrutiny of all things is syllogistic [...]
>   And yet
> I have forgotten my loves [...]
>   and I have lost what is always and everywhere
> present, the scene of my selves, the occasion of these ruses,
> which I myself and singly must now kill
>   and save the serpent in their midst (256).

Towards the end of the poem, the more memory is activated as that which constitutes the self through the many, and as syllogistic reasoning takes over poetic inspiration, the more there remains a constant in the act of knowing: that at the heart of things is the quietude of grace, and that nothing happens until love moves it. In Frank O'Hara we find a prophetic epistemologist. A seer who can tell us where knowledge is. All we need to do is allow ourselves to stumble over what we can invent. Between nothing and everything there is invention. To invent writing is to propose a program without a method, but keep it a secret for a while. This is the time when writing can consider itself occasioned, and if not, then at least invoke the mystery of numbers; The numbers that make up the sum of the experiences of a writer who learns through writing and of an epistemic creative writer who knows things because he knows paradox. It is my contention that paradox marks the language of the epistemic creative writer more so than it marks the language of poetry. While in poetry or fiction a paradox may be employed in order to highlight the possibility of the improbable, in epistemic creative writing paradox shows the realization of the impossible. At the heart of reasoning about creativity lies the idea that the epistemic writer is not just inspired but also conscious about where this inspiration comes from. He is mature enough, as it were, to be able to go back to a state of innocence. Gertrude Stein's language can be considered in this sense a prime example of the childish approach to metaphysical concerns. Yet, the way in which she formulates her questions opens the door to the paradox of existence. 'I am, because I can make myself dumb,' would be the kind of axiom she would agree with. In another context, we also have examples of such a take on writing in authors who practice academic writing that cuts across creativity and science. Let us look at Douglas Hofstadter.

Stumbling unto grace

Reviewers and critics of Douglas Hofstadter's much acclaimed book, *Gödel, Escher, Bach* (1979), all agree that the concept of invention runs throughout the book's multiple levels of narration. The book's central concern with the question whether machines can think is seen through the lives and ideas of famous mathematician Kurt Gödel, J.S. Bach, and the Dutch illustrator M.C. Escher. What is most known about these three people is their ability to combine simple thought with the creation of complex patterns that culminate either in a paradox or a puzzle. The subtitle of the book itself "A metaphorical fugue on minds and machines in the spirit of Lewis Carroll" gives the reader a hint regarding the different ways in which one can approach aspects of complexity through simplicity and vice versa.

For example, Hofstadter interprets Gödel's complex incompleteness theorem from 1931 through Escher's illustrations of strange loops. Thus, Gödel's theorem which states in Hofstadter's rendition that "all consistent axiomatic formulations of number theory include undecidable propositions" (Hofstadter 1979: 17), is seen through Hofstadter's definition of an Escher loop, which for Hofstadter is "a way of representing an endless process in a finite way" (15). Furthermore Gödel's statement, that it is impossible to design a formal system which would contain all true statements and no false statements, is also seen through Bach's formal compositions which were construed as "relations between separate sections" (28) that create patterns of unity between "true" and "false" beginnings and endings, in other words, strange loops.

What critics have not yet emphasized, however, is the fact that Hofstadter's *Eternal Golden Braid* is a reinvention of invention. The relevance of such a work for our study here is in its proposing that reasoning about knowledge cannot happen unless creativity enters a paradoxical loop. Invoking reason in creative writing is akin to summoning a witness who cannot be sworn. The epistemic creative writer submits willingly to being thrown by what he knows into a recursive structure. He also knows that every time he resurfaces a new aberrant thought is formed that yet makes sense. For, knowledge coming out the other way through the spiral is a poem. I want to use Hofstadter's example of a professor writing about writing but from the perspective of a writer who repeats himself in his reflecting corridors. Similarly, the epistemic creative writer is a writer who stumbles over his own inventions consciously. Furthermore, the epistemic creative writer is also a writer who is surprised all the time at his own acts of inventing without a method. Let us see what the implications of this is for the writing of literature that sings in its continuation of the line of thought about nothing through everything to listening and keeping quiet.

Hofstadter engages in inventing reconfigurations based on the imagination of Gödel, Escher, Bach, Carroll, and Hofstadter himself, which the reader is invited both to imagine and discover. Referring to his style employed throughout the book, the use of fables and dialogues, and the theme of tangled hierarchies and strange loops, which, as he says, "sometimes it will be hidden, other times it will be out in the open; sometimes it will be right side up, other times it will be upside down, or backwards" (10), Hofstadter gives a clear indication as to the nature of inventiveness that his book ultimately deals with on all possible levels. As he puts it: "Quaerendo inveniendis" is my advice to the reader" (10), thus implying that by seeking one will discover the place where invention can take place.

For Hofstadter, the relation between discovery and place is essential insofar as the question of invention falls within the category of its relation to place. For example, Hofstadter's discussions and fictionalizations via Lewis Carroll of Bach's two-part and three-part inventions, illuminate complex, yet simple, processes in aesthetic work: coming upon, stumbling over, and ultimately writing stories out of one's ideas and imagination have a relational function. The etymology of the word invention is here a good starting point. From Latin *in venire,* to come upon something, the word already suggests an element of accident: finding something that is already there. By 1500 the word has come to designate a made up story, whereas it is not until 1531 that the meaning shifts to defining an original device or method (OED). These etymologies all resonate in Bach's, Carroll's, Gödel's and Hofstadter's various inventions.

Looking at the book's fragmented patterns via Derrida's inventions of the 'other' (such as in his discussion of Leibniz and de Man) in this section here I argue that the relation between imagination and inventiveness in Hofstadter is mediated by propositions on incompleteness and their paradoxical relation to 'whole' fragments. The discussion of Hofstadter's book will be followed by a close reading of more recent study on a related topic in Brian Rotman's critical work *Becoming Beside Ourselves: The Alphabet, Ghosts, and Distributed Human Being* (2008). This book takes issue with how creative inventiveness transcends the boundaries of institutionalized discourse. Both these works also engage with method, the method of creative writing across academic disciplines, but blur the distinctions between the self-legitimation of the systematic academic writing process and that of potential for the creative process.

My aim then is to suggest that mental and aesthetic representations involve and draw upon a poetics of embedding – each mental image embeds its representation – thus making invention the matrix of the imagination. And why is this relevant for the writing which creates knowledge? Simply because writing relies on embedding purely geometrical forms – we recognize patters – often following a dialogical structure à la Socrates, or logical propositions that have space in focus, or rather operate with spatial forms. We have already seen how this comes to manifestation in Lacan's ideas about how we mobilize signs. The question of knowing, under which condition the proposition: 'now I write' is true, follows implicitly another question, especially where an academic creative writer is concerned – and Hofstadter embodies both capacities – namely, 'do I want to think or do I want to write?' Of course, this does not mean to suggest that there is writing that is ever devoid of some form of reflection, but in this context here, just how creative an academic can allow himself to be is relevant to consider, especially if creativity means allowing animals to speak, music to enunciate structures, and drawing to hunt. Thus, this question presupposes a straightforward answer regarding the question of what kind of space one inhabits and says yes to: 'yes' to the academic discourse and 'no' to fictionalizing; 'yes' to the academic discourse and SOME fictionalizing, or 'yes' to fictionalize it *all* and then give it the status of research.

As in both worlds, the world of logos and the world of mythos gatekeepers do their jobs, is it noteworthy to observe what strategies a writer uses when wanting to bypass conventions and thus perhaps answer a straightforward question that requires a 'yes' or a 'no' with a 'maybe.' Thus we may have this scenario that an academic may face by way of soliloquizing with himself when asking himself: 'in this research-based work, do I want to be an academic or a fiction writer?' If the writer merely answers yes, then the result of what the writer says yes to is easily marked by the very materiality of writing within a specific genre that will announce itself. But even when the writer says no, writing can still happen according to the precepts of one of the genres, and one which the writer may not set out consciously to make up his mind about using. There is, however, a different apprehension of what is going on, both in terms of agency and in terms of what one thinks is either excluded from or included in the act of writing, whether consciously or more unconsciously done. This latter situation, when unconscious writing happens, as it were, more often then not, also answers in the affirmative the following question: 'do I want to write or do I want to think?' But answering this with a 'yes' is often ambiguous, for what does one say 'yes' to: writing, or thinking? Inventing perhaps.

In logic making a distinction between inclusive disjunction (that which remains true if either or both of its arguments are true) and exclusive disjunction (that which is true if only one but not both of its arguments are true, and is false if neither or both are true) indicates that choosing to do one act over the other is exclusive – either you write or you think – a writer's affirmative answer to an either/or question suggests inclusiveness. My claim is that en epistemic creative writer would prefer both any time. An epistemic creative writer writes from within this paradoxical possibility, of always answering with a 'yes' to a question about choice.

What becomes even more interesting is the state when a creative academic answers the either/or question with a maybe. Thus, the proposition: 'do I want to write or think? – Maybe', is what calls for assessing to what extent such stretched creativity is useful in terms of what one learns about one's own craft first, but also about the world one is writing about. Logically speaking there is no explanation, unless we want to axiomatize undecidability. Following Urquhart, there is some logic with a finite frame property that is undecidable ("maybe one or the other"), such as we have it the following proposition: for any subset X of ω there exists a logic Ax with the finite frame property, such that Ax has the same "degree of unsolvability as X" (in Goldblatt, 1992: 58). Basically this means that if one answers an either/or question with a yes, no, or even a maybe, one shows a preference for spatial logics that allows for incomplete structures. In other words, one departs from the binary structure of the crossroad. Here, I want to pursue this line of thought in language games – first in Hofstadter's work and then in Rotman's – with view to answering this question: what does it mean to invent against the background of writing which presents itself as the result of a 'maybe' situation? In other words: 'am I making any sense?' Becket asked that, and so did all the others mentioned in this study so far. The intuitive claim is that an academic creative writer always finds himself in the bind of the structural 'either you are this or you are that', an academic or a fiction writer. Yet, what binds the seemingly incompatible and rigid state of either/or is precisely the more malleable 'maybe' or the idea that any either/or situation can be invented as an 'other.'

Between nothing and everything there is maybe

In his seminal article "Psyche: Inventions of the Other" Jacques Derrida emphasizes an aspect of the word invention claiming that invention is linked to a self-referential system in which the event of coming upon something is contingent on topos. While the act of invention can take place only once, according to Derrida, placing one's finding in context is a question of method. Taking his point of departure in trying to invent something that is already there, namely the work of Paul de Man – whose work in Derrida's essay is deferred recursively while still managing to create a context for Derrida's thoughts on the idea of invention – Derrida points to three meanings of the word invention in French. First, invention is the capacity to invent or the natural genius for inventing, or inventiveness; second, invention is the experience of inventing, or the "first time" of the new event; and third, invention is that which designates the invented thing. Thus we have a tension not only between the container and the contained, form and content, but also between form and function. Here Derrida identifies two competing meanings inherent in each of the three meanings of invention:

> "first time", the event of a *discovery*, the invention of what was already there and came into view as an existence or as a meaning and truth;

> the productive invention of a technical apparatus that was not already there as such. In this case the inventor gave it a *place* upon *finding it*, whereas in the former case its place was found there where it was already *located* (Derrida 1989: 49).

Invention then operates on two levels: on the one hand, it points to the act of unveiling discovery, and on the other hand, it involves production. Where discovery is concerned, the fact that stumbling upon something takes place accidentally suggests that invention happens in no time, as it were. Invention as production, on the other hand, is dependent on time insofar as it requires recognition and hence institutionalization. This leads Derrida to assume that invention is linked to the discovery of a general truth insofar as the object of discovery has to already be there, that is, it has to have a location which everybody can identify. The art of inventing then, or as he puts it, *"ars inveniendi* concerns the *searching* as well as the *finding"* (50). However, as one does not want to merely find a truth that is already there, it is necessary to invent a research program, or a method, "an analytic method that is called the method of invention" (50). Thus Derrida contends that "the truth that we must *find* there where it *is found*, the truth to be invented, is first of all the nature of our *relation* to the thing itself and not the nature of the thing itself" (51).

Derrida's discussion of Leibniz's interpretation of invention as seen in relation to truth, and in fact in relation to relation, as it were, is of relevance here when one considers Hofstadter's repeated insistence that invention is based on the formulation of propositions and that these propositions consist of certain truths. For Hofstadter, our relational relation to truth, or the thing to be invented, has to have proof, even if proof itself proves the incompleteness of truth, such as we have it in the case of Gödel's criticism of Bertrand Russell's theory of types in *Principia Mathematica* (1910–1913) which was developed as an attempt to get rid of all the paradoxes and strange loops in a formal system. Hofstadter defines proof as "demonstrations within fixed systems of propositions" and points out that the revolutionary aspect in Gödel's theorem consisted not in saying that Russell's statement of number theory was false, but saying that the statement of number theory did not have any proof. What Gödel then did was to find a truth there where it was already found, and therefore *invent* that Russell's fixed system, that of *Principia Mahtematica,* was incomplete. Thus what Gödel demonstrated was, as Hofstadter renders it, the fact that "there are true statements of number theory which its methods of proof are too week to demonstrate," and that "provability is a weaker notion than truth, no matter what axiomatic system is involved (Hofstadter, 1979: 18-19).

Gödel is for Hofstadter an inventor of truth. Says Derrida following Leibniz:

> When Leibiniz speaks of the "inventors of truth", we must recall [...] that he means the producers of propositions and not just sources of revelation. The truth qualifies the connection of subject and predicate. A person has never invented something, that is, a thing. In short, no one has ever invented anything. Nor has anyone invented an essence of things in this new universe of discourse, but only truth as a proposition. And this logico-discursive mechanism can be called *technè* in the broad sense. Why? For there to be invention, the condition of a certain generality must be met, and the production of a certain objective ideality (or ideal objectivity) must occasion recurrent operations, thus a utilizable apparatus. If the act of invention can take place only once, the invented artifact must be essentially repeatable, transmissible and transposable. The two extreme types of invented things, the mechanical apparatus on the one hand, the fictional or poetic narrative on the other, imply both a first time and every time, the inaugural event and iterability. Once invented, so to speak, invention is invented only if repetition, generality, common availability, and thus publicity are introduced or promised in the structure of the first time (Derrida 1989: 51).

Derrida thus points to an essential aspect of invention, namely, its institutional status, insofar as producing propositions relies on formal analysis and on procedure. When Derrida refers to repetition, transmission and transposition, he implies that what is inherently characteristic of invention is the tension between form, here the fictional or poetic narrative that scrutinizes the presence of motifs, counter-motifs, sequences, and developments, and method in the sense that what is emphasized in invention is the process whereby the poetic narrative is modified and thus turned into a model of inventiveness. Invention as an elaboration upon simple ideas is inventive when a process of repetition, transmission and transposition of these ideas takes place.

Hofstadter's book can be said to operate with all these strategies. His own inventions such as mathematical formulae, theorems, and axioms, while based on the elaboration upon themes, also counter and meta-develop these themes by re-articulating them as new. The technical expositions of set-theory, combined with Escher's visual illustrations of Bach's inventive repositions of simple ideas in his two and three part inventions culminate in the creation of 21 dialogues written in the form of fables. The first dialogue occurs in the first chapter and borrows the title of Bach's invention, more precisely the "Three-Part Invention."

Here Hofstadter explores Zeno's paradox of motion with its two theorems, namely that "motion is inherently impossible" and "motion unexists." Hofstadter repeats not only Bach's title, which he uses as a motif for his form but also Lewis Carroll's protagonists Achilles and Tortoise, whom Carroll himself borrowed from Zeno. The dialogue between these two unlike figures is shaped in Carroll's "Two-Part Invention" as a process which re-arranges the argument in Euclid's theorem and transforms the theorem into a paradox. While the first dialogue, the "Three-Part Invention," is mainly concerned with form, as Hofstadter's two protagonists plus Zeno himself engage in an elaboration and demonstration of Zeno's paradox, Carroll's "Two-Part Invention" is concerned mainly with process as the two protagonists engage in an elaboration of Euclid's theorem, yet whose final demonstration is postponed. Whereas the first dialogue posits invention as an example of reasoning in syllogistic form, the second dialogue offers an example of inventiveness insofar as it investigates the relation between reasoning, reasoning about reasoning, and reasoning about reasoning about reasoning. This regression *en abyme* of reasoning which is entangled with both invention and inventiveness shows that imagination itself is a relational form whose function is to communicate hypothetical variants of invention. "The Two-Part Invention," then, functions as an analog to Zeno's paradox about the impossibility of motion presented in the "Three-Part Invention" and on the possible consequences of imagining that impossibility.

These first two dialogues called invention set the tone for the rest of Hofstadter's dialogues which combine both form and process in an attempt to strike a balance between the two. And the fact that they are all construed as fables is not without significance. Going back to Derrida's rendering of Leibniz's thoughts in *New Essays Concerning Human Understanding*, one of the main tenets in Leibniz's expositions is that invention, insofar as it deals with a high degree of probability, had better be anchored in an examination of "games of chance." What invention, then, produces is for Leibniz a relation between discovery, searching, pure chance, and formal chance. Here, it is interesting to note what Derrida extracts from Leibniz's call for "a new species of logic," and from Leibniz's wish and conviction that "a clever mathematician would produce a substantial work, well detailed and well reasoned, on all sorts of games, as that would be very useful for perfecting the art of invention" (Leibniz in Godzich 1989: 56). Says Derrida, first claiming that what Leibiniz refers to when he says 'games,' is in reality a mirror-game:

> The game here occupies the place of a psyche that would send back to man's inventiveness the best image of his truth. As through a fable in images, the game states or reveals a truth. That does not contradict the principle of programmatic rationality or of the *ars inveniendi* as the enactment of the principle of reason, but illustrates its "new species of logic," the one that integrates the calculation of probabilities.
>
> One of the paradoxes of this new *ars inveniendi* is that it both liberates the imagination and liberates *from* it. It passes beyond the imagination and passes through it (57).

Hofstadter's fables construed in the didactic spirit of Bach's inventions counter in counterpoint the idea of invention as form and inventiveness as process. Discussions on inventiveness center on reasoning and method whereas invention is seen through the imagination of mathematical geniuses. The book's 21 fables are metaphorical dialogues which counterpoint the book's 20 chapters. What is interesting about these dialogues, which all have the names of Bach's musical works, is the way in which they reinforce the various paradoxes Hofstadter is interested in, including variants thereof, such as, for example, infinite regress in Lewis Carroll's paradox. The longest of these dialogues, which otherwise do not fill more than two, three pages, is "Little Harmonic Labyrinth." This dialogue acts as Derrida's *ars inveniendi* and shows how infinite regress both liberates the imagination and liberates from the imagination.

Achilles and the Tortoise find themselves on a trip to Coney Island and decide to take a ride on the Ferris Wheel. The Tortoise had a prediction of good fortune from a fortuneteller and is filled with anticipation when they are invited to go for an "Unexpected surprise." At the end of the ride, as they encounter a monster-like creature named Goodfortune ready to cook the Tortoise and eat it, they ponder over what chance and good fortune they might have in order to escape. Awaiting their fate in the monster's living room who had invited them to eat popcorn while himself preparing the sauce in which to cook the Tortoise, they stumble over a book entitled *Provocative Adventures of Achilles and the Tortoise taking place in Sundry Spots of the Globe*. While aware of their status as inventions of Zeno, Carroll, and Hofstadter in the first two dialogues, the "Three- and Two-Part Inventions," in the "Little Harmonic Labyrinth" the two protagonists are completely ignorant of the isomorphism between their story and the story they are about to read. Thus, when reading the book featuring an adventure called Djinn and Tonic, the Tortoise and Achilles decide to take on the roles of the Tortoise and Achilles in the book.

In the Djinn and Tonic story, Achilles had invited the Tortoise to see his collection of Escher drawings. Upon seeing Escher's illustration entitled *Convex and Concave* (1955), the Tortoise tells the story about his own adventures every time he would drink a potion that would transport him into one of Escher's worlds. Offering Achilles a guided tour in Escher's two internally consistent worlds, which, "when juxtaposed make a completely inconsistent composite world" (105), the Tortoise explains how by drinking a tonic they can return back to where they started. Soon thereafter they both find themselves sailing down a canal in a gondola. Not being so sure of whether it is a good idea to continue, they decide to jump out and exit through one of Escher's frames. As the Tortoise explains, once in one of Escher's drawings, one can always change the picture by going through one of the regressive and recurrent frame exits. Thus, once in *Convex and Concave*, and tempted to steal the lamp guarded by the lizards, Achilles finds himself holding the lamp in his hands after having fallen through a hole which turns out to be a groove in a record of Bach's *Little Harmonic Labyrinth*. The two protagonists are thus entangled recursively in the Labyrinth. From the tertiary level of the labyrinth the Tortoise explains that the lamp has a genie in it, and that this genie is able to grant three wishes to whoever holds the lamp. The following initial exchange takes place:

> *Tortoise*: [...] Go ahead Achilles, take the first wish.
>
> *Achilles*: Wow! But what should I wish? Oh I know! It's what I thought of the first time I read the Arabian Nights (that collection of silly (and nested) tales) – I wish that I had a HUNDRED wishes, instead of just three. Pretty clever, eh, Mr. T? I bet YOU never would have thought of that trick. I always wondered why those dopey people in the stories never tried it themselves.
>
> *Tortoise*: Maybe now you'll find out the answer.
>
> *Genie*: I am sorry Achilles, but I don't grant meta-wishes.
>
> *Achilles*: I wish you'd tell me what a "meta-wish" is!

> *Genie*: But THAT is a meta-meta-wish, Achilles—and I don't grant them either (110).

The story goes on to explain the notion of recursive and nested structures and modulations in music, which leaves both the reader and the listener "dangling," as Hofstadter puts it, without resolution. As Hofstadter explains, modulation is a setting up of a temporary goal without resolution. Paradoxically however, although the genie manages to grant Achilles a meta-wish by making recourse to a meta-lamp and a meta-genie, resolution is impossible to achieve, insofar as Achilles's wish gets to be formulated as a "Typeless wish" which reads: "I wish my wish would not be granted." As a consequence of Achilles's wish the two protagonists get thrown out of the story, or the story's contextual system. Achilles's wish thus created a paradox, which crashed the story. As the Tortoise explains: "for that Typeless wish to be granted, it had to be denied – yet not to grant it would be to grant it" (115-116).

What we can infer from this story is that, for Hofstadter, invention functions as a Typeless wish while inventiveness functions as an incomplete system. The recursions in the dialogue are analogs of invention as form and inventiveness as process. Invention as form is based on formulating definitions that may be recursive, while inventiveness as process points to incompleteness insofar as the imagination is able to create alternative variations of what is invented. Of recursive definitions says Hofstadter:

> Sometimes recursion seems to brush paradox very closely. For example there are recursive definitions. Such a definition may give the casual viewer the impression that something is being de-

fined in terms of *itself*. That would be circular and lead to infinite regress, if not to paradox proper. Actually a recursive definition never defines something in terms of itself but always in terms of *simpler versions* of itself (127).

The implication of the assumption that invention can also be elaborated as a typeless fragment is that in a recursive system one can prove the unknowability of truth. The fact that invention denotes stumbling upon something, finding something that is already there, furthermore leads to the assumption that invention perpetuates itself in fragments. What is remarkable about Hofstadter's book is the fact that he creates a form that locates the book within random fragments which further create patterns for the relation between imagination and inventiveness. Invention itself thus becomes the matrix of imagination insofar as invention is intertwined with the fictional world of the fables. As such, invention occupies the place between imagination and invention as form by inhabiting them both. The fictions that Hofstadter writes are thus based on creating a relation of sameness between formulating incompleteness and demonstrating it. The fact that we can formally have inventions in two parts, three parts, or an infinite number of parts demonstrates that we can formulate performative approaches to discourse by fragments. On invention, one can only write in fragments as did Beckett and Stein, Lacan, Hofstadter and Derrida, by making recourse to the foremost characteristic of the fragment, which is to open itself unto potential. It is for this reason that invention as form almost always comes in dialogue and searching questions. As when Hofstadter's last word "Ricercar" is given back to Bach, and Derrida asks in dialogue with his imaginary reader:

What am I able to invent again, you wondered at the beginning, when it was a fable.

And to be sure you have seen nothing come.

The other, that's no longer inventable.

"What do you mean by that? That the other will have been only an invention, the invention of the other?"

"No, that the other is what is never inventable and will never have waited for your invention. The call of the other is a call to come, and that happens only in multiple voices." (Derrida, 1989: 62)

We can perhaps appropriately say that invention is a fugue on inventiveness, that invention is a form of sameness in its difference which is precisely what gives stumbling the status of grace.

How do you spell G-R-A-C-E?

Brian Rotman's book *Becoming Beside Ourselves: The alphabet, Ghosts, and Distributed Human Being* (2008), ends befittingly with a number of hypothetical situations. As the book revolves around the question of what to do with the archaic, old-fashioned, and now useless system of alphabetization, from reason to affect, Rotman's attempt to envisage a new system of other possibilities that would end "the era of alphabetic graphism" is worth considering. Already the idea of the possible replacing certainty is an interesting idea, particularly if one is not familiar with the scientific discourse that cuts across pure mathematics, or the area in mathematics that deals with infinity, and digitalized technology that challenges the cultural prestige and dominant position of what Rotman calls "infinistic mathematics." If we thus take it from the end, as Rotman would probably approve, let us make the point that a book such as this one performs what it preaches, in terms of tackling head-on the interdisciplinary approach to the question of subjectivity, the person, or rather, the agent, and creative writing, all emphasizing the privileged and dominant position of the singular agent over the pluralistic agent as embodying a multitude of relations, or as announced in the title, agent as distributed human being. As such, however, the book can only make sense in a system in which the letter of the alphabet still rules the world, if it presents itself as a gesture, or rather, if it advances its argument about the plausibility of the possible over the certain as a gesture towards a potential.

Entangling the influence of Christian and Judaic doctrines for the advancement of the idea of monotheism, Rotman basically makes the Marxist claim that if only we would forget for a while about religion, then we would experience what it means to live in a state of the 'meanwhile.' As this 'meanwhile' can bring about a remediation of monotheism, it can thus open the space for reconsidering what concepts such as belief and faith may hold for the agent who is distributed, or who is 'many.' But let us remind ourselves first of where we are at this point and what we are trying to pursue, however linearly, for now: we went from 'nothing' to 'everything', and after a stint at the recursive crossroad of the 'maybe', logically speaking we now need to say something about what we 'meanwhile' need to consider before making a final choice.

Back to the end of Rotman's book. After a quick series of concluding remarks that have to do with what we can imagine is possible at the end of the entire tradition that has induced, or rather forced metaphysics into the straight-jacket of the writing culture, Rotman writes in the last paragraph, beginning with, yet also by way of returning to, two words which he uses emblematically, constantly, and uncompromisingly throughout the book, namely, 'the possible' and 'the meanwhile':

> Possible… but, meanwhile, here in the alphabetic, all-too-archaic present, science in the form of physics dreams of a 'God particle' and pursues a monadic Grand Theory of Everything; a God-saturated America in thrall to the Bible remains convinced of its exceptional and special relation to the monobeing; and Muslims fight holy wars against infidels who dare insult God's one true prophet (137).

Even without having read Rotman's book in its entirety, one can make the following inference from this very paragraph: that the ghosts of doctrinary and ideological ideas revolving around the constitution of subjective consciousness as that which relies on constructions of the inside of the real world, rather than beside it, and hence symbolic representations as 'really' is the case, must be put to rest. How one achieves this goal is what preoccupies Rotman. The book thus goes from considering theories of cognitive evolution – such as the development of the neural system as an alphabetized system of symbolic relations in which the self emerges always as symbolic, and is hence always virtual rather than real – to technologized mathematics as the gate towards considering the idea of parallel selves that emerge precisely within, yet also against the background of the ghost-world in which disembodied selves hover a-temporally over past forms of representations as well as future ones.

The idea is that the ghost is not a thing of representation but of enactment, which Rotman sees as an allegory for the existence of a parallel world of senses ruled by gesture to the world of reason ruled by convention. In this academic study, Rotman, however, allows himself to turn everything from a shadow into a ghost, following Shakespeare in Hamlet: "A dream itself is but a shadow," and indicating that the very distinction between doing academic work and writing a work of fiction is but an illusion. All is fiction. As is the case with pure mathematics that starts with the most gobbledygook ideas, all imaginary notions can also find proof in a symbolic language and thus be raised to the status of true statements in the real world. So, the relevance of mentioning such a work here has to do with Rotman's primary suggestion that as academics, we must begin with what is possible, what is in the meanwhile and the maybe of this or that, and end somewhere in the imaginary, so that we can start again.

But let us have a brief look at what is happening in *Becoming Beside Ourselves* and what it tells us about the epistemic creative writer. The book follows a tripartite structure. Part I and Part II each consists of two sections. Between them, we find an Interlude, consisting of just one chapter on more explicit mathematics. While Part I and Part II can be seen as instances of an analog world, the Interlude functions as an interstice for digitalized technology. This middle section can also be perceived as a performative act, that of a gesture, meant to enhance the idea that forms of communication are always mediated by sets of reductions: the reduction of the idea of becoming to being; an other, or pluri-selfhood to individual selfhood; multi-consciousness to singular consciousness; instances of the a-temporal or the 'meanwhile' to past and present; gesture to the alphabet. What Rotman sets out to do in his book is investigate the consequences of a reversal of these reductions, and look not only at how all media configure what they mediate, but also at what configuration and mediation each consists of in itself, if potentially removed from the context in which they are grounded by definition.

The three epigraphs beginning the book also support this idea, as they all enhance and perform simultaneously the potential passage from the dominance of the word to gesture, real world to symbolic world, counting to counter-counting, linear logic to the law of the excluded middle, and the material body to the immaterial ghost. The epigraphs are all attempts at formulating not only definitions of the dynamics of becoming, but also of being beside topos, as it were, seeing selfhood as a cultural and mathematical problem. They also suggest the implications of articulating alternative states for what can be perceived as the world's interminable discourses. Through these fragments, the reader instantly becomes acquainted with Rotman's methodologies all formulated along the lines of what can be thought of as off-beat, queer, and counter-evolutionistic poststructuralism. Thus we go from the signposts signaling shifts, fluid connections, and unending answers to unending questions formulated by Deleuze and Guattari, Eve Kosofski Sedgwick, and Raymond Barlow. On "becoming" say the first epigraph:

> Becoming is certainly not imitating, or identifying with something; neither is it regressing-progressing; neither is it corresponding, establishing corresponding relations; neither is it producing, producing a filiation or producing through filiation. Becoming is a

verb with a consistency all its own; it does not reduce to, or lead back to, "appearing," "being," "equalling," or "producing" (4).

The philosopher of 'the beside' tunes in in a parallel fragment – also typographically so rendered on the page – and thus intones, also by way of pointing to the aesthetic quality of concepts:

> Beside is an interesting preposition [...] because there is nothing dualistic about it; a number of elements may lie alongside each other, though not an infinity of them. Beside permits a spacious agnosticism about several of the linear logics that enforce dualistic thinking: noncontradiction or the law of the excluded middle, cause versus effect, subject versus object [...] Beside comprises a wide range of desiring, identifying, representing, repelling, paralleling, differentiating, rivalling, leaning, twisting, mimicking, withdrawing, attracting, aggressing, wrapping, and other relations (4).

To this, one can read the third epigraph from Barlow as a putting into motion the very idea of problematizing what motion itself is in relation to agency:

> But who is this "self"... and why is it at this particular juncture in the history of Western societies the very identity of the self becomes problematic? (5)

Now, there is a reason why I choose to quote from the marginal discourse of the paratext. Firstly, because Rotman's book invites the reader to adopt the very same gesture he makes, namely the one towards acknowledging 'the beside,' and secondly, because the key concepts that the epigraphs revolve around constitute in fact the backbone for all notions that Rotman develops thematically and then employs not only rigorously, but also efficiently in his own arguments. The book, in this sense, can be said to be as much about theories on the distributed human being, as it is about the distribution of concepts beside concepts.

Structurally, between 'becoming' and 'ourselves' there is, quite literally, an interlude; the interlude of 'the meanwhile' where Rotman considers going from the concept of the human – as formulated by a grammatology deployed within, distributed, and disseminated through the alphabet – to a gesture of dismissal which begins as a necessary condition for the re-assessment of the immaterial body, so that an understanding of the body without organs, for instance, – an idea imported from Deleuze – can be articulated.

The body thus submits to a set of re-mediations which have agency into focus. First, the body is seen as the result of indexical and iconic representational processes. Here, the emblematic phrase that captures subjectivity could be: 'I point to myself and others, therefore I am.' In other words, the agent here is the cogito, or one's mind. Then the body is considered as the result of abstracting from actual representation in which the body is paradoxically caught in a symbolic relation. The virtual and thus 'more real' body takes over the cogito as an external relation. The agent here is the body itself, and the phrase that we can employ to characterize this re-mediation could be this one: 'I'm wired, therefore I am.' In the third stage, the stage where Rotman is preoccupied with the immaterial ghost, one is invited to make the inference that insofar as the body is *not* and therefore it *is* precisely, what becomes redundant is the very idea of causality. Passing the causal 'therefore' through the 'meanwhile' suggests that if there is an agent here, then it is geometry itself. The 'meanwhile' indicates that if nothing happens here, a lot of things happen simultaneously with this nothing in the parallel worlds to the meanwhile.

Rotman's background as a mathematician, writing about such concepts as nothingness and infinity, does not deny itself at this point. The *Interlude,* which discusses math 'in the meanwhile' is also the chapter that is most fascinating as it opens towards the path on which the ghost treads, but as the ghost does, without leaving a trace. Taking his cue from the phenomenology of Maurice Merleau-Ponty and the mathematics of Gilles Châtelet, Rotman asserts that geometry is important for the "thinking flesh," to the extent that it provides a link for situating the body as a diagram between spatial logic, gesture, and the mathematization of space in which infinite possibilities are seen in a constant relation to gesture. As Rotman sees gesture as non referential, and, following Châtelet, as a "disciplined distribution of mobility" that enables one to know things before one knows them via intuition, he thus asserts that:

> [G]esture is outside of the domain of the sign insofar as signs are coded and call for a hermeneutics, an interpretive apparatus separable from, and in place prior to, the act of signification. Rather, the mode of action of gesture is enactive, exterior to anything prior to its own performance: it works through bodily executed events, creating meaning and mathematical significance "before one knows it" (36).

That mathematics is there to confirm that which is precisely not a concrete science is something that attracts Rotman. Central to his argument throughout the whole book is the idea that mathematics offers two modes of converting what Châtelet calls "the disciplined mobility of the body" into signs. For Rotman there is thus a movement which can be calculated from the body to a sense, or rather, senses, which is not reducible to sight. Thus he claims that the disciplined body is transduced into signs:

> [V]ia metaphors which "shed their skin" to become symbolic operations such as adding numbers; and capturizing it, freezing mobility in mid-flight to form a diagram [...] the source of mathematics is not itself mathematical; it arises from what Châtelet calls 'ruminative' or 'contemplative' and on occasions 'metaphysical' thought. It corresponds to what most mathematicians refer to simply (and opaquely) as 'intuition': the hunches, instincts, premonitions, convictions of certainty without evidence, and numerous other gut feelings that seem to hover over any engagement with the subject (37-38).

What makes Rotman's book a valuable essay on human subjectivity as it has particular relevance for our understanding of the epistemic creative writer is precisely this type of argumentation which takes into account the unreasonable element in reason, and ultimately claiming that if there is hope for us as a human species it is not because we can engage in calculating and predicting what can be seen, but because we can make a leap of faith and thus believe in what cannot be seen, or that for which there is no proof, technologically speaking. The argument is also that the best technology around is never the result of rational moves, but irrational ones, accidents, stumbles, and the like. This emphasizes not so much how subjectivity can be deployed in an algebraic dimension, as it were, when we can basically count our shifting identities by using addition and subtraction, but rather, and more so, how subjectivity is based on more complex relations which can be explained better via mathematical analysis, which, unlike algebra, is concerned with change and continuity.

Thus Rotman asks some seminal questions: What happens when the self becomes beside itself via a disembodied body as a result of the body being removed from communication? What is the function, precisely, of disembodied agencies in the face of losing God, religion, and some other such authoritative powers? Here he proposes that we shift our attention from what he calls the "lettered self" constituted through inscriptions in books, rules and conventions set up by sacred texts, to immaterial acts, such as silence. Here he suggests that we must value the importance of gesture, as signifying technologies also enable us to do; look, for instance, for infinity inside the computer.

The Deleuzian concept of the "agent-as-assemblage" has a parallel and analogous function to mathematics for the way in which Rotman understands what is at stake in the difference between mathematical imagining and mathematical 'reasoning' in relation to the way in which technology, or rather the computer, reconfigures both mathematical and human reality, namely not through a logic of representation but rather through a logic of enactment. What comes to our rescue is thus, again, the ghost. Especially Cantor's. Georg Cantor's infinite arithmetic and the theory of infinite sets inform the whole of Rotman's call for pluralized selves. As one such, if one can imagine oneself as a pluralized self, one is free to wonder why Rotman makes so many references to music in his book. My hunch is that if he continues a tradition here, one which has the significance of real numbers in sight as a love relation between man, machine, and the cosmos, then it is because of a singing tradition. This Jew has not yet left the building. He's still in there singing, embodying the ultimate *hazzan*, paying homage to the cantor.

In this study here I find it useful to look at how 'creative' scientists complement what the 'creative' humanist is trying to formulate at the junction between doing academic stuff and not making any claims to knowledge. To write without a method while using the creative process as a method is, in a way, a possibility to try out different states of embodiment and disembodiement. Only so can we understand why we even want to bother with pushing the margins of gatekeeping. We'll look more at this in the chapter on Kathy Acker to get a fuller sense of how we can employ Rotman's ideas for politicizing the epistemic creative writer.

Meanwhile, if we are to extrapolate a remark on the significance of these works, Hofstadter's and Rotman's, for the way in which an epistemology of creative writing can be devised according to precepts which allow for invention to take over only so that we can arrive at the inconclusive statement that that which creates knowledge is intuition, then we can further assume that the writing which produces knowledge, both as a method and as a process, through invention and inventiveness, necessarily must pass thorough an evaluation of sound, or structural music, as that is what comes closest to understanding the silent call of the gut, or the hunch.

Although neither Hofstadter nor Rotman mentions it, with the rise of the scientific discourse, some time around Newton's time, silence was instituted in academic institutions that were producing knowledge with view to astonish. This is not a bad thing in itself, if only people had not forgotten to communicate their astonishment in turn. Just look at Beckett again. He is one of the first writers to seriously consider the significance of silence for any epistemic creative act. In this context here, and while tuning into what the mathematicians are trying to tell us, we suddenly get an even better sense of what he meant when he shouted: Shut up. Keep quiet. And if you can't do that, then, hum!

Those familiar with the renaissance and pre-renaissance discourses will know that everything that surrounded celestial and earthly phenomena was explained at that point by learned men in terms of these phenomena's relation to sound. In fact, this interest in the relation of objects to scholars' formulation of a science which constructs them went through an evaluation of sound, and it goes at least all the way back to Solomon and David (who after having grown impotent and thus unable to explore the feminine power and voice wrote psalms and songs that celebrated a whole lot of noise in heaven).

In an interesting lecture by John Maynard Keynes, Newton, who was an avid astrologist, was called "the last of the magicians, the last of the Babylonians and Sumerians" (Keynes, 1942). Keynes pointed out that Newton's diligent reading of the bible grounded his formulation of his theory of gravity in his interpretation of signs according to their ability to sing the praise of singularity. In Keynes's view, Newton, the scientist, was a creative writer par excellence precisely because, although he put down his "magic books" in order to engage in 'serious' science, he never put them down from his mind. It is thus this imaginary possession of magic that makes the creative scientist more interesting than the rest, and who thus serves as an example to follow if one is interested in knowing what kind of knowledge the writing of magic and science together produces.

The epistemic creative writer is bound to be fascinated by the esoteric in the formulation of theories of knowledge, and here I would venture to suggest that a taxonomy of epistemologies of creative writing can include a serious consideration, if not of the exact disciplines, such as math, then at least of theories which pose relevant questions regarding precisely the relevance of exactitude in creativity, if this is even possible to achieve, ever. But as with Wittgenstein, we can perhaps think of devising strategies for a type of questioning which has both reason and creativity in focus, but only as these two are caught in the meta-house of knowledge ruled by the master of contemplative ruminations. Says Wittgenstein in his *On Certainty*: "Knowledge in mathematics: Here one has to keep on reminding oneself of the unimportance of the 'inner process' or 'state' and ask: "why should it be important? What does it matter to me?" What is interesting is how we use mathematical propositions" (Wittgenstein, 1969: 41). By the same token, we can contend that epistemic creative writing is thus the writing which uses intuitionist propositions, and that what this writing teaches is that there is no difference between an academic's priming the pump, and a poet's fall into silent dawn condensing musical links. Bash(o)ing haikus and sounding the primes.

5

I CITE CYBORGS
NIETZSCHE, MELVILLE, ACKER, ZARATHUSTRA

Find something you love, and let it kill you.
– Charles Bukowski

One of the main ideas in cultural studies that takes into account the transformative processes in society – an idea that has the potential to reconfigure humans – relies on the notion that individuals acquire agency only when they are narrated. It is thus through extension, through the agency of an other's body and language, and through networking that a sense of identity emerges. In other words, we are what we are because we are supplemented. This law of the supplement in poststructuralist discourse opposes traditional thinking that holds the notion that transformations come from within.

The body as a container for thought poses several contradictions. First, insofar as thinking depends on the ability to make distinctions through language, the assumption that thought arises uncontaminated and in pure form rests on fallacious ground. What characterizes language and its arbitrary relations is not a unitary form framed by the singularity of one thought, but a fragmentary relation of dependency between language and the body. It is through our bodies that we articulate whatever conventions we follow, and hence a second contradiction arises. If thinking materializes as it sometimes does (one hopes), it is not because it finds itself in an immanent relation to the body, but because it transcends the body on its own terms – the body's, that is.

The materialization of thought occurs only insofar as the body desecrates it through arbitrary articulation. Hence, one can concur that the relation between thought and the body as mediated through language is bound to situate itself in the inscrutable and the incalculable. This irreverential relation may be said to rely on opportunity rather than calculation, which means that the language of the body, if it chooses to articulate, is unpredictable. In this relation, if thought is capable of and hence retains any kind of singular manifestation, it will be a thought of the body's ability to express a desire for immortality.

Against this background the epistemic creative writer is capable of inventing cyborg thinking. According to cyber critics, the desire for immortality alone marks our entrance and ultimate belonging to the realm of the cyborg. Following some of the ideas of disembodiment that we found in the previous chapter, let us make a detour and compare such unlike authors as Kathy Acker and Herman Melville in the context of the epistemic creative writer working on how to effectuate a writing program for the cyborg. But first, ahem, a Nietzschean recollection.

A(h)nnunciation

One of the most interesting anticipations of the modern discourse on immortality is due to Friedrich Nietzsche. In Nietzsche's desire to act as a "physician of culture," he makes a most remarkable statement, which I suggest links the idea of immortality with immortality's recurrent return as grammar. In his *Twilight of the Idols* he thus states: "I am afraid we are not rid of God, because we still have faith in grammar" (Nietzsche, 1984c: 483), indicating the paradox of God's ethereal yet continual domination over the body through the materialization of language.

Nietzsche writes by fragments when he posits the hermeneutic idea that affirming one singular part of one's life means affirming it as a whole, in its entirety. How the part becomes a whole, and how the part bestows singularity over the whole is seen particularly in Nietzsche's *Ecce Homo* (1888/1979). In the paratextual subtitle of this autobiography, "How one becomes what one is," we find Nietzsche's attempt at translating description into an imperative that has the affirmation of a singular experience at stake: "become what you are."

As critics have already noted, there is a stringent correlation between the idea of immortality and the ability of an individual to create a 'singular' space in society that can be called his or her own and that can be ensured to be his or her own even after the person's death. Daniel Ahern, in his *Nietzsche as Cultural Physician* (1995), juxtaposes Nietzsche's concern with exhaustion, decadence, sickness and health – all constitutive of a "physiological dynamics" – with immortality and eternal recurrence – constitutive of what I would call "ethereal dynamics." I suggest that what informs both these dynamics is an attempt at formulating a singularity of presence through affirmation. As Bert Olivier also observes in his "Nietzsche, immortality, singularity and eternal recurrence":

> What makes a true or 'singular' individual, for Nietzsche, is precisely the ability to overcome the tendency towards a kind of disintegration of the self into incompatible components, reneging on the (admittedly formidable) effort to refuse and conquer this tendency. Such a refusal manifests itself in harnessing all the divergent traits and characteristics that comprise a personality, artfully coordinating their differences towards the goal of being an integrated, self-creating, self-created person (Olivier, 2007: 77).

What interests me here is the link between singularity, immortality, and the belief in grammar, and the way in which the epistemic creative writer makes use of this link in the work that sanctions instruction according to the rule of 'no rules'. In Nietzsche's work this link is formulated either as a demand, an imperative, or an apostrophe. When he exclaims in *The Gay Science*, beginning with an affirmation of a necessity: "One thing is needful. 'Giving style' to one's character – a great and rare art!" (290; 1984b: 98-99), he indicates, by making a proto poststructuralist gesture, that we are already 'other' the moment singularity institutes itself in parenthesis, paratext, and ellipsis, or one could also say, at the margins of grammar. Olivier provides a good definition of singularity (as opposed to the fleeting nature of particularity) by way of quoting Joan Copjec:

> This notion of singularity, which is tied to the *act* of a subject, is defined as *modern* because it depends on the denigration of any notion of a prior or superior instance that might prescribe or guarantee the act. *Soul, eternity, absolute* or *patriarchal power*, all

these notions have to be destroyed before an act can be viewed as unique and as capable of stamping itself with its own necessity. One calls *singular* that which, 'once it has come into being, bears the strange hallmark of something that *must be*,' and therefore cannot die" (Copjec, 2002: 23-24 in Olivier, 2007: 79).

One way in which one's character acquires style is at the moment when "faith in grammar" gets to be articulated while there is also an attempt at escaping the constricting rules of grammar. If style in its more archaic form means a reduction of things to the bare essential, to gesture, grammar in its most reductive form is manifested through interjections; a mouth gesture (speech) rather than a hand gesture (writing) is bound to have a different value stylistically. Interjections have no real grammatical value, and are known as "hesitation devices." It may be that Nietzsche, being well acquainted with rigorous philological approaches to language, was aware of the value of hesitation when he peppered his works, especially the aphoristic kind, with such interjections as 'Ah!' and 'Oh!' These interjections usually have no connection to the grammatical sentence which transmits a thought.

Such examples of interjective and interruptive yet supplemental kind, one might add, are nowhere clearer articulated than in *Thus Spoke Zarathustra*. I will engage no further with this work here, as I prefer to save it for last, but meanwhile let it ghost other examples of writing in which the faith in grammar, once it has come into being, cannot therefore die. Insofar as it can be postulated that Nietzsche was engaged in ghostwriting for Zarathustra, he was interested in the mechanisms of expressing himself in the margins of Zarathustra's eloquence through interjective interposition. In other words, he explored the possibility of expressing himself through contingency on the *must be* (Ah!) as a preference for *not dying* (Oh!).

In his book *TechnoLogics: ghosts, the incalculable and the suspension of animation*, Gray Kochhar-Lindgren advances the argument that the ancient dream of immortality is now realized through cloning, genetic research, and artificial intelligence. As he puts it:

> Ghosts. Machines. Cyborgs. All are figures that have crossed over, and that assist us in thinking the crossing of the old lines between the living and the dead. All are outlaws, renegades from the proper, going back and forth by day and night, sometimes in disguise, even though the border patrols are everywhere (Kochhar-Lindgren, 2005: 30).

What I find interesting in the growing body of literature and treatises on creative writing engaging with both ghosts and cyborgs is the idea that immortality, while implicitly expressing a right to never die, also takes refuge from itself in the guise of an ethereal body. Immortality is on the run, a refugee, as it were, materialized in the language of the body that would "prefer not to" die. As a departure from Nietzsche, but not in spirit, I want to look here at such different texts as Melville's "Bartleby, the Scrivener" and Kathy Acker's "The language of the body" and make the claim that the body, in its attempt to achieve immortality by ghosting either being, writing, or machine, violates its own right to remain in a state of becoming, or crossing over.

Melville's protagonist, a law-copyist, by repeatedly informing his employer that he prefers not to do any of the tasks imposed on him, institutes a crisis that has consequences for his body: he ends up starving to death in a prison, a situation induced by the state of never either refusing or accepting to eat. Acker's text posits a similar situation in which the language of the body is translated into rendering an absence. By having an abortion, the protagonist neither refuses nor accepts the potential of the extra body (the baby) to cross over into life. Here I want to suggest that the suspension of animation is contingent on the ethereal body as manifested in the figure of a ghost or a cyborg. I want to see this metaphor of crossing over as emblematic of what the epistemic creative writer is up against in her desire to bear 'academic' witness to her creative work.

O(h)ntology

One of the trajectories that the logic of the technological takes is to consider the separation of the living from the dead. This separation is often seen in cyber criticism as a relation based on annihilation: as bodies narrate their existence through language, at the same time they undermine that very existence through perpetual violations of language. Where bodies are concerned, language functions as a mechanical supplement subject to change, transformation, and improvement. In computer science, language is already seen as a machine which can be coded and programmed according to an object-oriented ontology, which is to say that desire is brought into the machine as a means to operate with the differential and binary character of language. As Aden Evans puts it: "The result is a fold in the code, which extends outside of its plane toward another dimension, to rub against the human world" (Evans, 2006: 90). This rubbing against each other of man and machine engages creativity that does not rely on a transcendental subject. This latter idea is traced back to Walter Benjamin by critics such as Warwick

Mules, for whom Benjamin's search for a fold in language that would embody experience as unmediated by form is an expression of materiality and plasticity. Benjamin's thoughts, claims Mules, are furthermore "a reflection on the singularity of experience itself, bereft of the certainty of formal knowledge, dangerous and ruined [...] Creativity is the release of singularity captured in form. To write this sentence as I have just done (but who is this "I"; at what time does this "I" write?) is to make a case for creativity" (Mules, 2006: 75). I venture here to offer this answer: The "I" writing out of creativity releasing singularity is the epistemic creative writer *par excellence.*

Some of the implications of considering subjectivity that is caught between experience and the body are seen by Kochhar-Lindgren through an ethical prism that filters an essential question: in the face of technology, to what extent can we talk about human nature? The logic of the technological is to compress existing definitions of human nature, which situate human nature in context à la Jose Ortega y Gasset: "Man, in a word, has no nature; what he has is history" (Ortega y Gasset, 2002: 217) with definitions that state that human nature somewhat has to do with the ways in which we define our fears. One could give an example that goes back to Cartesian thinking. "I think therefore I am" can be said to basically formulate all our fears of not having our thoughts embody our bodies – or our bodies embody our thoughts. This dialectical thinking is what prevents us from considering possibilities of crossing various thresholds and developing a cognitive awareness of a pseudo-identity.

If we go back to Nietzsche, however, we see a re-valuation of all values through the plastic figurations of the pseudo-self. This self is a-historical insofar as its constitution is not contingent on the dynamics of historical change but on the dynamics of crossing thresholds. Says Nietzsche: "Every profound spirit needs a mask: even more, around every profound spirit a mask is growing continually, owing to the constantly false, namely *shallow*, interpretation of every word, every step, every sign of life he gives" (Nietzsche, 1966: 51). For Nietzsche, the profound spirit, otherwise aiming to be free, follows a historical trajectory when it masquerades fear into knowledge.

Kochhar-Lindgren, who follows closely in Nietzsche's footsteps, puts it this way:

> There is a profound fear, in transepochal culture, of becoming incorporated into the Borg or of being attacked by the monsters spawned by technics, but, on the other hand, this is a moment of opportunity, for as Guattari argues, "A machine assemblage, through its diverse components, extracts its consistency by crossing ontological thresholds, non-linear thresholds of irreversibility, and creative thresholds of heterogenesis and autopoeisis." We are the aliens, we are already other, and the work of the *hetero-* and the *auto-* must be enacted, with as much panache as we can muster, keeping in mind that the logic of such a move must deal not with an imitation of the human form, much less an ideal Platonic form, but with a technologics of production that wills the perfection of nature along certain of its axes (Kochhar-Lindgren, 2005: 127-128; author's emphasis).

If we pause to ponder some of the words in this passage, written by means of borrowing "ontological thresholds, non-linear thresholds of irreversibility, and creative thresholds of heterogenesis and autopoeisis," we may conclude that some prevalent ideas passed down to us from the German Romantics are clearly obsolete. In spite of the Romantics' effort to elude the traps of dualism, when Herder, for instance, declares in 1774 that "The body is the symbol, the phenomenon [the real manifestation] of the soul in contact with the universe," he presupposes that there is no threshold to be crossed, and thus finds himself caught in another master's house. This house is however haunted by the notion that symbolism must sacrifice expression in the name of interiority. I suggest that what Kochhar-Lindgren is positing in his demand for the enactment of the 'already' – "we are already other through the workings of *hetero-* and *auto-* which must be enacted" – is the idea that in cyberspace there is only exteriority and singularity mediated by the dissolution of (symbolic) form.

Hegel, for instance, in the first volume of his *Aesthetics*, defined the *symbol* as "an external existent given or immediately present to contemplation, which yet is to be understood not simply as it confronts us immediately on its own account, but in a wider and more universal sense. Thus at once, there are two distinctions to make in the symbol: (i) the meaning and (ii) the expression" (Hegel, 1975: 303-304). For cultural theorists such as Brian Rotman and Kochhar-Lindgren, cybernetics offers a third element that supplements Hegel's dialectics: the idea that "we are all temps." A symbol in cyberspace, especially the ghost, consists of meaning, the expression, and the untimely (Kochhar-Lindgren, 171). Even chronologically, it takes time to get from the Ah! of existence to the Oh! of death.

But before I move on I should mention that in Gray Kochhar-Lindgren the grey zone occupied by the ghost is circular. His book is paratextually 'signed' by Nietzsche who autographs the beginning singularly and the end by proxy: Thus spoke 'Nietzsche' in the epigraph to the introduction: "The most concerned ask today: 'How is the human to be preserved?' But Zarathustra is the first and only one to ask: 'How is the human to be overcome?'" And thus spoke 'Zarathustra' in the epigraph to the conclusion: "Higher than love of the neighbor is love of the farthest and the future; higher yet than the love of human beings I esteem the love of things and ghosts. This ghost that runs after you, my brothers and sisters, is more beautiful than you; why do you not give him your flesh and bones?" Oh, between Nietzsche and Zarathustra it is all Gray. At this point, one is tempted to say that we are quite away from Beckett and Stein, Lacan's psychic structuralism and the formal mathematical structures of O'Hara and Hofstadter, but if we consider the gray zone they all operate within in formulating a poetics of creative writing under the sign of epistemology, we can begin to guess what they are all saying, namely that they all ghostwrite. But for whom?

Another

A great deal has been written about Herman Melville's story "Bartleby, the Scrivener: A Story of Wall Street" (1853), but only a few consider the relation between the character Bartleby and a cyborg. (I am thinking here of Klaus Benesch: *Romantic Cyborgs: Authorship and Technology in the American Renaissance* (2002). Benesch discusses, however, Melville's "Dollars Damn Me" rather than Bartleby). In Donna Haraway's definition, a cyborg is "a cybernetic organism, a hybrid machine and organism, a creature of social reality as well as a creature of fiction" (Haraway, 1991: 149). While the idea of cyborgs populating the American Renaissance exhibiting transcendental and Romantic concerns may seem far fetched, the truth of the matter is that authors such as Melville have been preoccupied, not to say obsessed, by the dialectic between nature and technology. However, if the Romantics considered the link between organicity and mechanization they still did so by looking for the sublime. This latter concept has undergone significant changes, and in the current age of the posthuman, the sublime has ontological rather than symbolic implications.

For a cyborg the sublime is a manifestation of a beatific state embodied by extensions such as prostheses that mediate between the desire brought into the machine and the singular experience that this desire yields (see for instance the work of Cypriot cyborg performance artist Sterlarc). As Klaus Benesch also puts it, the link between "cybernetic images" of man-machine in early nineteenth-century literature enters "more of a symbolic than an ontological lineage with their postmodern, posthuman relatives" (Benesch 2002: 27).

The reason why Bartleby is an interesting figure in this relation is because he embodies several contradictory states. Each of these states violates the other. After having acted as a automaton (which represents the first level of embodiment) – copying the same type of legal documents again and again – he discharges himself of his duty, not by refusing to work as such, but by assuming a position of enunciating a preference based on contingency. When the narrator of the story, who is also Bartleby's employer, asks him whether he *will* not continue with his work, Bartleby always delivers the same automated answer: "I *prefer* not to." Although Bartleby speaks in the name of his preference, one that in turn bespeaks him, the subject who speaks

(I prefer not to) and the subject who is spoken of ("I" as the body that prefers not to) are never identical.

Cultural theorists and creative academic writers such as Mules and Kochhar-Lindgren would identify Bartleby's predicament as that of a subject who has already joined the Borg by positioning himself in the context of the already Other, the already Alien enacted by heterogenesis and autopoiesis. The more Bartleby articulates "I prefer not to," the more the body becomes inert. This inertia can be seen as a moment of crossing over into ethereal immortality, which Bartleby experiences by becoming a ghost by proxy, an extension of the already Other language embodied in the phrase "I prefer not to."

In his essay "Bartleby, or on Contingency" (from *Potentialities*, 1999) Giorgio Agamben advances the convincing claim that the grammatical value of this sentence (a negative plus an infinitive), which traces and marks incompleteness, creates a space called "potentiality," and enables Bartleby to transcend both existence and nothingness. In Agamben's scheme, a potentiality is not just a potentiality but also a potentiality for the opposite. Bartleby thus actualizes and realizes at the same time Nietzsche's project of overcoming faith in grammar.

The phrase "I prefer not to" had already become a ghost, haunting Bartleby's colleagues who had started using it themselves quite unconsciously. While Bartleby finally dies from a violently slow death induced by inanition, insofar as he prefers not to eat, his "I" as the subject that kept enunciating itself in a potential state of becoming manages to transcend the limits of finitude. As Bartleby's singular statement stands out from the beginning, it nevertheless proliferates within multiplicity – it haunts all the others. This turns Bartleby's death into a secondary experience: his death is not an absolute death but what remains in experience after Bartleby has abandoned Being.

Insofar as Bartleby's death is mediated by the creative language machine, which in its folds is capable of making space for potential states rather than their actualization, it becomes a platform for other events to take place, such as becoming ethereally immortal. It is to this state that Bartleby's narrator makes an anticipated reference when he contemplates doing something for him: "I might give alms to his body; but his body did not pain him. It was his soul that suffered, and his soul I could not reach." The difference between Bartleby and the narrator here is that, unlike Bartleby, the narrator is unable to cross a creative threshold and imagine on his own what Bartleby's motives for his behavior are.

Warwick Mules states: "Creativity [...] begins from the contingent, the specific – wherever one begins. It takes as its starting point the medium of expression in which objects are made apparent in their singular 'givenness' to perception" (Mules, 2006: 77). Melville ends his story with the narrator's double exclamation: "Ah Bartleby! Ah humanity!" adding to the feeling not only that Bartleby has gone to meet his maker – himself, that is – in that space of autogenesis and autopoiesis – but that in the process he has also turned himself into an object apparent in its singular givenness to the perception of a virtual world, which the narrator cannot see. Or prefers not to.

Other

Kathy Acker's story thematizes some of the same concerns with how to write on subjectivity, a body which refuses to embody subjectivity, and a desire for ethereal immortality. A female, yet unnamed, narrator begins to narrate a moment in her life associated with the inevitable pain following an abortion. This pain is however suspended insofar as the event takes place in a dream.

> I got married when I was very young. I did not know my husband… The day after our wedding, I had a dream about the world: At the entrance to the world, I was about to have an abortion. I had had abortions before this. I had to decide whether or not I wanted an anaesthetic. I guess that the doctor had asked me, but I don't remember that anyone was there Thinking, I asked how much the abortion was going to hurt me. The doctor replied, "Oh, there'll be pain…" in a voice that was trying to dismiss such pain. Since I knew that that type of voice meant that there would be a lot of pain, I chickened out. The blanket that was lying on top of me was yellow. I hate pain. I decided on anaesthetic. All through the abortion, I was kind of conscious. While I was in this consciousness, a pillow, which was around my ass, inflated and I floated three feet up above the cot. After the abortion, my body was OK, so I left the hospital. This was the scene of my marriage (Acker, 1992: website source).

This passage sets the tone for the way in which the narrator shifts between narrative moments. One is tempted to say here: thus spoke Nietzsche: 'pain is the true metaphysical reality', insofar as Acker can be said to subversively re-interpret Nietzsche's *The Birth of Tragedy*. If pain, for Nietzsche, is the most powerful aid to mnemonics, as well as the main condition for all forms of creation, for Acker, pain is the experience of a metaphysical dream. If, for Nietzsche, pain reflects the burden of biological existence, for Acker pain is linked to the annihilation of existence, to death. In dreams, our metaphysical reality is transformed into metaphysical illusion, a form of death that is not final but delayed by the presence of ghosts.

In Acker's first dream – which specifies moments of which the narrator is conscious and hence can retell in a coherent way – we also find other dreams recounted either as they occur, simultaneous with the moment of telling, or as they are retold in hindsight. The simultaneity of narration at this second level is marked through direct speech and dialogue (usually between the narrator and her husband, Steven). The dialogue in turn launches other dreams, which are then retold.

These dreams follow both conscious and unconscious patterns and are the expression of fragmented feelings. What the narrator is interested in is the extent to which she can formulate what the body feels independent of cognitive subjectivity. As the "I" of the narrator deliberately situates itself outside reality – events take place in a virtual space –what the "I" embodies – the dream – becomes an object subjected to an autonomous sphere of knowledge. In other words, when, what, how, and if the body knows, the narrator will tell. This structure is followed by a "Masturbation Journal" in which the narrator provides entries for three days. So, the dreams are not only about telling and retelling stories, but also about writing. Just before the journal entries the narrator assesses her own position in relation to the stories told and in relation to her husband, who always wants to know how they end. Writing is thus anticipated by a call on the language of the body to disclose its secrets. Writes Acker:

> I've begun a journey to make sex live, to find the relation between language and the body rather than this sexuality that's presented by society as diseased. My body seems to reject ordinary lan-

guage. If I can find the language of the body, I can find where sex is lying. While I masturbate, I'll try to hear the language that's there (idem, website source).

The narrator's approach to searching for the language of the body so that she can locate sex points to the necessity of channeling experience through a singular moment that dissolves form (or rather the faith in grammar). This can be seen in the way in which the journal entries are put together, both at the level of form and content. The entry for "Day 1" begins with a sentence in parenthesis: "(This might not make any sense)" and is followed by a couple of other lines emphasizing movement and expectation. These lines have a performative character insofar as they lead straight into another sentence which can be read as a comment on movement and expectation: "there is nothing: it is here that language enters." "Day 2" begins with this line: "It starts with bodily irritation, but then one has to forget the body, leave the body, leave the body until the body quivers uncontrollably." While the body is here rendered incalculable, it is also seen as a space with levels, but no dialectic between them. In its singular existence the body does not belong to the text; rather it belongs to a textual multiplicity. In cyberspace the body is all about networking and regeneration, rather than system and reproduction (Haraway). This interconnectedness is what enables the narrator to offer descriptive images of some levels of the body. Likening the body to a room, she states:

> In this room, everything hangs out: nipples scrape against air; buttocks thrust out so that the asshole is open, and all that was inside is now outside now it starts. it: actual touching. This is the beginning of feeling (idem, web source).

The beginning of feeling is also marked by multiple choices. This is illustrated in one of the lines in the journal entry for "Day 3," which states: "While crossing the threshold, language is forbidden; having crossed, it's possible to have language." The threshold here can be seen as Félix Guattari's threshold of irreversibility. Guattari plays in an interesting way with some of the signifieds of the signifier threshold in his *Chaosmosis* (1995): liminality (limen = threshold), but also margin, outskirt, here in the sense of being cut off by interruption. One could say that precepts and affects are outside the notion of having "faith in grammar" insofar as they are not bound up with any preconceived subjective content or objective form. They are characterized by a singularly liminal quality insofar as they are able to cross thresholds and map potentialities of both, death and existence. Says Guattari:

> There is an ethical choice in favour of the richness of the possible, an ethics and politics of the virtual that decorporealizes and deterritorializes contingency, linear causality, and the pressure of circumstances and significations which besiege us. It is a choice for processuality, irreversibility and resingularization (Guattari, 1995: 29).

Once the crossing over is done, what is left behind is only the essence of the articulating or silent body. Whichever we prefer.

One of the passages in Acker's text that more clearly takes the question of ethereal immortality into account is the dream in which the narrator, her husband and two other women, one of them a countess, discuss the other two Hungarian countesses: Klara and her niece Ezebeth Bathory. These two 16th century historical figures have entered our cultural consciousness alongside characters such as Dracula and other vampires.

"Klara Bathory had married four husbands in succession. She had murdered the first two. Afterwards, she took a lover who was much younger than her…" Steven returned. "She smothered the boy in castles. Then, a pasha captured him; while the former was skewering and roasting him on a spit, the entire garrison raped Klara. They cut through the throat of the woman who was still living." "It is a violent society." "Klara's niece was Ezebeth Bathory, more well known as The Scarlet Witch." "She murdered almost 610 young women," her secretary added. "Yes, she kidnapped young girls in order to get their blood." "No." "She hung them up by their wrists, then whipped them until their tortured flesh was torn to shreds." My husband spoke for the first time. He, the Countess, and her friend were sitting together on a small sofa. I was perching on an armchair. "Oh yes, and she clipped their fingers off with shears," – the Countess. "Pierced their nipples with needles, yes, then tore out the tips with silver pincers," my husband. "Because human blood is an elixir,"– the Countess. "…she bit them every where and pushed red hot pokers right into their faces…" – my husband. "No!" "And with the curses of witches…," said the young girl, "And with the curses of witches, especially the sorceress Darvulia Anna, cut off pieces of their flesh, grilled them, then made them eat parts of their own bodies," "Go on go on go on." – the girl. "Kissed their veins with rusty nails," – the woman whom I had desired. "Go on go on go on," – her lover "…and when the young girls parted their lips in order to screech, she plunged the flaming rod into the caverns of the throats…" my husband began taking over… "No!" "Your wife is very much in love with you, isn't she?" the countess asked him. "How does the story end?" my husband replied. (Acker, 1992: website source)

While the narrator takes active part in the telling of this story based on the practice of Ezebeth Bathory who bathed in the blood of young virgins so that she could stay young and alive (a practice which Acker only alludes to), she also indicates at the end of the story that she feels this and other stories are all being talked to death. By exclaiming that she doesn't want sexuality, she articulates a preference for precisely that stage where the body enters a relation with what it prefers not: to be vampirized by language. In a parallel that recalls Nietzsche, it is interesting to note that in the 1962 film *The Slaughter of the Vampires* (directed by Roberto Mauri) the role of Bram Stoker's protagonist, Professor van Helsing, is here replaced by a Professor Nietzsche. This suggests a catachrestic relation between annihilating the vampire's eternal recurrence by using a hammer and the real Nietzsche's notion of philosophizing with the same weapon; for the latter the vampire even has a name, Spinoza, as we are informed in *The Gay Science* (372). In a cultural studies and creative writing context context we can further observe that Nietzsche's proclamation: "God is dead," is often echoed in pronouncements such as "Dracula is dead" (*The Brides of Dracula*, 1960), thus suggesting the irony in having the immortal overcome by the mortal.

As Acker's story ends with someone named Rodney waiting for her "beyond a door marked by a black O,"[1] which is also the last line in her story, it is clear that what the body prefers not to is also to continue being a body in any real sense. If we were to paraphrase one of Nietzsche's most condensed and charged maxims: "Man is something to be overcome," we could say that the body, in both Melville and Acker is also something to be

---

1   This may be a reference to *Histoire d'O* which was a controversial erotic novel published in 1954 about sadomasochism by Anne Desclos under the pen name Pauline Réage. The novel has been accused of representing women in an ultimately objectified position.

Overcome. What is further suggested in Acker's story is that in order for Rodney to be able to wait, the narrator would have to hold a promise that potentially she will cross over through the hole, suggested by the letter O. This roundness which we also find in Bartleby, when the narrator makes a consideration of his former employer's name, John Jacob Astor,[2] is the name Acker gives to her objective: to become immortal by placing her body in care of the ghost in the dream machine. The "Ah" in Melville and the "O" in Acker each constitute moments of singular expressions that eradicate language structures by undoing the NO, or O. (Nietzsche nods, and where is Beckett?)

The point of juxtaposing Mellvile and Acker here is to highlight the significance in writing of the ritual of crossing a threshold, particularly if the writer proposes to engage with the meta-dimenion of writing, when the protagonists in the fictional text are intended to write, and through writing, through their bodies, they become theories on creative writing. If Bartleby the scrivener can be seen vacillating as to whether he wants to cross the threshold of 'academic' writing into the fiction of living life as a scrivener, Acker's witches are all about performing magic while in a state of altered consciousness. Acker's text takes on the dimension of what can be termed spirited writing.

What I find relevant here is precisely this notion of spirited writing, as I suspect that what makes a writer epistemically creative is her courage to cross over into the world above the dual-

---

[2] "The late John Jacob Astor, a personage little given to poetic enthusiasm, had no hesitation in pronouncing my first grand point to be prudence; my next, method. I do not speak it in vanity, but simply record the fact, that I was not unemployed in my profession by the late John Jacob Astor; a name which, I admit, I love to repeat, for it hath a rounded and orbicular sound to it, and rings like unto bullion" (Melville, website source).

ism between creativity and science. And what can this magical conjunction be called? Nietzsche suggested the term "gay science." Perhaps we should finally turn to him for a more ample elucidation and for a more nuanced understanding of what exactly he did for Beckett, Stein and a host of other writing seekers, an understanding that made them proclaim themselves anti-writers of the ghost in the machine type.

Tightrope cyborg

In the "Prologue" to *Thus Spoke Zarathustra,* we read this passage: "The crowd, believing that Zarathustra was the ringmaster come to introduce the tightrope walker, gathered around to listen" (Nietzsche, 1961). This passage has always struck me as being about the idea of grounding in writing. Creative writing *par excellence* begins with a grounding of thought in what one has heard before. It often takes no more than a piece of gossip to put the writer on track. Epistemic creative writing is first grounded in what one has heard, and then in a processing of the information one has just received. For the writing to be deemed creative, however, one would have to allow for information to also be misunderstood, or at least relayed as a conscious form of miscommunication. Why miscommunication, one would ask, and the answer here would have to be simply because the epistemic creative writer is not interested in making any claims to knowledge. He writes for experience, for the process, rather than the method. The epistemic creative writer's heuristics is more than just pedagogical or philosophical. He writes for balance, for the tightrope. How writing gets across and to what effect is more important than accuracy and factual integrity.

The question that the epistemic creative writer poses is this one: 'how can I move the reader while I'm still thinking about it, while I'm still thinking about what to say?'

Let us look at Nietzsche's example. Nietzsche is misunderstood. Nietzsche has always been misunderstood. And although, given such established precedence, one would be justified in assuming that there is nothing that would prevent new interpreters of Nietzsche to go on with misunderstanding, the truth of the matter is that there is almost no new study of Nietzsche that does not purport the opposite. Thus any new book on Nietzsche claims to shed some new light on some thought or downright offer a definitive interpretation. Where Nietzsche himself is concerned, one could imagine that, as a philosopher, he might be tempted to worry about all these new revaluations of his thoughts. As a writer, a creative writer, *par excellence,* and one concerned only with the poetics of the borders between disciplines, one could imagine that Nietzsche would probably laugh all the way to the bank at the idea that writing is merely there to be either understood or misunderstood. Writing, he would tell people and critics alike, creative, prophetic, philosophical, cultural, or otherwise, is a currency used for consecrating thoughts, as they happen, in a time and space of when they happen.

There is in Nietzsche an insistence on nuance in writing, but a kind which can also be said to be consistent with its own internal contradictions. It is thus also inflexibly rigid. As a critic, which Nietzsche also was, one could imagine that his concern with interpreters that are more powerful than himself manifests precisely as a concern with how to hit the balance between timely thoughts and the ones which have the potential to become classics. What is thus worth tracing in Nietzsche is not so much the extent to which his writings invite the invention of new interpretations of his thoughts, but rather the extent to which Nietzsche's creative impetus can be said to rely on encapsulating a *zeitgeist* within the form of unending, yet already existent within itself meta-interpretation of this *zeitgeist*. And what does this mean exactly? This means that a writer, if any good, must formulate aphorisms which combine literary aesthetics with keen cultural awareness in such a way so that one leaves room for expressing a type of knowledge that one would not be ashamed of having attained. As Nietzsche puts it pertinently in *Beyond Good and Evil*, in which epistemology is explored to the fullest by way of interludes, maxims, epigrams, and aphorisms:

> 64. 'Knowledge for its own sake' – that is the last snare of morality: with that one becomes completely entangled in it once more.

> 65. The attraction of knowledge would be small if one did not have to overcome so much shame on the way. (Nietzsche, BGE, 1964: 79).

One of the chief characteristics of the aphoristic style is the reduction of a set of ideas to an essential minimum. When the practitioner of the aphorism, a fragment, or a maxim, is successful, it takes, however, not only skills to produce elegant bottom-lines, but also a sense of how far such bottom-lines can be stretched. Readers of Nietzsche appreciate the philosopher's capacity to encapsulate complex ideas in a simple form, which is yet quite complex in itself. This being the case, I want to look precisely at Nietzsche's elasticity when it comes to articulating his well-known desire to ignite established ideas, and blow them to pieces with his own dynamite. Quite literally, can an elastic set things on fire, survive the fire? Can a truth be final even when it is elastic? What does it mean to write, for Nietzsche, when writing presents itself as a sin against silence, as a fire that burns the very abstract that is supposed to transcend and even the very production of meaning? Thematically, I'm interested in looking at how Nietzsche formulates epistemologies of creative writing against the background of such stylistic devices which have the genre of the aphorism and the fragment as primary media for expression.

The other claim that I want to make is by way of reminding the readers of Nietzsche of that which they already know, and this without being too presumptuous, namely that one cannot dissociate Nietzsche's concern with writing from his concern with culture. The more nuanced take on this claim consists of suggesting that although Nietzsche relished bashing the literalism of culture, he himself wanted to be taken literally where his writing was concerned. To give an example, in the songs of Zarathustra, after he goes from 1 to 12 on the depth of eternity – and woe to all those who don't take Zarathustra literally – he sings "the 7 seals or the yes and amen song." I read what Zarathustra has to say literally simply because he makes sure not to have any nuance between his yes and his amen. Thus each seal ends appropriately with a desire for eternal recurrence and 7 repetitions of these lines: "Never yet have I found the woman from whom I wanted children, unless it be this woman whom I love: for I love you, O eternity! *For I love you, O eternity*" (Nietzsche, Z, 1961: 244-245).

Now, what is implied here is that although Nietzsche sees himself not only a product of his culture but also its keeper and promulgator of counter-ideologies, he is also interested in proposing that there is no clear-cut relation between an individual and his environment. There is thus no "us," neither individually in terms of interrelations, nor pluralistically in terms of the mass vis-à-vis culture. There is only eternity, pure, formal, and non-nuanced eternity, and man as an individual is a walker on a tightrope that's rigged between the here and now of one's culture, and eternity as one's dream. Against this background, when Nietzsche declares that writing needs to be consecrated through love – the love for the woman who bears no children – makes more sense, as the woman can be seen as an allegorical figure, albeit of a literal nuance, if such a paradox is possible, of a culture that bears no fruits other than its own contradictions. In a seminal passage from *Untimely Mediations,* Nietzsche illustrates perfectly his own versatility in terms of always being consistent with himself even when he contradicts himself. Nietzsche's contradictions can also be seen to parallel those the beloved woman in *Thus Spoke Zarathustra* is accused of; a woman who seems to say, on the one hand, there is no 'us,' there's only writing – a statement uttered as a meditation given in response to the philosopher who resolves to place himself within, what he calls, 'the circle of culture' – and on the other, she clearly invites the philosopher to become her, the woman, who says: 'and yet, there *is* 'us,' here's the *übermensch.*' Thus says Nietzsche:

> [C]ulture is the child of each individual's self knowledge and dissatisfaction with himself. Anyone who believes in culture is thereby saying: 'I see above me something higher and more human than I am; let everyone help me to attain it, as I will help everyone who knows and suffers as I do: so that at last the man may appear who feels himself perfect and boundless in knowledge and love, perception and power, and who in his completeness, is at one with nature, the judge and evaluator of things.' It is hard to

create in anyone this condition of intrepid self-knowledge because it is impossible to teach love; for it is love alone that can bestow on the soul not only a clear, discriminating and self-contemptuous view of itself, but also the desire to look beyond itself and to seek with all its might for a higher self as yet still concealed from it. Thus only he who has attached his heart to some great man receives thereby the *first consecration to culture* (Nietzsche, UM 1997: 162-163).

What Nietzsche does here that is fascinating is formulate an epistemology of creative writing which can be defined along the lines of an immediate transgressive act, that of associating culture, a given and constructed thing, with love, which by virtue of its being straightforward and simple, almost of horizontal dimensions, is also precisely transcendental. Yet, love, for Nietzsche, is not transcendental in any religious sense, as it rests on a desire for inner power constructs, and is as such the very result of a struggle for power. Love is thus the sole entity that can bypass our rational thinking about the construction of self-knowledge as dictated by culture, while itself a construct. But love as a construct is precisely also desired beyond judgment and evaluation, as it is a matter of acceptance. Love is thus extravagant in its very thrust. When Nietzsche insists: "for I love you, O eternity," what he says is that if love is accepted, and there is participation in the world suggested by the lover to whom love is declared, then this lover becomes one's very possession, uncompromising and unending for as long as the mind perceives it as such.

We have already seen how for Gertrude Stein the economy of love, the love of self, defined the epistemic creative writer as a writer of everything. The guiding axiom that was formulated along this line: 'I love myself, therefore I can write for myself and strangers.' For Nietzsche, who is not merely interested in everything but in the eternal return of everything, love acquires a different dynamics, and it has specific consequences for the act of writing. He seems to suggest that one cannot love anything before one loves eternity.

Nietzsche loves eternity, because it is the only thing that doesn't disappoint. Hence, the thought of eternity can be perceived as an immediate transgression of the very thing that constructs it, be that time, or culture. Nietzsche is interested in immediate transgressions, especially as they take place on pages first – the first real test for thinking anything worth the while, and without which no realization of any act worth the while would be possible. Here, then, one can make the inference that any epistemology of creative writing begins, for Nietzsche, with whatever body parts that can be said to enhance the balancing act on the tightrope to infinity. The body, color, emotion, sound, and reason are all activated in motion and in equal measure. Writing thus becomes writing on the body, with the body, and for the body that perceives all that which touches it. The body is seen as the ultimate container of both, the most abstract thought in the mind, the thought that stretches to infinity, and blood in the veins, the material test of how endlessness can be grasped at a rigid level. Writing, for Nietzsche, thus situates itself between such elastic states of the mind and the rigidity of the body, and it approximates each in relation to the other.

Through the love of eternity Nietzsche succeeds in approximating the assurance of writing, but as with any assurance, it is not the thing itself, but rather a phenomenological perception of the thing. Through the mouth of Zarathustra this is made clear, yet one can notice the unambiguous internal contradiction that the juxtaposition of love and writing elicits where stretching the elastic of infinity is concerned. Nietzsche was, after all, not a phenomenologist, hence he didn't have a problem measuring the intensity of his gut-feeling, even if this meant going in two opposite directions at once, or *ad infinitum*, actually. Says Nietzsche:

> Of all writings I love only that which is written with blood. Write with blood: and you will discover that blood is spirit.
>
> It in not an easy thing to understand unfamiliar blood: I hate the reading idler.
>
> He who knows the reader, does nothing further for the reader. Another century of readers – and spirit itself will stink.
>
> That everyone can learn to read will ruin in the long run not only writing, but thinking too.
>
> Once, spirit was God, then it became man, and now it is even becoming mob (Nietzsche, Z, 1961: 67).

This passage illustrates that the desire to be "perfect and boundless in knowledge and love" becomes a realization of this bottom-line: 'write and die.' If we stretch it, we could even say, 'write as an individual and die a mob.' For Nietzsche, pure formalism is not a question of nuance. How can one inflect that which is or is not? Either you are this, or you are not. Either you're a writer, or you are not; a philosopher, an *übermensch*, or a prophet, or not. And yet. What interests Nietzsche in equating the different types of impersonation with the 'not' of being is the possibility of going purely formal in the middle of things, as it were, where the state in between the culture of the individual and the culture of the masses clash, crash and burn, or simply explode through the double repetition induced by causality: "For I love you, O eternity. *For I love you O eternity.*" As this line itself can and goes on eternally, it thus enacts not only one but two potentials: to return (to culture), and to consecrate (to culture). Taken once, "For I love you, O eternity" is the beginning of self-knowledge. Taken twice, "For I love you, O eternity," is dynamite knowledge, for what it ultimately does is place an injunction on the very act of seeking as it relates to individual agency: seek not yourself so that you can know yourself, but *cherchez la femme.* And make sure you do it in writing that is also highlighted (the second, *"For I love you, O eternity"* is italicized). Furthermore, in the middle of *Thus Spoke Zarathustra,* Nietzsche equates woman with eternal truth, mystery, profundity, and fidelity (132).

This is a good strategic move on his part, for if he were to proclaim that, indeed, now he has found the truth as such and for itself, independent of temporal predicates and free of context, then he would have a problem with the very idea of consecration. Once truth is found, what is there to search for in the future? And be consecrated to what? There would be no need for the writer to sacrifice anything, and least of all shed either blood or ink for anything. Eternal truth linked with woman, however, manages to induce at least a temporal crisis, thus allowing the writer to change his mind as he goes along, and as a woman does, if we stick to the cultural time in which the book was written and its contaminating idea that if woman is anything then she is fickle not faithful.

With culture as history and woman as eternity Nietzsche is well equipped to explore the territory beyond good and evil, particularly in the genre of the aphorism, as aphoristic language is the only kind of language that bypasses the censorship of tautology. If things are as they are, they can also get better. There is thus always a graduation of nuance even in things which are otherwise declared beyond inflection due to a constant state. Nietzsche is one of the very few writers who can pull off the constancy of nothing, nuanced nothing, in relation to movement, even the standstill kind. For Nietzsche, the law of physics which dictates that nothing happens until something moves is tightened with the law of busted morals: good, better, best is only as good, better, best if situated between love and indifference.

In *Beyond Good and Evil,* all Nietzsche's aphorisms that deal with knowledge – how we acquire it, what we pay for it, and how good it is – deal in fact with formalizing to the point of getting rid of nuance the bottom-lines of the beyond that nonetheless stretch between love and hatred, ancient and modern, man and woman, here and there. What is suggested is that in these binary relations, hatred is more elastic than love, and so are woman, the modern thinkers, and the abyss. Their elasticity goes to the infinite. If I were a mathematician, I would say at this point that Nietzsche is simply just beautiful in this thought as he places equal passion and scorn in such declarations which are seemingly incongruous. But then, such is the nature of the aphorism: to approach in formulation the state of ultimate reduction of thought as is the case in pure mathematics. Thus says Nietzsche in the following aphorisms pertaining to knowledge, woman, and unending traps, suggesting once more that the proof of good writing is not in the eating as much as it is in the thinking about it.

64. "Knowledge for its own sake"—that is the last snare laid by morality: we are thereby completely entangled in morals once more.

115. Where there is neither love nor hatred in the game, woman's play is mediocre.

146. He who fights with monsters should be careful lest he thereby become a monster. And if thou gaze long into an abyss, the abyss will also gaze into thee.

152. "Where there is the tree of knowledge, there is always Paradise": so say the most ancient and the most modern serpents.

153. What is done out of love always takes place beyond good and evil (Nietzsche, BGE, 1964: 115-130).

Relating to Nietzsche's ability to stretch bottom-lines, what is also remarkable from the point of view of the epistemologist interested in how knowledge is produced and to what effect is the fact that his formal approach to language and genre is filtered through an awareness of how phenomenology works. In this sense he anticipates some of the best contemporary work on such elusive notions as love, and gazing abysmally into the territory of the other. I'm thinking here of Jean-Luc Marion.

What Nietzsche anticipates in the phenomenological discourse that can be seen to converge with a certain formalism found in analytical philosophy and logics is the idea that there are obligations that impose themselves on us and that are constituted by something other than our own intentionality. In one of his earlier works, *The Idol and Distance* (2001), Marion posits a similar idea to that of Nietzsche's genealogy of morals, which suggests that the conceptual idolatry of morals generates its own downfall and deconstruction. For Marion, distance creates the greatest intimacy, and the dynamics of the gaze is a form of love's intentionality that acquires a moral dimension à la Nietzsche, which is to say that distance, love's intentionality, and the gaze are modes of knowing induced by a kind of perception that anchors knowledge in a gradual certitude that is more decaying than edifying. Here I would venture to suggest that what binds Nietzsche's writings together, or rather functions as a glue, is the idea that love is a form of intentional morality, and we therefore have a hard time devising strategies around it that do not compromise it outside the moral dilemma: To love or not to love? Knowledge by decay. Certitude by *décalage*. Marion's later work, *The Erotic Phenomenon* (2007) implicitly credits Nietzsche for the beautiful death he arranged for God, so that love can rise, or be resurrected from metaphysical death. As with Nietzsche, if it's not the woman who does it, inspire writing about birth and death, then eternity certainly puts it in perspective. A perspective of the assurance of time in relation to the other. Says Marion:

> Only eternity responds to erotic reason's need for the assurance of the present – knowing definitely whom I love [...] 'Will I have the strength, the intelligence, and the time to love you to the end, without remainder or regret?' for the one that I love clearly imposes herself upon me as a saturated phenomenon, whose endless and measureless intuition does not cease to overflow all of the significations that I attempt to assign to her, beginning with the first among them, 'Here I am!' Seriously facing the face of the other, or more precisely, the face of this unsubstitutable other of whom I claim to be the lover, requires that I give without end a new meaning to the intuitions that never cease coming to me, and thus that I say all the words and pronounce all the names I am able to mobilize, or even that I invent others, so as to accomplish

the indefinite interpretation. The lover never finishes telling himself of the beloved, telling himself to the beloved, and telling the beloved to herself. The lover, in front of the intuitions that the beloved inspires in him, must deploy an endless hermeneutic, a conversation without endpoint; thus he needs a period of time without bounds in order to carry out his discourse without conclusion. Love demands eternity because it can never finish telling itself the excess within it of intuition over signification. I will only know whom I love in the final instance – by eschatological anticipation of eternity, the sole condition of its endless erotic hermeneutic. Thus, only eternity answers the need of erotic reason concerning the assurance of a future – being able endlessly to tell me whom I love and to make it known to her, since without me, she would not know it (Marion, 2007: 210).

If asked, Marion would say the same as The Beatles, 'all you need is love.' Perhaps this is so. But it seems that the continuity of love, insofar as it needs constant reassuring, is dependent on the incentive to give nothing to itself. How else to understand endlessness? As reassurance comes in fragments, impulses, nods, and lexia, it supplements continuity with 'everything' which is also 'nothing' at the same time. In other words, if the proposition 'all you need is love' is correct, then it can only be so if it runs counter to time as a matter of necessity. Thus we don't operate with either the past or the future, but with their assurance. Perhaps this is what Marion means to suggest, when he further says: "To love requires loving without being able or willing to wait any longer to love perfectly, definitely, and forever. Loving demands that the first time coincide with the last time" (211).

When Nietzsche goes against systems of morals, what he says is that because morals never coincide with anything other than temporal normative codes that are contingent on time, morality is in fact never radical enough. As he puts it: "systems of morals are only a SIGN-LANGUAGE OF THE EMOTIONS" (Nietzsche, BGE, 1964: 138). Hence, the only thing that saves man from engaging in creating a useless typology and science of morals is if he obeys only love, since love, as in Marion's rendition, demands that polarities converge in the extremes. In other words, morals go 'boom' in the middle. On this, Nietzsche also comes close to post-structuralists such as Foucault, for whom consecration to culture through dynamite love rather than exploded morals equals knowledge that is not made for comprehension but for awe. Try and look at an artifice made out by blown morals, and we all go, awesome! Yet Foucault can't bring himself to be as radical as Nietzsche. He reaches for the knife rather than fire. "Knowledge is not made for understanding; *it is made for cutting*," he says, thus emphasizing indirectly the idea that the fragment is the thing. Go for the fragment (Foucault, 1977: 154). Nietzsche burns it up. His fuse goes to infinity. If he's into cutting, it's the emancipated woman's balls he wants to cut. As he suggests it in "Why I Write Such Excellent Books," writing is indissociable from woman – "they all love me," he says, "excepting the abortive woman" (Nietzsche, EH, 1979: 75). This statement is quite unconscious on Nietzsche's part, in spite of the fact that he claims to be "the first psychologist of the eternal-womanly" (75).

Where woman is concerned, precisely as a vehicle for knowledge, as a carrier of knowledge, Nietzsche is not mistaken to assume that as a writer who knows his privileges, as he boisterously heralds, those privileges of ruining taste, he must be careful around the 'complete' woman who has equal power in terms of realizing the value of the fragment in relation to totality. The fragment is faithful to eternity not totality, and fragmentation can go on infinitely. Totality has no such dynamism. It's just there to enforce a diabolic constancy. It awaits blowing up. In contrast, the fragment has active agency: it combines fear and trembling, the sublime and the profane in paradoxical ways. Therefore, says Nietzsche, joyously retreating from the attempt to dynamite the fragment and the woman, its guardian: "Happily, I am not prepared to be torn to pieces: the complete woman tears to pieces when she loves" (75). Here we get a glipmse into how Nietzsche anticipates the cyborg, namely by building into the woman's body writing itself. This writing, however, comes back to haunt him, dictate to him, as if from a mechanical source. Nietzsche feels that he is in need to perform cord magic, and he feels the urge to walk on the tightrope himself. He walks without stumbling, but what maintains his balance is not his commonsense but the constant whisper from the woman to whom he is tied.

For Nietzsche, it is with this fear of the "amiable maenads" that dangerous writing begins, and with it the formulation of an epistemology of creative writing, the writing that places the prophet on the highest of thrones, the only seat that legitimizes beyond even legitimation itself the performative enunciation: "Thus spoke..." Says Nietzsche:

> The art of *grand* rhythm, the *grand style* of phrasing, as the expression of a tremendous rise and fall of sublime, of superhuman passion, was first discovered by me; with a dithyramb such as the last of the *third* Zarathustra, entitled "The Seven Seals," I flew a thousand miles beyond that which has hitherto been called poesy (75).

Immediately after these lines, we have the bashing of the abortive woman, and one can almost sense Nietzsche's anxiety at imagining the woman saying: 'Nietzsche talks too much,' and then demanding: 'let's have some silence now.' Thus silenced, Nietzsche has to borrow Zarathustra's mouth, and say, in anticipation of nothing, and before the woman's injunction to love the fragment to pieces: 'I did it. I invented it. Writing. I blew this whole setup surrounding morals and truth. With style, and rhyme, tropes and wit.' The woman is pleased and Nietzsche is appeased. Thus spoke Zarathustra. Writing is knowing by fire, by cutting the philosopher's balls, and by becoming a woman with a mustache. For, as Nietzsche seconds, "one can simply no longer endure other books, philosophical ones least of all" (72). Shall we say amen, or shall we go dancing in the double-forked artifice? Nietzsche's specter shouts beyond the grave: 'never trust a dead body.' Indeed, where are the philosophers when you need them?

The point of invoking Nietzsche here, almost as an interlude between man ghost, machine, and love, is to demonstrate that the epistemic creative writer, unlike the traditional academic, always has 'nothing' to consider. And then there is the love of writing. How to bear witness to it? How to say you do research, when in fact it is words that fascinate? The well-turned phrase, rather than findings? At this point in this book I can safely say that what attracts me to the writers mentioned so far is the fact that they are all tired of the dogmatism of writing for the purpose of cutting it to the bone. If one wants to keep it simple, one can say nothing, as Beckett went on and on about it. Or just repeat yourself as Stein insisted. Or how about slashing your throat, as Acker would have it. Or postponing it indefinitely in preference of not preferring anything?

So here is a suggestion: the epistemic creative writer is the writer who writes about minuses not pluses. On this, I like what the popular writer on creative writing, Robert Pirsig, has to say in praise of Natalie Goldberg's work on creative writing, on the cover of her acclaimed book: *Writing Down the Bones* (1986/2005): "The secret of creativity, Natalie Goldberg makes clear, is to subtract rules for writing, not add them. It's a process of 'uneducation' rather than education." Following this line of thinking and extrapolating a thought from it, I think that I like the idea that perhaps what drove Beckett, Stein, and Nietzsche to formulating an almost anti-writing stance is their realization that what stood between them and the writing without the *epi* in the *st(e)ame* was the philosopher.

Let us see in what follows whether we can stop thinking, and yet still end up with a treatise on knowledge as it formulates itself in (some) writing. Exits bloody Acker. Melville prefers not to. Enters David Markson. Andrei Codrescu says: *non serviam*.

6

EPISTEMOLOGISTS OF SITE MARKSON AND CODRESCU

There is a danger, even in Wittgenstein, of talking things to death.
– Geoffrey Hartman

David Markson is a writer who, in a series of "novels" entitled *Wittgenstein's Mistress* (1988), *Reader's Block* (1996), and *This is not a Novel* (2001), explores some of our basic conceptions of genre. Can we call a book of fragments a novel? Is a novel still a novel when the characters are given names such as Author, Protagonist, Reader? What are we left with, when critics resort to labels such as "novel of intellectual reference and allusion... minus the novel" and "seminonfictional semifiction" to categorise his texts? Through an apparently endless list of anecdotes and facts regarding the deaths of composers, authors, philosophers, etc., Markson, designs a topos of the graveyard where his fiction can rest. I intend to offer a reading of these texts as postmodern epitaphs, both evoking the tradition of epitaphic writing, and playfully subverting our expectations of this genre. Furthermore, I see Markson's texts echoing Beckett, but whereas for Beckett the epistemological project fails to fail more and better than the previous attempt, for Markson epistemic writing is history writing. But not the kind that we encounter in the catalogue of historical texts. If Markson has a project at all, then it is this: to declare the death of God and the author insufficient in relation to creative writing. For Markson, insofar as it is knowledge itself that is dead, the only thing that remains and is worth considering is the writing that accounts for the circumstances in which men of knowledge died. Unlike Beckett, who suspected that breath is significant in writing, even more so than words, Markson believes that the voice beyond the grave cuts it. In the following, let us first look at a performance of unconventional epistemic creative writing that is written in the vein of 'don't listen to me,' and then move on to another writer, the popular Andrei Codrescu, whose novels, poetry, and radio appearances take epistemic creative writing to non-conformist heights.

The tomb repeats

Of epitaphs says Debra Fried: "Epitaphs make us see ourselves as doubles – perhaps incomplete or imperfect doubles – of the dead, as living dead, as readers awaiting our epitaphs" (Fried, 1986: 617). The function of the epitaph is to perform silence. The dead's last voice, as it were. The epitaph is a false oracle, however, for the writing on the tomb is in fact an iconic double sign: on the one hand, it represents the voice of the dead, which is endowed with the capacity to say something important, final, and 'complete', and on the other hand, it activates the memory of the passer-by who seeks a truth in his own contemplation. To be reminded of one's own mortality by the 'living' voice of the dead – Fried gives an illustrative example of an epitaph that works every time: "Prepare yourself to follow me" – seems to have one effect only: the realization that there is nothing sacred about being dead. Epitaphs, then, can be said to mediate a profane relationship between the dead and the living. As Fried writes: "What death does to men, the style of the epitaph does to language: makes it repetitive, incantatory, static, self-righteous but stunned, unable to untie the strands of cause and effect, literal and figurative" (618). Insofar as there is an identification with the spoken-word of the epitaph, the reader finds her/himself in a state of 'expecting' to read for the literal or figurative interpretation that the epitaph elicits. What the epitaph does is repeat what the reader already knows: that as far as the dead are concerned, thought and action, writing and living, are not opposites, but fragments of opposition between the sacred and the profane, between the disembodied voice and the 'gramophone'-like plaque on which it is inscribed. While the dead go on being dead in spite of acting being living through the epitaph's performative voice, the reader goes on living in spite of the contemplative thinking about mortality. Here, I would argue that what makes epitaphic writing epistemic writing is its inciting to participation. You hear the voice that draws you into the void, and lo and behold, you know things. How? 'Through repetition, of course,' we can almost hear Gertrude Stein offering her opinion *in situ*.

Let us see what Fried also further says, following Shlomith Rimmon-Kenan: "Repetition in epitaphs presents a graphic instance of the way in which 'although repetition can only exist in time it also destroys the very notion of time.' Inscribed repetitions undercut the notion of time in the same way that any monument both preserves and erases the event, person, or idea it is erected to commemorate" (621). Applied to explaining writers such as David Markson – whose works, *Wittgenstein's Mistress* (1988), *Reader's Block* (1996), and *This is not a Novel* (2001) will be the focus of this section – Fried's insight can be suggestive of a textual practice which takes a fragment out of its context in order to make that context an actual possibility in time. The fragment is thus endowed with the highest authority. However, Markson's 'stories,' for instance, have no authentic relation to actual time in spite of operating with actual facts. Therefore, what we are dealing with is a case of the fragment, which, if it were to perform the truth of actual events, it would do so only at the expense of making context completely beside the point. The fragment itself, then, acquires the function of the epitaph to perform beyond the grave the 'complete' text's last rights/rites. The epitaph is thus the real existence of the complete text. Perhaps what Markson intuitively knows is not that the author must die at some point, but that the text should. Fragmentary situations which rely on the structure of the 'undone,' such as the one Markson creates in all his 'novels,' refer perhaps to the kind of authorship that questions itself and 'undoes' itself by never asking the same question.

As the epistemic creative writer is always concerned with the degree of awareness that goes into asking precisely the question of what one is doing exactly, looking at the fragment and fragmentary writing as a genre helps us to understand how the epistemic creative writer makes use of the mind's capability to always believe in whatever story he invents and the intent to love the story (here echoing Pascal's observation that "It is natural for the mind to believe and for the will to love; so that, for want of true objects, they must attach themselves to false." In this sense, and because of his ability to listen (à la Beckett and Gertrude Stein) the epistemic writer is the creator of invented knowledge *par excellence* (we recall here as well Hofstadter's idea that links invention to a conscious act of stumbling unto grace). But what kind of genre would epistemic creative writing follow, if we were to place it in a category? Let us look at this more broadly before we take the plunge into the tomb.

Lid on genre

There is no such thing as a great definition of genre. From Aristotle onwards, attempts to describe works of literature in terms of their shared characteristics have been limited to few, yet fundamentally different ideas. Classical genre theory defines genre in terms of regulations and prescriptions, whereas modern genre theory attempts to avoid hierarchies, genre being a matter which can only be described, for example, by identifying a set of structures in a given work. Genre however, whether purely regulated, prescribed, or described, is performative of its own mode of existence.

We could say that genre manifestations occur in two modes: monologic and dialogic. When monologic, genre assumes one of the four most agreed upon manifestations: epic, lyric, dramatic, and satiric. These four, like the monologue, are most powerful when they are indicative of an inner form. On the other hand, when genre is dialogic, in the sense that the inner form of a dramatic structure enters a dialogue, for example, with a satirical element, the inner form assumes an outer expression. We have an instance of this in what is called 'dramatic irony' (Empson, 1973: 38). We have a case of dramatic irony when the narrator makes direct recourse to the reader's participation in the events, for instance when the character is portrayed in a situation that to the character himself seems heroic, and the reader is told beforehand that there are other solutions. The character's actions are thus rendered pathetic. And most often the reader's participation is manifested in the reaction: "how stupid, the idiot is doing the wrong thing!" At this point then we can say that genre enters a self-reflexive mode, it is marked by the plurality inherent in dialogism, and it becomes a definition of writing that is addressed to nobody. Now, this assumption is problematic in the context where genre, although considered the most culturally and historically located of categories, is also seen as fixed, in the sense that it is representational rather than performative. From Bakhtin onwards genre categories were extended to represent not just literary forms but also modes of subjectivity. These modes are seen as transformative interventions in the way genres are being systematized. Emile Benveniste's "shifters" relying on the capacity that pronouns such as the "I" have to combine "conjunctions of past usage(s) with present appropriation" (Benveniste, 1971: 291) point to the fact that what is at stake is also the question of how to determine generically forms of subjectivity that are not manifested in genres that are context situated.

I propose to look at the type of writing that situates itself between genres, between subjectivity and speech acts, between generic history and literary representations. Such writing, I argue – by making the claim that it is seemingly addressed to no one ("myself and strangers") – designates a non-genre that is nevertheless a genre that contains a contradictory meaning: as a topos of a graveyard for words, genre is a sublimation of its own constitution as non-generic and is thus contingent not on historical and cultural development but on their possibilities. Insofar as this kind of writing, however, still takes for granted that there is an audience, and hence purports some ideology, it would have to subscribe to a genre which is thus in a constant mode of being renegotiated, especially in the sense of laying old values to rest.

In their introduction to *Romanticism, History, and the Possibilities of Genre* (1998), Tillotama Rajan and Julia M. Wright take issue with the "conservatism of genre" and call for a revaluation of especially Romanticism since the Romantics developed genre from a "taxonomical given into a cultural category, so as to make it the scene of an ongoing struggle between fixed norms and new initiatives" (Rajan and Wright, 1998). As Romantic literature is characterized by a concern with "generic representation" and the redefinition of literature that seems to be performative of acts of writing especially as manifested in the fragment (see Schlegel), I find the criticism on the Romantic period relevant to any discussion of the performativity of genre. As Rajan and Wright write:

> Genres are often seen prescriptively as a means of interpellating the subject into existing norms and hierarchies. Tzvetan Todorov, however, may well be closer to articulating the essential fluidity of the category when he argues that genres often originate as speech acts, though not all speech acts are immediately institutionalized as genres. If genres are confined to "the classes of texts that have been historically perceived as such," their classification is inevitably bound to the ideology of a society that chooses to encode only certain forms of genres. On the other hand the

fact that there are uncategorized speech acts with the potential to become genres leaves a space for individual or collective intervention in existing system(s) of genre which must therefore be considered highly unstable. This situation is further complicated because the discursive and meta-discursive existence of genres do not necessarily coincide: a genre may have existed in the early nineteenth century but may not have been named until recently. Both in literary practice and in our discussions of it, genre is thus the site of a constant renegotiation between fixed canons and historical pressures, systems and individuals (1).

What is to be emphasized here is that both genre and its representation occupy a "highly unstable" position when it comes to categorizing, and that genre first occurs as a "possibility", which may include its own falling out of categories of communication especially when the latter are rendered as taxonomies. Insofar as there is such a thing as a genre which falls outside of categories of communication that define literary texts in terms of author, text, and reader, or addresser, message, addressee (Jakobson), genre can be said to perform its own failure at the level of definition while successfully being preoccupied with the question of writing itself. Genre in this sense is as profoundly historical and cultural as are the ways in which it is being systematized. However, if genre begins as a possibility transcending a certain "form" that can be conceptualized as "representation" (Lyotard), then genre can be said to perform its own history and typology. When Schlegel initiated a theory concerned with writing "literature," he proposed that the fragment be both the mode and the genre which best reflects how literature is to be both represented and conceptualized. More contemporary writers have expressed a similar concern with writing that addresses genre as a question of writing, with writing designating a specific topos from which the audience, while excluded from making pronouncements on the kind of writing at hand, is brought in a state of 'attendance.' This is epistemic creative writing in a nutshell.

A most notable example is David Markson for whom writing is really reading, and the audience is contingent, meaning here, accidental. Markson does not write for the sake of the author, the text, or the reader, but for the sake of making genre a question of a performative possibility. Writing as a performative potential means having readers embody the dialogic nature of several epitaphic voices. In his "novels" Markson does not define genre, but circumstances when genre becomes the text itself, that is, literature. He employs a style that fashions his writing always as an engagement with the declarative, either in the form of what is already communicated in the words of others, or as a dialogue with another voice that mediates between the written and the spoken word. For example he writes:

> There's no such thing as a great movie. A Rembrandt is great. Mozart chamber music. Said Marlon Brando (Markson, 2001: 148).

When we read such lines, we identify the voice in the first line as that of Markson's. Three lines down, however, we realize that Markson is double voicing Marlon Brando. This is, by the way, an example of dramatic irony. While Markson does not tell us anything beforehand about Marlon Brando, he does get us interested in what else of the kind Marlon Brando said. And while we may not say, "how stupid," we most certainly could exclaim, "really now!" But Brando exits the scene, with Markson leading us into temptation. If double-voicing is allowed, how about triple-voicing? Markson's intervention here, and one that marks him as an epistemic creative writer, indicates what is momentous in writing, the 'now I write about what was said' moment that has the potential to suspend our critical faculties in favor of considering the stupendous, the fantastic, the sublime, the extravagant, the extraordinary, the knowledge that has it all, the etcetera, and the so on of writing. Through writing we know.

For postmodern writers such as Markson, dialogism between various forms of writing, belonging to as many forms of genre, is a way of individualizing one's own style precisely as text. One of the ways for genre to achieve its performative quality, and thus let itself go ahead of structures and definitions, is to appropriate another's voice and turn it into propositions for a style which renders the text unique. Markson puts into practice the close relation between text and genre as mediated by uniqueness. Theoretically this relation has already been dealt with, quite elegantly I would say, by Michael Riffaterre. Says Riffaterre:

> The text is always one of a kind, unique. And it seems to me that this *uniqueness* is the simplest definition of literariness that we can find…. The text works like a computer program designed to make us experience the unique. This uniqueness is what we call style. It has long been confused with the hypothetical individual termed the author; but, in point of fact, *style is the text itself* (Riffaterre, 1983: 2, author's emphasis).

What Riffaterre identifies here as style is what I would call epistemic creative writing, insofar as uniqueness in writing does not come to expression without a heightened awareness of what is proposed epistemologically, or knowledge-wise. Furthermore, what is interesting in Riffaterre's definition is that while he does not distinguish between text and literariness, he does point to what the text is by saying what it is not, that it is definitely not the author. For Riffaterre, the text's uniqueness is a path the reader can walk on, this side of the extraordinary, to get to what goes beyond the text's frame into the realm of aesthetics, the other side of the extraordinary, where uniqueness is not subject to definition. Or so one likes to think. Contrary to Riffaterre, for whom literary phenomena are a question of the relation between the text and the reader, rather than the text and the author, Hugh Silverman's definitions of the text involve the disclosure of the author in a state of in-between-ness: "The text is in the in-between of the artwork and the artist [...] The text embodies the disclosure, but it does not fulfill it. The text is, in a sense, a fragment of that disclosure" (Silverman, 1994: 54-55).

Now, the form of the fragment, in Markson's case mostly as quotations, functions as a performative definition of genre. Markson's works suggest that we ask with Markson himself operative questions related to genre, such as – and repeating ourselves –: can we call a book of fragments a novel? Is a novel still a novel when the characters are given names such as Author, Protagonist, Reader? What are we left with, when critics resort to labels such as "novel of intellectual reference and allusion... minus the novel," or "seminonfictional semifiction" to categorise his texts? Markson's readers are concerned with Markson's character Reader, who, while a reader himself, is acting as a protagonist. Brian Clark makes a pertinent point when he calls Markson's work, particularly *Reader's Block*, a case of "surphysical narrativity." He writes:

Reader, like a *gomi* boy or a bag lady, stumbles into territory of his own creation and finds himself defined, not as *self*, but as *everything else*. What the novel suggests is that categories such as reader and protagonist are never "I" but rather *we*. The form of the commonplace book, with its demonstration of a life spent reading, already gives the novel narrative movement: toward death, the end of a life of reading. But of course reading is also an act of reincarnation; or, better, the dialogue never dies, it is merely we who find our way into the conversation (Clark, 2001: website source).

Here Clark characterizes the epitaphic genre. Through an endless list of anecdotes and facts regarding the deaths of composers, authors, philosophers, etc., Markson, passes on knowledge about the significance of where invented knowledge and factual knowledge can rest together. This fiction genre, which is performative, operates with categories such as Writer, Protagonist, Reader, as appropriated categories of writer, text, reader, with Markson's Protagonist as the adopted child of Text. Writer can provide Reader with an appropriated idea of a Protagonist, who in turn is being adopted by Writer as his Text's alter-ego. Here I would argue that the relation between text and genre, literature and literariness is marked in the equation where the "I" of the text does not become a plural "we," as Clark suggested, but a graveyard topos. Insofar as there is such a genre as "writing for no one" (Gessen), this genre is necessarily performative of a narrative which moves forward in the form of fragments. It is thus not the text which is subsumed by genre. Genre itself elects the text, does the text 'in' as it were, attests to its funeral, and writes the epitaph.

Genre that is determined by entering a dialogue with a voice beyond the grave marks dialogism as a set of legitimate questions that can only be answered by other questions. For example, how does one understand the notion of a 'graveyard of genre'? Does the writing which is inscribed by the topos of the dead automatically subscribe to the epitaphic genre?

The epitaph becomes a function of "writing for no one", and operates with the actualization in genre of a text written *as if* on nothing. This is the genre of the "nonbook." *This is Not a Novel* (2001) is an example which posits the *as if* (I know what I'm doing) as an actualized possibility of having *nothing* (to do with it) combine the autonomous in genre with the general in a text. Markson's novel begins with an instance of the *as if* as a double in his epigraph from Jonathan Swift: "I am now trying an Experiment very frequent among Modern Authors; which is, to write upon nothing." Here Markson assesses to what extent the nothing is worth investigating, as the first couple of lines in the book suggest:

> Writer is pretty much tempted to quit writing. Writer is weary unto death of making up stories (Markson, 2001: 1).

What follows is a tirade on death, who died of what, where they got buried, and even more importantly, information on whether they have been worthy of the events of the day. The epitaph is in the process of emerging out of nothing. It is thus not 'nothing' that needs to be examined, but the fragments that have 'nothing' rest in peace. Says Markson:

> Lord Byron died of either rheumatic fever, or typhus, or uremia, or malaria. Or was inadvertently murdered by his doctors, who had bled him incessantly.

Stephen Crane died of tuberculosis in 1900. Granted an ordinary modern life span, he would have lived well into World War II.

This morning I walked to the place where the street-cleaners dump the rubbish. My God, it was beautiful. Says a Van Gogh letter.

Writer is equally tired of inventing characters (1).

What can be said of the epitaphic genre, and how does it relate to epistemic creative writing? In Markson's case the narrative line concerning the question of writing can be seen as a difference between the fragment and the fragmentary. In writing the fragment Markson writes for the dead. When writing the fragment fragmentarily Markson writes for the living. When the difference between the fragment and the fragmentary is conflated, the writing is for no one. Keith Gessen has suggested that Markson's writing for no one is a dilemma which confronts the modern writer. "If you never do anything" – Gessen asks – "but read and write – how can you then write about anything else?" (Gessen, 1999). While Gessen's point is significant, I would suggest that the textual space marked by the difference between the fragment and the fragmentary in the gathering of quotations, trivia, and facts, opens up a means of communication which goes beyond establishing what genre Markson's writing subscribes to. When genre is performative, when it construes itself as a graveyard for the writing that is done for no one, it defines the text as a space of imagery on which a final statement is made as a description of what limits, delimits, and conditions the text in question. And yet, insofar as we could argue that because Markson writes on death in the way in which he does, he writes for everybody. As an ode to *memento mori*,

Markson pays tribute to all of us who share death, whether we think about it or not. On this, he aligns himself with Gertrude Stein, for whom writing is never for no one but for everyone, especially oneself and strangers.

The idea of an epitaph fulfills the significance of the death of the author. Roland Barthes's argument for the death of the author opened a space for questioning to what extent an author's authority dies with him/her. Barthes' claim was that there is no reason to believe in the author as a point of origin, the author merely fulfilling some authorial categories. But what authorial categories can an author fulfill when he presents himself as three categories, Writer, Protagonist, Reader? What authorial categories are there at work when the writing presents itself as an epitaph for no one? Authors who choose to make their texts analogous with other texts or contexts exercise their authority beyond the grave, as it were, while authors who make their work exemplary exercise an extension of their own autonomy to the margins of writing. Debates on the authority of texts, however, still revolve around the question of who dies first. But it does not occur to writers – except for Markson and the non-comformists, perhaps – that if the text itself dies first, then authority must be confronted differently. Are there remains, and if yes, how do they survive? As fragments, as a faint breath? As a trace of nothing?

Pseudo-epistemics

Let us consider the epitaph as less than marking a spot, a topos, and more than a ghost-voice. Let us look at how it might function as a means for inducing the performativity of the fragment as a graveyard of genre. Insofar as authors can become authors as readers, and thus evade the possibility of dying, the writing that is produced can legitimately be called "reader's block" as a means for shifting between the writing out of memory to writing *in memoriam*.

Markson's *Reader's Block* (1996) is a book made up by an assembly of, more often than not, unrelated fragments. These fragments, while playing and toiling with the idea of forwarding into focus different points of representation, make representation as such secondary to the real process at work, which is to do the text 'in', as it were. The epitaph then emerges as a text put into a perspective similar to dramatic irony. The agency that I assign here to the fragment is akin to what I see the epistemic creative writer does: namely, call into question the premise for interactive knowledge. Here, particularly the question of embodiment is relevant to consider. If the author is dead the text that he leaves for posterity embodies him. If the text dies, formally, so to speak, its words are free to form a platform for some other interaction than was initially intended. Death constrains the form, but the spirit of the word carries on a new content. The epistemic creative writer conflates the production of knowledge with the creative act in the obvious; yet not in the obvious that is out in the open, but rather in the obvious that is right under the surface of writing. Let's have an example.

Markson's narrator – if that is indeed what he is – an author called Reader, considers writing a book. However, the endless gathering of information comes in the way of the actual writing process, Reader thus ending up presenting a list of themes that Protagonist would go through in the eventuality of writing the novel. We read Reader's records and notes, and hear from time to time his voice when he poses direct questions as to the possibility of writing not a work but a representation of a work: "Nonlinear? Discontinuous? Collage-like? An assemblage?" (Markson, 1996: 14). First and foremost, though, Markson establishes an affinity with a certain corpus of writers, mainly the Greeks of the classical period, and the continental modernists, novelists, poets, and philosophers alike. The encounter with unrelated juxtaposed fragments of biographical facts and acts makes reading a move towards performing an act of acknowledging human experience in its intertextual and interactive mode. However, I believe that Markson's work cannot be contextualized as a work of collage, nor can it be made to fit the group of well-established postmodern authors who have collage on their writing agenda, for instance Kathy Acker. Markson's work is precisely not a collage but deals with the emblematic manifestation of the epitaph as a performative genre. His repeated questions throughout his work: "Nonlinear? Discontinuous? Collage-like? An assemblage?" referring to the construction of a work that would fit specific norms of genre, is a simple dismissal of all those attributes as they are devoid in themselves of the ability to generate a topos where writing for no one would become readable independent of context. Markson's postmodernism here is more aligned with that of Mark C. Taylor (especially in *Hiding* (1999), a work emphasizing surface as a topos *par excellence*) than with that of Fredric Jameson who distrusts anything called surface.

Markson's book produces a certain sense of familiarity as the reader is able to recognize references to works and authors of interest. These references are, however, contingent on the reader's participation in the realization of an absent coherence at work through the transcendent formulation of a context of the imagination, which would allow, say, for a synchronic reading of a text Markson has in ellipsis. Markson's fragments as ellipses are indeed epitaphs to both 'complete' and 'incomplete' works that he happens to refer to. For example, these fragments, while seemingly fleeting, are, at closer inspection, not fleeting at all. They appear in fact to be grounded, or inscribed in a context of origin which draws on the epitaphic sense of topos.

Central to Markson's voice is the voice of impersonation which lends reading visiting rights, as it were: one re-visits the site of literature where it merges with other arts. Music and painting are inscriptions reminding one that things happen. Death happens; works of art happen to live longer than their artists; writing happens even in spite of itself; questions happen. It all resonates in counterpoint, or in what Markson calls a "fugue":

> What has happened? It is life that has happened; and I am old.
> Said Louis Aragon.
>
> If an ox could paint a picture, his god would look like an ox.
> Said Xenophanes.
>
> Laurence Sterne's corpse was sold to a medical school by grave robbers. It had been completely dissected before someone chanced to recognize it.
>
> How much of Reader's own circumstances or past would he in fact give to protagonist in such a novel? (12)
>
> [...] Heraclitus did not say that one cannot step into the same river twice. One of his followers did.
>
> Heraclitus did say that praying to statues of the gods was like talking to a house instead of to its owner, however (23).

[...] It took eight years to sell the first printing of six hundred copies of *The Interpretation of Dreams*.

Perhaps one solitary mourner appearing, regularly, at one grave. Here again, a woman. Young. In fact too young to have a connection with anyone buried here that protagonist can fathom.

Or are some few of the graves more recent?

Roland Barthes died after having been hit by a laundry truck (23).

The task that Markson sets himself as an epistemic creative writer is obviously to ring the church bells. It is with sheer delight that one attends Markson's mass for men of stylistic, existential elegance and wisdom, such as Louis Aragon, Laurence Sterne, Heraclitus, and Roland Barthes. The reader is given a chance to experience a sense of finality. Here, Markson's project is successful insofar as it confers to death the quality of being 'final,' yet 'undone.' The epistemic creative writer is caught creating knowledge by undoing its sting.

What was that all about?

In *Reader's Block* Markson thus sets up relations that are analogous to both writing and dying, knowing and knowing creatively. Following, quoting, ghosting, and hosting the 'undone' formulae of Wittgenstein, Markson's practice of writing is a performance of epitaphs in the form of 'undone' fragments to 'complete' texts. Markson undoes himself, and thus raises himself to the level of the creative and imaginative critic. "The world is my idea" (11), says Markson/Wittgenstein performing rituals of textual appearance, genuineness, truth and sacrality, marvellous inconsistency, and funerary finality. It can be contended that for Markson, the construction of the fragment in the epitaphic sign forms and follows a cortege behind the complete text's final way. Following Wittgenstein's voice and letting us know nothing else about Wittgenstein's writing is a way of re-inventing Wittgenstein's work *in absentia,* for we know it exists. Markson's narrating voice in the fragment about Barthes is similar to a prayer that one likes to imagine is said by the one leading the cortege. One also likes to think that the prayer involves words on a *corpus Christi incognitus*, as it were, words which go beyond the representation of *memento mori*, and yet inform the "interminable undecidibility" that the deconstructive move from representation to representation posits. On this relation Karen Mills-Courts writes in a relevant passage in her work *Poetry as Epitaph*:

> This movement opens up a text to the "the danger itself". This danger is death: ... abyss that Derrida calls the death of presence and the death of meaning that must accompany the death of voice. In this situation the critic is, like Eugenio Donato's Baudelaire, "constituted by an accumulation of memories, an archeological museum of fragments of the past, haphazardly juxtaposed, each a synecdochal textual representation ordered by the accidental metonymic accident of proximity." And, as Donato points out, the count less than their emblem, the pyramid, ... collection of memories which we are now in a position to read as the symbol of linguistic representation itself... [The critic] then, being nothing more than a set of representations, is reduced to a cemetery containing nothing but funerary monuments (Mills-Courts, 1990: 7-8).

The significance of Markson's work lies in its concern with the possibility of representing in writing both the author and the critic, yet without making recourse to either of them. Insofar as Markson poses questions in an inverse order, the critic and the author appear in a perspective which inscribes voice within an economy of representation. It is not Donato's perspective, in which the critic is the warden of the churchyard, nor Mills-Courts's perspective in which voice is endangered and must settle with accompanying the "death of presence" and the "death of meaning."

Markson's approach to the text is by saving it from itself and its appearances. It is neither criticism, nor the text or the author that is subjected to Markson's questions, but rather, the mutual relationship between them, which puts emphasis on the fragment as a unique form of literariness. For Mills-Courts, for example, it is criticism that fulfils the characteristics of finality in death, whether textual or otherwise. Criticism is raised above "voice" and is turned into a principle for epitaphic functioning. Here she says:

> Criticism becomes the epitaph of epitaphs. Nonetheless, we can experience the "death" of voice, of the "principle of intelligibility," the loss of this kind of significance, only by conjuring its "afterlife" as an echo that inhabits the inscription that points to its loss. We understand the death of "presence" by virtue of a maker that "presents" and "describes" its loss through a peculiar reincarnation of presence in the form of the voice of meaning. This too is epitaphic (8).

Now, Markson's work is remarkable for its mediation between the author and the critic, the author's death and the author's function, as he creates an intimate canon of literary theory which is made up of quotations in the image of Wittgenstein. Not of Wittgenstein's thought to be sure, as that would mean to render a 'world, and what is the case' as insignificant, but Wittgenstein's style which seems to be ever commanding, "prepare yourself to follow me." Relations of epitaphic representation are posed in Markson's works as questions to the text and the premises behind it. "Wittgenstein, it is you who are creating all the confusion!" (Markson, 2001: 141), 'he,' the 'character' named Writer, exclaims in *This is Not a Novel* going on to trace in the words themselves the meaning of having incompatible, yet juxtaposed fragments of deaths, natural and not so natural. And while these words seem to inaugurate their writers, they nonetheless usurp the authority of their writers. Markson's epitaphic fragment is the complete text's undone doing. The writers, painters, musicians, and other artists whose deaths and mishaps Markson refers to are all there not to form an entire oeuvre – a literary canon, monographs or otherwise – but to inform the fragmentary in the fragments that Markson finds worthy of his own work. These fragments elect the ceremonial master. Examples abound.

This is Not a Novel rejoices in planning the funeral ritual over writers with whom we find affinity and correspondence. The book's record of registered suicides, madnesses, antisemitics, has only one point: to go nowhere, while still "getting somewhere" as Markson himself puts it. As the dead person goes nowhere, yet occupies a space both in memory and in the ground, so does Markson's 'novel.' While it goes nowhere, in the sense that there is neither character development, nor climax, it progresses through voice and style. It cuts the reader's need for plot to the bare epitaph, found in a triple-voice, echoing Beckett, Wittgenstein and the other Stein, Gertrude. One finds a breath suited for Laurence Sterne:

And who are you? said he. – Don't puzzle me, said I.

Says *Tristram Shandy*, VII 33 (12).

In between one passes by other mentioning of some other 'passing' as well as passing remarks on Writer's agenda:

A novel with no intimation of story whatsoever, Writer would like to contrive.

And with no characters. None (2).

Plotless. Characterless.

Yet seducing the reader into turning pages nonetheless (3).

[...] Actionless, Writer wants it.

Which is to say, with no *sequence of events*.

Which is to say, with no indicated *passage of time*.

Then again, getting somewhere in spite of this (4).

[...] Indeed with a beginning, middle, and an end.

Even with a note of sadness at the end (4).

[...] A novel with no *setting*.

With no so-called furniture.

Ergo, meaning finally without *descriptions* (5).

[...] A novel with no overriding central *motivations*, Writer wants. (6).

[...] Writer sitting and/or talking to himself being no more than renewed verification that he exists.

In a book without characters.

As noted, not being a character but the author, here.

We are and we are not.
Said Heraclitus.

Even with innumerable obvious likes and/or dislikes and central self-evident preoccupations.

[...] Knowledge is not intelligence.
Heraclitus additionally said (82).

[...] Laurence Sterne's realization roughly a third of the way through *Tristram Shandy* that the book lacks a preface. Whereupon he inserts one right where he is (106).

[...] Laurence Sterne died of pleurisy, after years of lung hemorrhages (128).

[...] Writer incidentally doing his best here – insofar as his memory allows – not to repeat things he has included in his earlier
work.

Meaning in this instance the four hundred and fifty or more deaths that were mentioned in his last book also (147).

[...] Roman Jakobson in opposition to a novelist, namely Nabokov, teaching literature at Harvard:
Should an elephant teach zoology?

Arnold Schoenberg and George Gershwin were tennis partners.

John Donne. Anne Donne. Undone (149).

[...] Words, words, words (165).

Markson's performative enumeration of "words, words, words," others' words, ends in a gathering of voices whose sound is similar to the writing on the cenotaph. The epitaphic fragment answers the question, "what is a fragment" in a wholesome voice representative of the words of the imagination. In postmodernist writing the fragment is manifested as a history which is impossible without a theory. In other words, the fragment as text in history does not exist as a textual content (form) unless it is rendered as form (content) in a specific discourse. In the context of the epistemic creative discourse what happens is that the fragment as an instance of formal epistemics gives us a semantics that produces useful analogies, or metaphors. Markson's fragments make up a whole world of silences, thus achieving what Beckett wanted. This epitomizes in fact Markson's contribution to the postmodern discourse that uses a modern voice (à la Stein and Wittgenstein) to dismiss the collage or what in modern discourse went by the name of "incompatible juxtapositions" (à la Acker).

Thus, one cannot stop using words, in the sense of quoting, in the same manner as one cannot stop turning pages. Markson's intimations become one's accompanying mistresses. Of course, before Markson wrote *Reader's Block* (1996) and *This Is Not a Novel* (2001), he wrote *Wittgenstein's Mistress* (1988). There the narrator, Kate, a middle-aged woman, seemingly the only person left on earth, initiates what for Markson became the genre of the dead novel. Or the death of the text. The complete text, that is, the text with a beginning, a middle and an end. Without any governing fragments, ruins, and other detachments. Markson's contribution to the construction of the fragment as formal epistemics[1] proceeds from assuming that the complete text

---

[1] Here formal epistemics should be understood as the use of literary methods, tropes, and devices to elucidate epistemic problems, including decision theory, agency, and framing.

is a text without questions. A good text should travel among quotations and pose questions.

Throughout *Wittgenstein's Mistress*, Kate is an example of the Wittgensteinian mode of questioning without being either affirmative, or propositional. All the questions in the book become a mode of putting themselves into a perspective that is inscribed within a hypothetical, yet certain framework. The question is a perspective that language sees itself through. Therefore there can be no complete texts. There is no such thing as a great complete text. Only musings, such as Kate's, who in turn acts as a pseudo-epistemic creative writer, writing for both Wittgenstein and Markson. Says she:

> Once, Turner had himself lashed to the mast of a ship for several hours, during a furious storm, so that he could later paint the storm. Obviously, it was not the storm itself that Turner intended to paint. What he intended to paint was a representation of the storm.
>
> One's language is frequently imprecise in that manner, I have discovered. Actually, the story of Turner being lashed to the mast reminds me of something, even though I cannot remember what it reminds me of (Markson, 1988: 12).

Turner becomes Odysseus' epitaph. What Markson achieves in his work is ground the concern with defining the fragment in the form of an epitaph to a once 'complete' text, or more precisely here a defined text, and thus redeem writing from itself. That is to say, by creating a corpus of fragments which seem to perform the function of quoting themselves among themselves, Markson assumes for himself the task of the creative critic who has no tasks, but who indeed fulfils the function of producing a body of literature which has the effect that imagination ought to have on/for a theoretical level. Markson converges to the horizon of perspective, both the modernist concern with defining via style the difference between creativity and knowledge and their mediums of expression in the fragment and the fragmentary, as well as the postmodernist concern with the same difference, yet expressed in a concern with hypothesizing definition that is based on predication.

For postmodern epistemologists, the fragment does not seem to exist unless it is named something else other than itself, unless it performs genre. Here particularly the idea of having an epistemology of creative writing as underlying a genre is interesting to consider, as such an epistemology of creative writing does the job of fusing what we know (based on facts) with how we know it (based on belief and the imagination). Markson, however, is a postmodernist writer who puts the fragment into a perspective which elongates it, as it were. This is the epitaphic perspective. What Markson does for the text is provide it with a condition for the possibility of looking at itself as a dead text. As a dead text, whose voice emerges through the epitaph, the text poses its own questions as to what makes it a literary matter. Every epitaphic question becomes its own answer, to paraphrase Debra Fried. Thus the text IS, because it has an epitaph. In this perspective, the epitaph provides the fragment with an identity that replaces the text in which the fragment itself appears with what is unique and extraordinary. It is the voice of the epitaph which makes the unique decipherable. The epitaph speaks for itself. And the epistemic creative writer takes dictations.

Speeding the reading

For Markson, the construction of a complete text is contingent on the fragment insofar as the writing process is based on gathering fragments of facts and information with which the writer's imagination engages. Conversely, leaving the fragments to themselves, as it were, presenting them as an *assemblage* engages the reader's imagination. The *assemblage* is Markson's matrix for the "nonlinear," "discontinuous," and the "collage-like" truth of the fragments which complete themselves in accordance with how far the reader's imagination can stretch itself.

When recognizing the writers for whom Markson writes imaginary epitaphs, one follows Markson's going ahead of the epitaphic perspective. When coming across names one has never heard of before, one invents stories about Markson's following behind the epitaphic perspective. The truth of Markson's text, then, is not interpretable in *appearance*, but *in lieu of appearance*, namely in perspective. This perspective combines the emergence of an 'idea' of a complete text, which the reader is able to imagine against the background of Markson's fragments, with the fragments that prompt imagination in the direction of completeness. In other words, this perspective is epitaphic, as the epitaph's function can only be actualized, or fulfilled, in perspective; or in the perspective which reading posits, one could contend. Hence, Markson's art goes ahead of itself as a text by writing imaginary epitaphs in a way which *appears* to celebrate, but actually refuses to follow the reading practice of such critics as Harold Bloom. In *This is Not a Novel* Bloom's reading speed, which is presented to appear to be something of a fright, something one must beware of, something one must guard oneself against, is lampooned:

> Harold Bloom's claim to The New York Times that he could read at a rate of five hundred pages per hour.
>
> Writer's arse.
>
> Spectacular exhibition! Right this way ladies and gentlemen! See Professor Bloom read the 1961 corrected and reset Random House edition of James Joyce's *Ulysses* in one hour and thirty-three minutes. Not one page stinted. Unforgettable!
>
> [...] What's this? Can't spare an hour and a half? Wait, wait. Our matinee special, today only! Watch Professor Bloom eviscerate the Pears-McGuinness translation of Wittgenstein's *Tractatus* – eight minutes and twenty-nine seconds flat! Guaranteed (Markson, 2001: 130-132).

The epitaph goes ahead, and the reader follows. It is this act of following – where Markson follows others by being ahead of them, ahead of their death, so that they will follow him, follow Markson's epitaph on them – which thus 'completes' the picture of how fragments are defined, how genre is defined. What we read is a topos, a graveyard of genre, when we read his epitaphic fragments. What does Markson do with his fragments, one would like to ask, apart from preparing himself to follow, as the epitaph dictates? Perhaps guard himself against the influence of others, or else welcome it. Welcome to Writing. Read in Peace. And don't think too much about Knowledge.

Exquisite crossings: Andrei Codrescu's rules of conventions

In the final bit here, and keeping with Markson's multitude of voices against the background of hollow tombs, let us go even more pluralistic and democratic and look at the popular with the US critical *intelligentia* Andrei Codrescu. His attempts at formulating a poetics of nonconformity against the background of influences from the Beat Generation and The New York School Poets demonstrate what it takes to be an epistemic creative writer. My argument is that Codrescu's poetry, prose poetry, and fictional work map a geography of the imagination in which the creative past is reconfigured through the recordings he makes of the present *zeitgeist*. All the writers discussed so far did that, heeded the *zeitgeist*, but not all thought of returning to the form of the aphorism via the fragment to indicate that the creative matrix of a culture generates its own rules and conventions.

Insofar as writing is a social method of creative imagination, it is worth considering to what extent speaking in slogans of nothing, by making detours through everything that happens in the meanwhile, discloses how knowledge is a social act of the 'expressivist' type. And what are the consequences of a social epistemics of creative writing that is devised in the name of refusing to methodologize writing? One may even wonder: what was the point of going through writers who resist contemporary attempts to classify epistemologists of creative writing according to their capability to instruct in schools? While reading Gold, Hobbs, and Berlin's essay "Writing Instruction in School and College English" from *A Short History of Writing Instruction* (2012), I came upon this passage: "James Berlin has critiqued expressivist rhetoric, particularly in its later manifestations, for what he considered its subjectivist epistemology, privileging the private and personal vision of the author at the expense of the public and the social" (243).

Now, while trying to understand the writers I've looked at here from the viewpoint of their poetics of epistemic creative writing that did not favor conformism, I came to the realization that in order to see how just how an epistemic system of creative writing works as an interactive model, one has to look precisely not at authors who invite to expression through imitation, but to writers who, as I've kept claiming so far, instruct by consciously making a gesture towards renouncing claims to methodical knowledge. By constantly posing the question: 'why write?' while showing stamina, resilience, and vitality doing just that, the writers here, from Beckett to Codrescu and beyond, invite us to consider this lesson: that writing is no effective mechanism for knowledge without the acknowledgement that the "I" writing is in fact doing nothing than showing the "I" citing. 'I am a writer because I quote,' one could just as well say it, and then get on with the program. Writing epistemically creatively means here that if there is any value in the writing that instructs without a method, then it is found in the personal expressivity that traces its steps back not to what others 'tell' you so that you may 'know,' but to what you discover yourself in this very act of tracing.

Let us look at Andrei Codrescu more closely to get a better sense of what is at stake here, also where the difference between a pedagogy of celebrating the self and a social heuristics is concerned.

Epistemics of the past

Every time Andrei Codrescu writes a new book critics unanimously agree upon one thing: Codrescu's voice is not only a voice of his time, but a voice capable of going in and out of cultural perspectives and contexts. Robert Olen Butler puts it thus in his review of Codrescu's latest novel *Wakefield*: "No one – and I mean no one – is more deeply in touch with the zeitgeist of this obsessive, lunatic age than Andrei Codrescu." The rave reviews coming from established scholars, poets, and novelists alike all see Codrescu as absolutely essential for our culture and literature. What is less noticed is the fact that while Codrescu's voice renews itself all according to which directions our postmodern culture moves towards, his ability to say something essential about literature and culture comes from the fact that he writes from within the past. He shares this with Raymond Federman, but whereas for Federman writing from the past is writing the past in formal recollecting terms that gather the experiences of the survivor with those of the immigrant, for Codrescu the past constitutes the invention of the future that consists of double perspectives.

In all his works Codrescu makes recourse to his experience as an immigrant writer who learns first to observe and then to subvert the customs of the new territory. Bringing a double voice to one's investigations of a literary scene involves a mapping of cardinal points in what constitutes the geography of the imagination of the said literary scene. Here I want to argue that Codrescu's mapping carries with it an element of nonconformity, insofar as it simultaneously relies on, fulfills, rejects, and partakes in the poetics put forth by his precursors.

In the context of our concern with epistemic creative writing here, we could say that Codrescu articulates the following question: 'how can I write like myself when in fact I want nothing more than to write like Allan Ginsberg?' A writing program emerges and we see Codrescu passing on the lessons he has learned from his masters as they are now his own. Unlike Beckett, however, who is also a model, and who rejected himself as a writing guru, Codrescu reminds his readers not to kid themselves about what they are reading, namely, that they are reading 'Codrescu' (here, as he follows the poet Ted Berrigan) and not themselves as inspired readers who see themselves already as writers of the future.

Codrescu's message here and advice to potential writers is this: 'do not conform; if you really know things do not say too much; and do not expect me to teach how (not) to write.' It is against the background of nonconformity that Codrescu's voice emerges as a recorder of an invented future that enables him to register a real present, or a *zeitgeist*. I furthermore want to suggest that Codrescu's concern with the past in a society that is marked by a desire to forget the past formulates itself as a poetics of epistemic creative writing that has return, revision, and reconfiguration on its agenda.

Ever since Codrescu came to America from communist Romania in 1966 his literary works have developed and maintained a nonconformist poetics. One of the central points in his poetry is that escape from conformity facilitates a mapping of conformity which proves useful in the process of reconfiguring and transforming the geography of conformist thought into a geography of nonconformity. The lesson? That one can write, teach writing, and proclaim at the same time that there is no method.

As a student of mathematics who crossed over to philosophy only so that he could write poetry, Codrescu's intentions from the beginning of writing at age 10 was to find out how poetry maps its incursions into cultural phenomena both against the grain of culture and along with it. We find the mapping of directions in Codrescu's impressive oeuvre in all sorts of manifestations. He has written more then 20 books of poetry and novels, started the influential journal *Exquisite Corpse* in the late 70s – which gathers the voices of cutting-edge poets – made the prize winning documentary *Road Scholar* in 1993, and has appeared with regularity on National Public Radio's program "All Things Considered." Along with mapping what is American in American poetry *par excellence* and American culture in general, Andrei Codrescu's writings engage, on the one hand, with returning to the poets whom he is still determined to learn from (especially the New York poets and the Beat poets), and on the other hand, with making his writings declarations in a manifesto form on the state of the imagination. In his short piece from 1999 in the journal *American Demographics*, "Zeitgeist: Making Up America" Codrescu returns to an episode about the notion of the poetic self which constitutes itself in and out of a perspective of optimism. The essay, whose subtitle reads: "Optimism at all costs is the price we pay for prosperity," is an example of how Codrescu's double perspective on American optimism both enforces the notion and also subverts it. The essay begins with recalling an episode that is also told in his autobiography, *An Involuntary Genius in America's Shoes,* albeit there the emphasis is on a different context (this practice of repeating oneself, or even better, quoting oneself, is very much at the core of what an epistemologist of creative writer does):

I have been a commentator on National Public Radio's "All Things Considered" for 16 years. During that time, the audience for the show has tripled. Obviously, this wasn't my doing, but I am often referred to as a "popular commentator," which should give pause. What are 7.7 million people thinking when they listen to the rants of a guy with a Transylvanian accent who didn't even grow up in the United States? What does that say about the United States?

Not only do I have weird accent, but I spent the first 19 years of my life without American television, American products, or the American language. My first sentence in English was composed in 1966 in Rome, while waiting for a visa to the U.S. My friend Julian and I composed this sentence: 'why don't you kill yourself?' we were so proud of this question, we took it to the streets and asked various Romans: 'Why don't you kill yourself?' The only people who tried to make sense of these words were a bunch of guys loitering by a fountain near the train station. They thought we were asking them how to get to the self-service machines at the station, those things that dispense soft drinks. Ever since, I have associated the idea of 'self' with a self-service machine. You put in a quarter and out pops a self (Codrescu, 1999: 24).

What this passage suggests is that nonconformity, for Codrescu, is a return to oneself by means of language. If language is the means for the re-invention of the self, then the self that is begot by language is a self of the future. Codrescu's further remark that "the chief characteristic of a new American self was its forward-looking ability, also known as optimism" (24) stands, on one hand, as a diagnosing of the American optimism, and on the other hand, as a critique of it. Codrescu's double perspective comes to expression when he contrasts the chief characteristic of optimism with another equally important trait thereof, namely, forgetfulness. Says Codrescu: "The number one ingredient in the melting pot of a successful American identity was amnesia" (25). Identifying paradoxical relations inherent in the notion of optimism constitutes for Codrescu a reminder of the implications of repressing a history that includes the vanquishing of the Native Americans, slavery, and labor struggles.

Codrescu's double take on optimism ultimately constitutes a belief in the necessity of a return. Yet this return usually marks either belatedness or anticipation, or both at the same time. For example Codrescu's repeated line in the evoked episode "Why don't you kill yourself' can be seen as both, an anticipation of America, and a belated expression that echoes Allen Ginsberg's poem "America." Ginsberg's questions after having demanded that America go fuck itself resonate with Codrescu's own feelings. In a tone, both similar and unlike that of Codrescu's, Ginsberg makes an appeal for a return to the things that have been repressed in America. While the outer frame of Ginsberg's plea is optimism, the inner tone is that of lamentation. Writes Ginsberg:

> America when will you be angelic? When will you take off your clothes? When will you look at yourself through the grave? When will you be worthy of your million Trotskyites? America why are your libraries full of tears? America when will you send your eggs to India?" (Ginsberg, 1956: 31-34)

Codrescu's complex optimism regarding America's simplistic optimism overrides the discourse of the unknown and contributes to his desire to map nonconformist poetry. In this he acts both as a critic and as a poet himself, thus embodying the epistemologist who wants to know how knowledge is produced in poetry by spotting the relevant analogies between others' poetry and his own experiences as a poet as they are fused at the collective creative writing horizon. Thus he brings to his discourse a double voice: his works are praised for their ability to observe with accuracy current cultural manifestations, yet the tone carries unmistakably the stamp of the 50s and 60s.

What is more, the more 'accurate' Codrescu's writings are, the more they also exhibit a fascination with what is mysterious and mystical in the obvious. As a mathematician, he goes about writing in the same way that Hofstadter does, by emphasizing the quality of hunches, contemplation, and what is beautiful in the banal observations. As a poet interested in the spiritual state of the US, Codrescu is also finely attuned to what ticks the soul, and what fuses the poetical bomb of sensibility. The epistemic creative writer 'knows' by virtue of his being able to identify the irreverent in writing, what it is useful for, and where it gets the poet.

Naked rebels

Codrescu identifies Ginsberg as the father of three generations of rebels. Having visited Ginsberg at his place in Lower East Side as the first thing to do in 1966, Codrescu has since concluded that Ginsberg is "the king of this capital of Bohemia that shelters the poet and artist refugees from the American dream, as well as the literal refugees who are looking for It" (Codrescu, 1993: 43). This suggests that Ginsberg's America is for Codrescu the art of invention and the locus where literary maps can be represented against the grain. Since their first meeting he realized that Ginsberg, while embodying a multitude of presences, is also anchored in the past that invents the future, which determines a whole generation and its time. As he recalls in his autobiography, the first impression of Ginsberg was of an erudite man who would talk to him rapidly in French and said "Kerouac, Cassady, San Francisco, Prague, Andrei Voznesenski, pot, and Umberto Saba in one sentence" (Codrescu, 2001: 133).

Ginsberg is also the poet whom Codrescu 25 years later visits in New York in connection with the literal mapping of the American landscape and poetics of spirituality presented in the documentary *Road Scholar*. The making of this documentary that took Codrescu from coast to coast in a '68 red Cadillac convertible had the purpose of investigating just how conformist nonconformity is. Visiting anything from utopian communes in upstate New York to old New York poets in East Village, from the ruins of Detroit to the riches of Chicago, from New Age and Native American groups to the gambling groups of Las Vegas and the poets of San Francisco, Codrescu is not only on the road haunted by Jack Kerouac, but insists that what makes the road interesting is its ability to plant an idea in our heads. This idea is America itself. On the road Codrescu learns that if one wants to map America as a land (of opportunities or otherwise) one has to do it through ideas, particularly the *'non serviam'* kind.

Each group of people that Codrescu visits, every poet, and every old friend contribute to letting Codrescu in on a secret. And one of the first lessons that he learns is that there is a relation of interdependency between a secret and nonconformity. One such secret is revealed by Allen Ginsberg in New York when, following Kerouac, he tells Codrescu that "the Land is an Indian thing" (Codrescu, 1993: 43). Since Codrescu is a fast learner, one of the first things he proposes to Ginsberg is that one should make a motion for acknowledging Ted Berrigan's right to have his statue erected in New York instead of that of Peter Stuyvesant, the Dutch governor of New Amsterdam who, in around 1655, wrote a letter to the queen in which he demanded the exclusion of Jews from the colony, now Manhattan. As Codrescu reasons, Ted Berrigan is much more suited to have a statue right on Stuyvesant square because Berrigan was an "includer of people" and not an excluder.

As an includer of people Berrigan is the kind of poet who is capable of inventing a future that becomes someone else's present. Such anticipations open the gate to the actualization of a potential, namely the potential to devise what is not conventional. Thus Codrescu quotes Berrigan: "People of the future / While you are reading these poems, remember you didn't write them, I did" (Codrescu, 1993: 45). Codrescu's scholarship on the road in the 90s concludes with a visit to Lawrence Ferlinghetti and a recollection of a past episode which involves Codrescu's literary ambitions in '66 and his subsequent claim to fame. He writes with the full conviction of having achieved the mapping of a past that reinvented itself as a future in which particularly lines such as these were valid: 'if you want to make it, don't listen; if you want to find it, don't listen; if you want to know it, don't listen.' The secret, however, to knowing how *not* to listen is in paying attention. Says Codrescu, hinting at some paradoxes of publishing:

> Lawrence Ferlinghetti published Allen Ginsberg, Jack Kerouac, and Frank O'Hara under the imprint of City Lights Books. Out of his hands came the small spring of rebel writing that became the mighty river of the sixties. I had but two ambitions when I left Romania: to be published in English by City Lights and in French

by Gallimard. The first one is done. City Lights published my memoir, *In America's Shoes*, and an anthology from my literary journal *Exquisite Corpse*, called *The Stiffest of the Corpse: An Exquisite Corpse Reader* (183).

City lights are not natural lights. They make you see, but what exactly? Kerouac's road had its terminus point in San Francisco and so had Codrescu's, although as Ferlinghetti puts it "the road hardly exists anymore, it's all up in the air" (183). Ferlinghetti's statement has implications for Codrescu whose intention, however, was to map the earth not the heaven. This earthly mapping had a concrete purpose: to constitute Codrescu's own contribution to continuing the line of nonconformist thought by taking the potential expressed in Ginsberg, Kerouac, and Berrigan to a realization of what is to know about these poets. Codrescu's initial aim was thus to turn a potential into a geography of the imagination that was still capable of accommodating such notions as the "road in the air."

An earlier poem titled "Toward the end of 1969" maps Codrescu's double-edged optimism and illustrates how the geography of the imagination of the time can be mapped onto an epistemic creative project that can be read both in the context of the 60s and that of the 90s, thus establishing the role of the poet as a subverting recorder of his time. Writes Codrescu:

> suddenly toward the end of 1969 everything is
> "objectified" after a fashion that leaves
> you in your clothes but not in your mind
> and every day sees
> the birth of new instruments, wooden and
> metallic, born out of circumstance, conjecture,
> and plain absence. not to under-

> estimate these things a new set of values
> is also born and not only one does not under-
> estimate but one praises
> lavishly, completely, with the dedication
> of a saint to the cross. sets of
> paternal and maternal perception knock
> patiently at the doors of the brand new cubicles
> like infant birds in eggs with a right
> to this world, but, really, what right
> to my world does a cane, a shoe or a hat have
> what right except part-time presence?
> i wonder but it all comes to this: even i
> see no wrong with the 90 per cent "alien-
> ness" of the world and i
> should know better because i am a poet
> (Codrescu, 1977: 13)

A brief look at the formal features of this poem discloses the same desire at work for mapping and formulating a geography of the imagination against the grain of convention. This mapping occurs precisely in the interval where the lines break off. Arguments are also disposed of in favor of the more convivial, 'because I say so' pragmatism. The poet just knows what he knows. The conspicuous ellipsis marked by the empty space after lines such as "everything is, "a fashion that leaves", "everyday sees" is there to diagnose what ails presence. The only two words contained within inverted commas, "objectified" and "alien-ness" mark the constraints of presence, insofar as presence only exists as part-time in relation to rights and objects. In particular, familiar – as against alien – and perhaps subjective – as against objective objects – are constrained to a part-time presence. What is called forth here is the right to return to a time before 1969, reconfigure 1969, and establish a road map for what comes after. What a poet should always know better is the fact that any act of revision takes place both in the break with the conformism of the past and in acknowledging the potential in conformist thinking to subvert its own ideology.

In a poem, "Sexual Politics," which appears in a novella from the collection of stories written between 1970 and 1978 under the title *A Bar in Brooklyn,* we find again a mapping of time and its influence on imagination which constitutes itself against the background of a double perspective:

> The things that made me come in 1966
> are now as different as
> America is in 1974
>
> In 1966 I liked to fuck straight on top
> Or bottom
> mostly women
> mostly men
> and America was an active country
> with men at the top
>
> In 1974 the government is collapsing on TV
> while the country watches from the bottom
> as I fuck boys, women, men, and girls
>
> and a new lyrical dimension opens
> in both of us
>
> My sweet juices, where are you leading the world
> (Codrescu, 2000: 159-160)

America is not what it used to be, as the message seems to suggest, yet one senses that liberation, whether sexual or otherwise, is not so much unleashed by activist movements as it is instituted by rules of conventions. Here you have two possibilities: to fuck on top or bottom, with more variation where the subjects are concerned: men or women, boys, or girls. It is all the same, the country is still going down the drain. Having sex does not change the knowledge of that.

The epistemic creative writer seems to say, 'write it like it is, but make sure not to leave out the self-delusion in the act of making claims to knowledge.' Codrescu adds here to the general stock of beliefs, makes the necessary changes to maintain consistency, and then considers to what extent the consequence is still true and aligned with what he hypothesizes. In logic this situation is identified with possible world semantics for counterfactuals. We 'know' by testing our beliefs against the background of what is consistent with our antecedents.

The epistemologist's compass

Is it perhaps not a coincidence that some of Codrescu's own formulations of rules regarding the poetics of nonconformity appear not only in journals that bear such names as *American Demographics* but also as addresses, such as the one delivered to the American Geographers' Association in 2003. The essay, which is in fact a prose poem, begins by asserting a change in the program: Codrescu will not lecture but go around and ask every geographer to "confess a cardinal sin," a confession that will earn each geographer Codrescu's poetic absolution. He then proceeds to explain the necessity of poetics by invoking Ted Berrigan:

> *Poets*, my friend Ted Berrigan used to say,
> Should endeavor to make at least four directions
> In their poems: Up and Down and Sideways
> And that's a cross
> The rest of the dimensions will take care of themselves –
> When my friend and colleague Kent Matthews approached me
> To speak to you people I wasn't too sure.
> I wasn't too sure what geographers were
> I looked it up in the OED and it said something like
> Geographers study physical boundaries
> But then the secondary definition said that people boundaries and
> economic ones were involved too
> But obviously not very much because that would be anthropology
> And economics
> Which kind of reassured me because that's just like poets
> Who get to study everything but not enough to call it anything else
> Though – to tell you the truth – many poets today don't really care what
> you call what they do as long as they get to do their best thinking about
> whatever it is in the most provocative language available –
> Maybe geographers are like that now – [...]
> (Codrescu, 2003: website source)

One of the points in Codrescu's address is to point to differences and similarities between two poetics – that of a geographer's and that of a poet's – which share a common ground where the mapping of an imaginative field is concerned. Letting the geographer know what poets do or should do, and putting signposts as to how one can identify and then go against a rule of convention, Codrescu's poetics relies on the geography of the imagination as a "prime mover" that both geographers and poets share each in their own investigation. As the talk was delivered on Mardi Gras in New Orleans, the poem takes a romantic turn and suggests that the landscape itself gets poetic whenever natural conventions are crossed. New Orleans is thus called the American Venice, and Codrescu describes its impetus by drawing parallels between the life of the city and that of the poet for whom the task of poetry is not only to devise a poetics of nonconformism, but also one of epistemic creativity.

> A city that refuses to conform to anything that is known about it
> And has had its geography redrawn and reimagined
> First as a creature of the lower Mississippi
> A river that has no intention of conforming and never has
> To the designs of those that'd fix its course and propensities.
> (idem, website source)

Codrescu's central point in his geographical epic is to emphasize the idea that nonconformist writing can be measured by the mappings that we create in the image of mapping. The image of mapping is a going in and out of territorial perspective. In his 'poem' "What is American About American Poetry" (1999), based on questions posed to prominent poets by the Poetry Society of America in connection with a major festival, Codrescu gives a clear indication of how nonconformity is bound up with history and why returns are necessary. More specifically, what bothers Codrescu is questions about literary traditions. While these traditions are worthy of following, his message seems to be that once a tradition is recognized, one has to move on. What is at stake in getting on with things is the fact that a tradition can only gain recognition if it is acknowledged and refuted at the same time. As Codrescu puts it in the following exchange that begins with a question by the interviewer:

Are there essential ways in which you consider yourself an American poet?

yes – i walk the walk and talk the talk & the talk came to me from living americans not books, so that their hands & mugs & hips put the english on it.

When you consider your own "tradition," do you think primarily of American poets?

i think of romanian, french, german, english romantics, and americans – in that order.

Do you believe there is anything specifically American about past and contemporary American poetry? Is there American poetry in the sense that there is said to be American painting or American film? Do you wish to distinguish American poetry from British or other English language poetry?

duh. of course there is. the specifics are in the poets, but not all of them. american poetry, film, painting, yes. i certainly distinguish american poetry from all other poetry written in english. the particulars of the american language are not, however, "national" because america is not a nation but a collection of impulses proceeding from a fundamental writ.

Which historic poets do you consider most responsible for generating distinctly American poetics?

whitman, pound, williams, mina loy, gertrude stein, hart crane, louis zukofski, carl rakosi, george oppen, kenneth rexroth, allen ginsberg, gary snyder, robert creeley & television.

[...]

What significance does popular culture possess in your sense of American poetry?

it renews the language. i'll take bart simpson over many of my contemporaries any day.

What about the American poets who lived primarily in Europe (Eliot, Pound, Stein)? What about the European poets who have recently lived or worked in America (Heaney, Walcott, Milosz)?

what about them? the americans who lived in europe found out just how american they were; the europeans who live in america usually find out just how american they wanna be.

[...]

Do you believe you could readily distinguish a poem by an American poet from a poem by other poets writing in English?

yes, especially if McDonald's comes up.
(Codrescu, 1999b: website source)

This 'prose poem' that formally continues Codrescu's predilection for the form – one he developed against the background of incorporating the style of the greatest aphorists in the American Romantic and Beat tradition – sets an agenda for analyzing a culture and its history against the grain of what has been naturalized.

Codrescu's analysis of the impact of literature that derives from various cultural manifestations can be seen as an attempt at identifying how the present maps its history in the image of future reinventions. For example Bart Simpson is not only seen as a poet, but also as a culture philosopher, who not only observes but produces a poetic discourse that mediates between myth and reality. What Codrescu means to imply is the fact that there are always Bart Simpsons who embody as many multitudes as did Whitman. This line of thought has been explored by Ginsberg, Berrigan, and Frank O'Hara since the 60s and achieves full flare in the form of the prose poem. O'Hara's pronouncements in his poem "Ave Maria", which starts with an imperative: "Mothers of America, let your kids go to the movies!" (in Paschen and Mosby, 2001), illustrates moreover the relationship between earthly roads and heavenly ones. Ferlinghetti's road "in the air" may well be represented here by the impact of television and its visual multitudes on poetry.

In a poem from 1973 "De Natura Rerum" we see again a desire to return to the past and its conventions but only so that a future can be reinvented as a space where potential nonconformist poets will operate. While the state of this nonconformity is however not explicit, it is rendered a secret whose revealing holds mythical promises. Writes Codrescu, either anticipating or following poets such as Bart Simpson, Allen Ginsberg, and Ted Berrigan:

> I sell myths not poems. With each poem goes a little myth. This myth is not in the poem. It's in my mind. And when the editors of magazines ask me for poems I make them pay for my work by passing along these little myths which I make up. These myths appear at the end of the magazine under the heading ABOUT CONTRIBUTORS or above my poems in italics. Very soon there are as many myths as there are poems and ultimately this is because each poem does, this way, bring another poet into the world. With this secret method of defying births controls I populate the world with poets (Codrescu in Lehman 2003: 185).

The title line which Codrescu borrows from Titus Lucretius actually reads "De Rerum Natura". Codrescu's inversion here is a pun which illustrates the essence of nonconformity: the poet's task is not to write on the nature of things but on the things of nature. We thus find in Codrescu's poetics a preoccupation with how poets say what they say, why they say it, and when they say it. This epistemic creative writer has a method after all, but it's still a secret. As all Codrescu's works are concerned with sources of inspirations and the means to map imagination and the creative matrix of a culture onto how knowledge is produced, we can argue that, for Codrescu, every act of creation generates its own rules of conventions, and the nature of convention is to create a platform, first for nonconformity, and then for knowledge.

Traveling texts

Here I want to turn to an even earlier text written by Codrescu in the late 60s in order to illustrate how the poetics of epistemic creative writing draws on nonconformity. Furthermore, I want to show how nonconformity enforces its own rules of conventions by drawing up a geography of both inspiration and imagination, grace and invention.

"Monsieur Teste in America: an arrival and the necessity of it" was first published in 1973 in the *Paris Review* and features two protagonists: a first person unnamed narrator who, having recently come to America as an immigrant from Europe, and having become tired and bored with the struggle for a new language, invites his mentor Monsieur Teste to visit him in New York. The 29 year old narrator hopes that Monsieur Teste will help him to not disclose more secrets, but formulate some of his own. As the narrator muses, one can only have about 6 "simple" secrets in one's life, to find, hold and cherish, yet when one comes to a new country the search for secrets slows down. As soon as Monsieur Teste arrives, the two embark on a journey of discovery. Monsieur Teste, however, does not seek enlightenment as he already embodies the voice of reason. Teste speaks only in aphorisms and epigrams and his utterances testify to his erudition and wisdom. But Teste's observations about America, however poignant, are not conventional. Lines such as "the infinite is a great influence on unfinished sentences," combined with observations whose interpretations involve a breaking of metaphors, point to the complexity of mapping simple secrets in foreign contexts. For example, when Teste explains why he wears an expensive watch, the message, while intended to express a universal, is passed through the filters of consumerism and capitalism that characterize America. "Value," says Teste, "is the defense of the unattainable. All things must be expensive. Things are an admission to a man's impotence. They must not come cheap" (Codrescu, 2000: 25). After a short exchange in which Teste makes a reference to the importance of minding his own business the narrator exclaims:

> With great pleasure I proceeded to describe to him how minding one's own business was not possible in America and how this wasn't really a bad thing because while it was true that others delved into one's business it was also possible for one to delve into others' business and that, you will grant, is the supreme pleasure of democracy (25).

The novella combines several genres: it goes from realist accounts to travel writing via aphorisms and maxims and the diary form, and finally it culminates in a full fledged magical irony, with Teste becoming a furnace in the end that burns reason, logic, and the narrator. What I am interested here in pointing out is the way in which Codrescu maps the imagination of his precursor poets and their implicit observations regarding the importance of creating a poetics. The narrator in "Monsieur Teste" prepares a menu for Teste which consists of dishes made out of American poets. Some axioms of nonconformity emerge, as the narrator explains in an entry in his diary:

> American poetry came to lunch today. Many poets were missing but I made do with the ones who were there. The poets there were mostly from the New York School which I attended in the hope of finding out the simple secrets the ignorance of which so handicaps a foreigner in America. These poets knew a great number of simple secrets which they spread around generously, unlike the rest of the schools which bored me to death with their European pretensions. I had learned, among others, such notions as "Clear the range! (Ted Berrigan), "If it fits in your mouth it's natural!" (Ted Berrigan), "Take it easy!" (Anne Waldman), "What's up Doc!" (Tom Veitch), "Why not Egypt?" (Dick Gallup) (33).

The narrator's lunch consists of 15 dishes beginning with the *entrée*, which is made up of new poetry movements bearing names such as Aktup, Metabolism, the Bowel Movement, and Syllogism, Actualism, Essentialism, and Infantilism. Such excessive labeling is the result of the narrator's observation that American poets are afraid of labels primarily because labels stem from critics and not themselves. The entrée provides the explanation that the reason why American poetry has a wide range of "cultural eclecticism" is because it started as a "race to elude the critics." The *soup* consists of pure meaninglessness and clichés as "nobody has yet written a perfectly obscure poem," while *Paté de foie gras* is served in the form of Ted Berrigan and Tom Veitch. The first is seen as a writer of a purer form than the latter is capable of, and we learn that "Purity [...] is really the degree of dedication to one's obsessions. Ted is obsessed with voice, Tom with God, and each of them does it by shifting things out of their conventional place" (34-35). *Gravy* consists of do's and don'ts and of reality seen through a grid, while a *medium-sized suckling pig with an apple in his mouth* comes in the form of lamentations over the poetry of Michael Brownstein and John Ashbery. Writes Codrescu as if from the apple's perspective:

> There are poets with a distaste for reality.
>
> These poets are insane, meaning that they have no defined territory with which to reshuffle their world, so they wonder through their imaginations and bring out things that, on first sight, nobody has ever seen. These poets have to be intelligent, however, and if they are, they usually notice that what they brought back resembles some quite common thing that everybody sees every day. At this point they form a method by bringing intelligence to bear on romanticism. These poets have no style. They are mechanics of celestial pornography. Michael Brownstein is one of these. I have never seen anything of his in which a subtle apology isn't made to some secret search. All his works say: *Look, I am sorry, dear God, but as I was coming through the stratosphere half of you burned up so I put a shoe in the missing place*. John Ashbery does the same thing but he keeps his terms abstract. This is a terrible disadvantage because abstracts tend to make one re-examine one's shakiest assumptions, and if this were done, it would take twelve years to correctly read a John Ashbery poem (35-36).

After Monsieur Teste gets acquainted with American cuisine, he calls for some refreshments. On the fruit plate consisting of *peaches, melons,* and *blackberries* the narrator makes the important, yet obvious observation:

> It is a monument to the stupidity of American criticism that all references to the New York School have, so far, spoken of a collective voice when, in truth, it is precisely the New York School that has brought the largest number of methods, attitudes and trends into a scene dominated by uniformity and boredom. There are at least fifteen poets in this set who embody essentially fifteen major philosophies (36).

Here I would suggest that the narrator playfully combines two biblical references: the forbidden fruit and the unwanted prophet. The fruit plate is served in response to critics' stupidity and their rejection of poets or prophets whose sin is not to have performed miracles but eaten from the forbidden fruit of knowledge. References to poets who all know something, who all possess simple secrets, continues in the menu list which includes final relishes such as cocaine, yoga, pot, Napoleons, Rhum Babas, Eclairs, Bakhlavas, Cigars, Coffee, Honey, and A Final Joint, each embodying more activist poets, such as Anne Waldman, Tom Clark, Aram Saroyan and Joe Brainard. It is clear that the menu is not intended for critics, but as the culmination point of the dinner consists of Whipped Cream, some room is made for more. The symbolism of whipped cream as the *crème de la crème* opens up for generosity and the finding of solutions, as the narrator explains:

> There is a lot more. Some resident critics would now be in order. Poets, as a rule, see themselves defined by their works and the

critical intelligence brought to bear on their contemporaries is almost always oral. America is, however, in great need of some new directions and a translation of these poetries into easy-to-follow computer programs, could conceivably, save the world a hundred years of sterility (37).

"Monsieur Teste in America" is a text which tests the validity and strength of American poetics against the idea of having poetics always follow a method. Although Codrescu acknowledges the significance of the New York School poets to have come up with neat philosophies, he is also suspicious of their teachings in that form, namely, as a philosophy. We can almost trace this suspicion back to Beckett, as we hear Codrescu bashing the poets who see themselves as instructors in the art of metaphor, and yet forgetting to make the metaphor an analogy to what is most fascinating in writing, namely, the ability to shut up.

The pun on the word "Teste," which also means head in French, is intended to suggest a crossing between reason and time. While reason itself is tested at a crossroads, time measures the path of nonconformity. Codrescu's overall remarks regarding the ethos of his generation of poets are formulations of a poetics that renders itself as a rule of convention that speaks both for itself and against itself. Thus, what interests Codrescu is how to revise and reconfigure not only the poetics, but also the geography of the imagination as it stumbles on cultural preconditioning. Codrescu's path is not the one least traveled but one which maps best the potential of one's generation. The 50s and 60s influence on Codrescu's work is mapped as an exquisite crossing of poetry against rules of convention.

Creative epistemics under the sign of nonconformity

Here, then, I want to suggest that the point and scope of any poetics of nonconformity in literary endeavors is to formulate precisely a poetics of epistemic creativity. So, we know who inspires us, but how do we go from what we know that the poets who came before us knew to what *we* know? This is still an open question. Markson saw the answer to this question as embodied in the attempt to read the writing on the wall. Codrescu's writings demonstrate that nonconformity as the method *par excellence* of the epistemic creative writer is at its best when it expresses itself according to a principle that favors no borders. This way we haven't said too much. At least not too much that would go against our own claim that an epistemic creative writer is the writer who creates knowledge but refuses to teach method. Within this principle, the first rule of the poetics of nonconformity is to express neither a need for critics nor poetic elaborations. Nonconformity, in this sense, is the grasp of avant-history, and as such, a basic innocence which re-invents the past as a relish for the future.

But why conflating a creative epistemics with nonconformity, one may still ask, and to this I would offer the following: insofar as the epistemic creative writer is a writer who exhibits a heightened awareness of the importance of instructive writing, he also understands that one way in which he can create space for the reader to understand himself in the act of reading is by making sure that no conventional methods for writing are proposed. The epistemic creative writer is not merely an expressive writer, a writer who writes for creative writing programs at diverse university colleges. Rather, the epistemic creative writer is the writer who understands that in order to say something useful you must step out of the space that engages your ego.

Awareness of what really matters comes from the contemplation of the futility of words. Before the word there is silence. After the word there is silence. But during the word there is knowledge that can be made crystal clear.

From Beckett to Codrescu, we've had a few examples of writers who are very much engaged in demonstrating how writing always cuts across the bridge between creativity, expressing it in writing, and academic knowledge about creativity. The very question, 'how do we know what we know?' is already a highly creative act, and one that, in the context of writing, presupposes reliance on contemplation. But what kind of contemplation? Of the learned type? Since Beckett, and depending on context and situation, since long before that, writers connected to the idea of passing on a writing tradition, though crafted in an individual voice, have realized that the only way the knowledge of what one is doing can cross the bridge of interaction is by allowing for 'nothing to be done' to be part of the interaction.

My final suggestion here is to say that the epistemic creative writer is good at creating a situation and then embodying it. It is through what is suggested visually that one learns. Therefore, and inspired by Nietzsche, Beckett ended up with ditching the words. His humming thereafter was heard by the few mentioned here, who all started intoning to the new music about how academic creative writing is all about teaching silence, and seeing it on site in action.

7

EPISTEMOLOGIES OF CREATIVE WRITING AXIOMATIC REDUX

For Enrique Enriquez

1. To breathe words that others can learn to write with.

2. To attempt to recover the unknown at the horizon of knowledge.

3. To define things without being too pedantic.

4. To dare to dream epistemic creative writing as a system of thought.

5. To realize that knowledge derives from what is formulated in the gaps, in fragments of memory, and in the kinds of discourse that are, above all else, contradictory, and hence silencing.

6. To emphasize a form of transgressive parody in which philosophy formulates an epistemology of creative writing almost in the guise of a fool's lament over the decay of history and morals.

7. To be a self-proclaimed literature philosopher *and* an epistemic creative writer who tells herself: 'I can feel it in my gut that I am an epistemologist. Even if what I hear (from others) may be a different opinion.'

8. To know how to combine the intention in creative writing with the knowledge of how to formulate a good question.

9. To stand creatively in an asymmetrical relation to the *whatness* of knowledge, or the meaning of knowledge.

10. To think about the logic of empty masks, the belief in the nothing that is, and the performance of quietude.

11. To always answer 'yes' to a question about choice.

12. To get a sense of where to place the 'meanwhile' between everything and nothing without being besides yourself.

13. To begin from the contingent, the singular givenness to perception.

14. To cross the threshold and find language forbidden.

15. To be there, beyond the threshold: 'Hello, who are you?' 'I'm language.'

16. To let love and writing walk the tightrope.

17. To write epitaphs in order to incite to participation.

18. To understand how the epistemic creative writer makes use of her mind's capability to always believe in whatever story she invents and her intent to love the invented story.

19. To express concern with the writing that addresses genre as a question of writing, with writing designating a specific topos from which the audience, while excluded from making pronouncements on the kind of writing at hand, is brought in a state of 'attendance' – in other words, to put epistemic creative writing in a nutshell.

20. To call into question the premise for interactive knowledge.

21. To conflate the production of knowledge with the creative act in the obvious; yet not in the obvious that is out in the open, but rather, in the obvious that is right under the surface of writing.

22. To create knowledge by undoing its sting.

23. To represent in writing both the author and the critic, yet without making recourse to either of them.

24. To allow criticism to be raised above voice and be turned into a principle for epitaphic functioning.

25. To allow the fragment as an instance of formal epistemics to give us a semantics that produces useful analogies, or metaphors; a whole world of silences.

26. To allow the epitaph to speak for itself, and the epistemic creative writer to take dictations.

27. To realize that writing is no effective mechanism for knowledge without the acknowledgement that the "I" writing is in fact doing nothing other than showing the "I" citing.

28. To 'know' by virtue of being able to identify the irreverent in writing, what it is useful for, and where it gets the poet.

29. To write things like this: 'if you want to make it, don't listen; if you want to find it, don't listen; if you want to know it, don't listen.' The secret, however, to knowing how 'not to listen' is in paying attention.

30. To place a myth in every poem. And as the poet says: "To let these myths appear at the end of the magazine under the heading ABOUT CONTRIBUTORS or above my poems in italics. Very soon there are as many myths as there are poems and ultimately this is because each poem does, this way, bring another poet into the world. With this secret method of defying births controls I populate the world with poets."

31. To make references to poets who all know something, and who possess simple secrets.

32. To sit and watch: while reason is tested at a crossroads, time measures the path of nonconformity.

33. To embody silence: in cite.

(NO)TT(ON)

I'm here

Beckett from across three pages, which I try to read at the same time – while three candles burn, while Bach pumps the organ, while my friend updates his status on Facebook emphasizing that he likes to listen to Rabbi Elias talking incessantly, but that he also likes the Rabbi to get crushed by Bach, so that some silence would occur, while I listen to my friend and get astonished again and again because he gets it, all of it, and more so, while reading lumpy poems on the silly lumpy pudding website, while the organ suddenly takes over and the *toooootally* fat sounds hit you in the *guttest* of your gut, especially the uterus as the more anatomically specific oriented would have it, while the body sinks under heavy-weight thinking, and yet also floats in the air at the idea that all we have is words, performance, and costumes to enact the sublime, man, what bullshit, but we buy it, we buy all of it, because we sense it, man, how we sense it, that it almost makes us think that there must be more between heaven and earth, but there isn't really, it's all projections and mirrors, and man, how we want the best, the very very very best, the absolute best, the highest best, even Jesus said verily verily, the best exists, because we believe in it, man, can you believe that, that is just so astonishing, believing while remaining silent in the face of knowing that the other knows that one is ready already for the already, the already that has already happened, fuck man, where is Derrida when you need him to tell you that it's all very unique in that very deconstructive way, and sublime too, and verily, verily worth the while, but then he was a Romantic – Beckett says on the first page, because I can't really read three pages at the same time, it's all a bluff, Beckett says: "You're on earth. There's no cure for that."

Fleshed out

The pathology of big breasts is going out. "Who do you want to look like?" the head plastic surgeon asks me. I know exactly so I answer unhesitatingly. "Well, like those two gnomic gnats, Beckett and Bob Dylan." "Who," he asks again? "Beckett and Bob Dylan," I say, and refrain from offering additional information. This strategy is also part of the program, to keep it simple. I go for the slender androgynous look. My hair will also turn completely white in six months, so I'm ready to face the world in this final phase of my meaningful or meaningless existence. "Say what?" Beckett asks me, and he never makes any conversation that is not based entirely on body language and no words. I say nothing. Ten vectors of ten-second thoughts go through my mind. Number two has this in it: *O, yes, yes, of course, why not, how excellent, this is just brilliant, it can't get any better that next time, when men tell me that they respect me, they will not mean the exact opposite. And they will not look at their watches in my presence either.* Dylan intercedes on thought number five: "*A poem is a naked person. Some people say that I am a* poet." *Good then, we go with that,* number one thought dictates, as number one never has anything original to say. My scurrilous intelligence is being performed on at the level of the flesh. The less of it, the higher the ground. "Have you been reading about Estragon and Vladimir on the verge of hanging themselves only so that they can get a major erection?" Beckett wants to know. But all I say is this: "I disappear a lot," just when my hand is being twisted by the good doctor who says: "Not bad. Not bad at all." Dylan goes, "Pressing On," and I think, *fucking Freud is home.*

Musketeer logic

Between us, giving and taking is a relative matter. Precisely. Einstein said to make things as simple as possible, but not any simpler. On precision he couldn't have put it more relatively. All precision that has to do with measuring how much we give and how much we take is relative. "Yes," he says, "musketeers were very good at figuring that one out, but only when they were dressed androgynously." "What's that supposed to mean?" I ask, feeling offended by having the picture of my heroes ruined. I expect him to say "nothing," but instead he says, "double and everything," paraphrasing a modern musketeer. Raymond Federman's American book, *Double or Nothing*, which is more of a fragment of a paradox – a French book dressed in Jewish clothes – is all about measuring giving and taking. What bothers me is the "everything." Relativity in androgynous dress has a special kind of gravitas. Not every matter of simplicity is simple. Some are chosen to be complex.

Checkmate

Ola, ola, ola, bola, bola, bola. This is not exactly *Parsifal*. Moinous and Namredef like Parsifal. After a lot of singing, there is a lot of dying. "I don't want to go to Dachau," I tell them. I just want the singing. Namredef blurts at me and almost tells me to go fuck myself. "Don't get so worked up," he says, "I'm Jewish too, you know," he further says. "Yeah, sure," I say, and start thinking about what would have happened to Malcolm X's philosophy had he gone to Europe to visit the old concentration camps instead of Mecca. I'm getting twofold vibrations. I wonder if Federman's family had a brief encounter with Max Ernst and Peggy Guggenheim while in there, at that place, the place that Wagner never wanted to mention. Peggy and Max got out. Then Max married Peggy and then he married that American who still wants a lot of colors in her dreams. I see them playing chess in one of Inverarity's framed photographs. Malcolm said: "Be peaceful, be courteous, obey the law, respect everyone; but if someone puts his hand on you, send him to the cemetery." Moinous and Namredef understand this very well, but only when pronounced in another language. They love their reactions to such statements to end with *Halleluiah* and *Amen*, but since they are more cultivated than most Baptists, they like an ending that goes Latin. Thus their favorite is: *nec plus ultra*. Oy, boy! Before the King goes into checkmate, the Queen gives him a kiss under their gazes. M & N approve.

Federman dies

Nobody ever waits. Waiting is the hardest. And you decided to die on me just like that. Well, you have been dying for some time now, just like a few people I know. Mother was dying before she actually did it, some 20 years before. The same with Beckett. By the way, say hello to both. Perhaps you can instruct mother to start reading some Beckett while there, wherever it is that you've all gone. She was a Beckettian to the bone, only she had no idea. I've also been dying since the day I was born, so we have that in common. I came into this world two months before my time. Mother was sure I was going to die right then and there. Me too. And then with all the operations, it's a miracle anyone survives. Three times I've had to spread my legs for the gynaecologist and anaesthesiologist. And then the energy thing. The ablation, they call it. Pumping up the heart to 400 beats so that they could guess where the current was and burn its many passages. Six places they've burned it, chasing it in the dark. Which is why the current comes back, I can feel it. I'm ergodic proof of what instability means. And now I also want to get rid of my big breasts. I have plastic reasons for it. I'm into the arts now. I want to seduce only myself, not others. And I fancy a splash of imitation. Beckett, whom we both love – that's right, I want to look just like him. I wonder what you'd say of that, that I may die, finally, with my chest cut open. Who's to say, indeed? We all die anyway. But meanwhile on your death, I've no idea why that obscene song sung by Serge Gainsbourg and Brigitte Bardot comes to my mind. *"Moi non plus,"* he says. *"Je t'aime,"* she says. But he insists. *"Moi non plus."* Ah, well, people come, people go. You were never sentimental about that. And yet you made me soft in my knees. Your texts still vibrate through me. The words. I'm doing a painting for you now. I use mostly the color called viridian. Can you believe such a name? You would like it, particularly because I got the inspiration from my favourite perfume, *YSL Rive Gauche*. Total viridium. So, who will read at your funeral? I'm busy writing and feeling sorry for myself, so I'll absent myself. Goddamnit, Raymond. You could have waited for me. You make me say, *"moi non plus."* You exit, but I promise, I'll take care of the X.

Topology

Gertrude Stein is pulling my leg: "Remember narrative is continuous." And then there's Wagner, and Cantor, and Bach, and all the others. I was thinking that the only thing that beats 'and yet' must be 'both, and.' And then thus there are the others, specialists in quantum grammar. What do we do with 'and then?' – Then suddenly? Transform the status of 'nothing' into 'all?' 'All are welcome.' To do what? Transform topology into a vocabulary of thinking? Thinking about it. A direct address is a ready-made costume. "You, I'm addressing – and my witnesses are 'all' here" – Or not. The gaze can also go blank, terrified by the potential No. Not yet. So 'Nothing' would come for nothing. And yet. All that writing can vibrate for! Sense it all written on the body! Gertrude hands me a cookie made by her lover, and orders me to shut up. In transfinite arithmetic, both nothing and everything have a higher status than otherwise. The set of signification comprises the oath: *Here I Am*. We keep counting. Alice keeps the score. And then hands touch and the kiss is hot. We love the logic of insufficient reason.

In praise of pandemonium

He said: "To be or not to be, that is the question." I'm tired after moving, which involved reading all the books again before putting them back on the shelves. The Shakespeare book – all works in one – is sticking out, and I'm tired of thinking of that one line. "Why can't I think of another," I ask myself? I'm tired of dying people asking questions. Gertrude asked Alice: "what is the answer?" and when Alice didn't say anything, she said, "in that case, what is the question?" At least Gertrude was smart and didn't procrastinate her own death for a philosophical question. My books have arranged themselves while I closed my eyes and thought of England. Agamben should come before Artaud in the alphabetical order. But I don't want to ask myself whether I should follow the compulsion to letter or not. I reason that since Artaud kept it simple, he should get the honor of beginning theory. *Here then the Question* is the first book on my first theory shelf. After Derrida, who makes it in the first round, the first shelf ends with Leslie Fiedler's *Waiting for the End*. "This shelf means serious business," I tell myself. "I need a break," I tell myself again. Hamlet follows, and I ask him whether he wouldn't mind laying it off. I don't want to be fucked in the middle of putting things together. From my vantage point I see the paperback section. Some tall books stick out, and I'm happy to procrastinate helping Hamlet out. The titles that I can read are these: *Re-search* (Burroughs), *The Torch in My Ear* (Elias Canetti), *The Woman who is the Midnight* (Terence Green), *The Greek Way* (Edith Hamilton), *Scratching The Beat Surface* (McClure), *Tropic of Capricorn* (Miller). "Whoa, this is even more serious," I tell myself. What's eating Miller after all that sex with Anaïs Nin? His first was *Tropic of Cancer*. Gertrude died of cancer to her stomach. "That's it," I say, and yell to Hamlet: "Hamlet, fuck philosophy! Off we go." He's happy to procrastinate, yet again. We want our books to be crazy about us, just the way we're crazy about them. Their authors? (here then the question) – we don't mind them dead. *Fin*, as they say in French movies. *Finitto*, in Italian. *Tutti morti*, if you want to dramatize. The other Gertrude, Hamlet's mother, has nothing to say.

Zorn's lemma

When the mathematicians hit you, be ready. It may not be only numbers that they have in store for you. Here I was, thinking of the growing intensity in the ping-ponging that I play with my genius friend, and laughing at the idea that the more I think that I can handle the biggest infinity around, imagining also that I sit on the edge of the universe where there's a lot of space between the galaxies – that's it, no more clutter, just as I like it up there – not even dust – so, yes, thinking at the edge of the universe of how beautiful it is to add one more zero to the one, and thus get further and further away from screwed up perspectives and verbal animations, I think, yes, with the biggest infinity around, the only ordinary thing that will happen is seeing the emergence of patterns that replace the world of words with images and symbols, and yes, the obvious itself will also occur like magic, and the obvious is that soon I'll change my profession, and so will he, the genius, that is, I mean, here at the edge of the universe, with space in between the ordinary occurrence of the obvious, yes, what will happen is that I'll take up his job at Aalborg University, a mighty universe indeed, and he will take up mine, an even bigger universe, as I'm always into bigger things than anyone else, and we'll improve the world from within, we'll go from the 10 raised at the power of minus 16 to some other 10 raised at some very nice infinity, to destroy numbers, crush them, to make some light, so ok, we'll need some help, I think Caravaggio is a good bet, and so is Zorn's 11th axiom of set theory, yes, we need to fix first some existences, even Gertrude Stein was into redemptive acts, so why not us, get past the obvious but not losing it out of sight, and also past the Bible, but not losing it out of sight either, and then we'll pause 5 minutes into the film that H, the genius, has been circulating around for our instruction into Zorn's Lemma, which says that, well, Zorn says a lot of things, that there must be a yes somewhere in it, there's for instance a very nice yes in the very fifth minute, after the alphabet and the creation, and after the facts: "In Adam's fall we sinned all;" "Thy life to mend, God's Book attend;" "The Cat doth play, and after slay," when the camera takes a break from all that infinite obviousness of ordinary things, and when it pauses on the yes, lo and behold, not on anything else, in fact it does so quite stubbornly, pause, that is, or hesitate, to be more precise, and yes, of course, before you know it, H and I will have a lot of fans, we do already, and they will all shout, *oy*, or perhaps, *oh my, how clever of you two, by Jove,* but then by then Jove will be out of sight, I mean, with all this infinity in the provisional who's to say what we'll get out of changing professions, but then again, at the edge of the universe, whether H will be a mediocre poet, and I a lousy mathematician, the question is, will it make any difference, no difference at all, we'll be so spaced out, and totally Muybridgian, beyond analogies, beyond the laws of attraction, beyond the laws of correspondences, beyond the laws of causality, beyond the laws of end results, and, I'm sure that I'm missing some laws right now, I'm sure of it, but, in any event, and even beyond 'whatever,' there is light, there's lots of light even there where there's lots of space between the lightning stars, and yes, even though I hate it, I think that I'll pick up the phone and ask the genius what the hell he's thinking about, although between the two of us, I know it already, so perhaps to the fans then, yes, we promise, we'll do it, we'll hit this one. Let there be 11 of them.

The socialite

AT ROSKILDE UNIVERSITY

— So, you're a PhD student?
— I was one 10 years ago.
— Me too.
— Any children?
— No.
— Then you'd better hurry.
— I can't have any.
— You can adopt.
— They'd have to be special.
— I was 8 when my father died, some 55 years ago.
— I was also 8 when mine died, some 35 years ago.
— And your mother? A feminist?
— No, a Marxist.
— Marxism is artificial.
— But useful.
— I've seen my mother doing things that were not artificial.

— You mean, like hammering?
— Yes. What do you hammer on?
— Poetry.
— Why?
— I'm interested in death.
— But you're not old.
— Didn't you just tell me to hurry?
— Wait until you're old.
— Old age has nothing good in it.
— Sure it has.
— Like what?
— Well, err, wisdom, I guess.
— Isn't wisdom a myth?
— No.
— Then, you have it?
— I suppose.
— How do you pass it on?
— Well, through my writing and teaching.
— About physics?
— Exactly.
— What else?
— Well, I don't know. You'd better ask my son.
— But I'm not asking your son. I'm asking you. What else?
— I need some air. Will you excuse me?
— Sure. Are you all right?
— No. Err, yes. I think so.
— You think so?
— I think so.

AT TROMSØ UNIVERSITY

— So, you're a writer.
— Not really.
— But you write.
— I analyze.
— Like that?
— Like what?
— Like Beckett.
— I like Beckett.
— You look great.
— Thanks.
— I mean, for a Beckett scholar.
— I'm not a Beckett scholar.
— You're not?
— No.
— You're really smart.
— Thanks.
— I can recite a poem for you.
— You can?
— Yes.
— About what?
— Death.
— What's it called?
— *Death, Death.*
— Go ahead.
— *Døden, døden...*
— Nice.
— Aaargh, you know, I could... you're... I would...
— I know.

— You'd also?
— Yes.
— You can have anything. I'll give you everything. My whole life is on this phone. You can have it. Take it. Take me. Steal all my texts from it. My publishers...
— If I didn't already, have everything.
— Then you would?
— I would, for all the 15 years between us.
— Live and die.
— Your poems are so young.
— Love and die.
— And beautiful.
— Love. Love me.
— You'll have a good death.
— You think so?
— Yes.

AT DUBLIN UNIVERSITY
— So, you're going for professor now?
— Yes.
— Your hair turned white.
— Yes.
— But, your body.
— Yes. I look better now than at 16.
— You bet. What's the philosophy?
— In your old age, the only good thing going for you is your light weight. Be ethereal.
— Like Beckett?
— Yes.
— His stomach curved inwards.

— So it did.
— What about Gertrude?
— She didn't believe in weight.
— She must have believed in something.
— Gertrude said: "I rarely believe anything, because at the time of believing I am not really there to believe."
— Do you believe?
— In what?
— In love.
— What kind?
— The total kind. The all the way kind. The interminable kind.
— I like infinity. My own.
— My girlfriend... you're a psychoanalyst, right?
— Sometimes.
— My girlfriend, she wants commitment.
— Sure she does. Don't they all?
— Yes, so you understand?
— Sure I do.
— Then, why doesn't she?
— Because she's not so smart.
— She is.
— Then what are you afraid of?
— Children.
— Do you want them?
— Well, yes.
— Then go for it.
— You think so?
— Sure I do.
— Why?
— Do you believe in life or guarantee?

— Life.
— Then, as I said, go for it.

AT HELSINKI UNIVERSITY
— So, you're still doing mathematics?
— No. Never have.
— Sure you have, at all our gatherings.
— I'm more of a priest now.
— You are? What doctrine?
— The loving kind. Love thy neighbor kind.
— Whoa, Norway messed you up again?
— No.
— You're cool.
— No, really, if anything, it's arithmetic.
— Whoa, such passion.
— You think?
— Yeah, a priest with a cool head and passion for counting. Churches need that. And that body of yours!
— Yes, they allow whores in the temple now.
— I've heard.
— Isn't that neat?
— Absolutely.
— "Shall we go all wild boys,
   Waiting for the end?"
— Just a smack at Auden.
— With a smack of leaf and eagle, girl.
— Professor, to you. I qualified in the Arctic.
— "Waiting for the end, boys, waiting for the end.
   What is there to be or do?
   What's become of me or you?

Are we kind or are we true?
Sitting two and two, boys, waiting for the end."
— What end?

"Where'er we tread 'tis haunted holy ground"

I think I look beautiful in my Lagerfeld creation of a white silk dress that goes all the way to the floor spilling over my brown Birkenstock trekking boots. I have a *rendez-vous* with Zarathustra on top of *Predikestolen*. He sees me from atop, waves at me and shouts: "you look like a parachute in all that mass of soft satin. Off somewhere?" He's jealous of my beauty. He's thinking of ways to possess it, but the whiteness blinds him. With his eyes closed he can't think properly. So it's very easy for me to just fuck him, and get it over with. But I have come for the natural solutions that lead to singularities. He wants gravity in vacuum. He speaks "Of the Virtue that Makes Small." I lose my native tongue, and start speaking in one I don't understand: *"Das Wandern" "Wohin?"* – *"Der Neugierige"* – by the time I get to – *"O Bächelein meiner Liebe,* how silent you are today" – oops, language is back – I see Jack Kerouac down on the road translating: *"Ungeduld"* – *"Dein ist mein Hertz,"* but then he also gets it mixed up: "Behold, think of Dean Moriarty!" "Did I say *Behold,* he asks, horrified? "Yes," I say. "That's Zarathustra's line," and then I explain: "when he's sexually frustrated he stops prophesying all that nonsense about unholy simplicity, and starts singing Schubert songs instead." I take off my dress, and all the men go: *"mein,* mine, *mein."* I follow the gravity. The transvestites go with the vacuum.

Marginally yours

He thinks I should write more on David Markson. My specialty is male authors, except for Gertrude Stein. But I leave it to Lynn Emanuel to handle it. Her typewriter is better than mine. And she knows the inside of Gertrude. "It is dark in there," the other Lynn says. She separates my interest for periods with a comma borrowed from Gertrude. Gertrude, as we all know was a master at repeating, and saved loads of punctuation for critics to come. I used to be into tormented modernists. Except Eliot. I leave that to Søren. He has infinite patience. I don't. Today the modernists get the ax, my ax. Except Celan. I rest my case where the others are concerned. The judge is happy that we waste no time, so the verdict can fall: dismissed, dismissed, dismissed, dead, dead, dead. Enters Markson. Needless to say, his *Wittgenstein's Mistress* is Markson's specialty where woman is concerned. But he leaves it to her to choose living with men in pictures. She then leaves it to the pictures to make it perfect. Lynn knows a thing or two about pictures. She showed me when we were standing in front of the *Book of Letters* in Libeskind's museum. We make fun of Wittgenstein in Markson's other novel, *This is not a Novel*. Says he: "Among Wittgenstein's spelling when using English: Anoied. Realy. Excelentely. Expences. Affraid. Cann't." Lynn and I can spell. Also backwards. Picture perfect.

"Hello!" he yells from refraction. "I said, you should write on Markson." But Lynn and I are watching Wittgenstein, who, "like a patient etherized upon a table," rocks the proof.

BIBLIOGRAPHY

1. Epistemic adventures: cool creative writing

Barrow, John D (2001). *The Book of Nothing.* London: Vintage.

Barthelme, Donald (1991). "Not-Knowing." *The Art of the Essay.* Ed. Lydia Fakundiny. Boston: Houghton Mifflin.

Beckett, Samuel (1986) *Endgame.*

Bunting, Basil (2006). in *The Great Modern Poets.* Michael Schmidt, ed. Quercus Publishing.

Brown, William S. (1998). "Power of Self-Reflection through Epistemic Writing." *College Teaching,* Vol. 46, No. 4 (Fall, 1998), pp. 135-138. Heldref Publications.

Caillois, Roger (1961) *Man, Play and Games.* Trans. Meyer Barash. New York, Free Press of Glencoe.

Chiaramonte, P. (1992). "Journalizing techniques for self-reflective leaders." *Western Business School Case #9-92-L004.* London, Ontario Canada: University of Western Ontario.

Elias, Camelia (2010). *Pulverizing Portraits: Lynn Emanuel's Poetry of Becoming.* London: EyeCorner Press.

——— (2009). *Eight Senses Plus Two.* EyeCorner Press.

——— (2010). *The Logician.* EyeCorner Press.

Fenton, James (2001) *The Strength of Poetry. Oxford Lectures.* New York: Farrar, Straus and Giroux. Salamander Press.

Huizinga, Johan (1955). *Homo Ludens: A Study of the Play Element in Culture.* Bacon Press.

Leibniz, Gottfried Wilhelm (Freiherr von) (1989). *Philosophical Essays. Ed. 2.* Edited and translated by Roger Ariew and Daniel Garber. HPC Classics Series, Hackett Publishing.

Moretti, Franco (1998). *Atlas of the European Novel: 1800—1900*. London and New York: Verso.

Schmidt, Michael (2006). *The Great Modern Poets*. Quercus Publishing.

Simic, Charles (2003). *The Metaphysician in the Dark* (Poets on Poetry). Ann Arbor: University of Michigan Press.

Shakespeare, William (2009). *The Winter's Tale*. The Cambridge Dover Wilson Shakespeare. Edited by Sir Arthur Quiller-Couch and John Dover Wilson. Cambridge: Cambridge University Press.

Tzara, Tristan (1973). *Approximate Man, and Other Writings*. Wayne State University Press. The University of Michigan.

Wittgenstein, Ludwig (1922/2007). *Tractatus Logico-Philosophicus*. The Ogden bilingual edition. Translated from the German by C.K. Ogden with an introduction by Bertrand Russell. New York: Cosimo, Inc. Classics.

2. No-site criti-cite: Beckett and Federman

Arnould, Elisabeth (1996). "The Impossible Sacrifice of Poetry: Bataille and the Nancian Critique of Sacrifice." *Diacritics* 26.2 (1996): 86-96.

Bair, Deidre (1990). *Samuel Beckett: A Biography*. London: Vintage.

Bataille, Georges (1988). *Inner Experience*. Albany: SUNY Press.

Beckett, Samuel (1953) *Watt*. New York: Grove Press.

——— (1958). *Three Novels: Molloy, Malone Dies, The Unnamable*. Trans. Patrick Bowles in collaboration with the author. New York: Grove Press.

——— (1967). *Stories and Texts for Nothing*. New York: Grove Press.

——— (1983). *Worstward Ho*. The University of Michigan: John Calder

——— (1986). *Samuel Beckett. The Complete Dramatic Works*. London: Faber and Faber.

Connor, Steven (1992). "*Absolute Rubbish*: Cultural Economies of Loss in Freud, Bataille and Beckett." In his *Theory and Cultural Value*. Oxford: Blackwell, 1992. 57-101.

Cronin, Anthony (1997). *Samuel Beckett: The Last Modernist*. London: Flamingo.

Derrida, Jacques (1978). "From Restricted to General Economy: A Hegelianism without Reserve." In *Writing and Difference*. Trans. Alan Bass. London: Routledge & Kegan Paul, 1978.

Elias, Camelia, ed. (2008). *Federman Frenzy: the 'cult' in culture, the 'me' in memory, the 'he' in history – encounters with Raymond Federman*. EyeCorner Press.

Federman, Raymond (1976). "Chronologie," *Samuel Beckett*. Eds. Federman and Bishop. Paris: Editions de l'Herne.

——— (1975). *Surfiction: Fiction Now and Tomorrow*. Swallow Press.

——— (1993). *Critifiction: Postmodern Essays*. Albany: SUNY Press.

Foucault, Michel (1977) "Preface to Transgression." *Language, Counter-Memory, Practice: Selected Essays and Interviews*. Ed. Donald F. Bouchard. Trans. Donald F. Bouchard and Sherry Simon. Oxford: Blackwell, 1977. 29-52.

Frow, John (1995). *Cultural Studies and Cultural Value*. Oxford: Clarendon.

Van Hulle, Dirk (2004). "Worstward Ho!" *The Literary Encyclopedia*. 4 October 2004.

[http://www.litencyc.com/php/sworks.php?rec=-true&UID=8883, accessed 21 December 2009.]

Hunter, Ian (1992). "Aesthetics and Cultural Studies." *Cultural Studies*. Lawrence Grossberg, Cary Nelson and Paula A. Treichler (eds.). New York: Routledge.

James, Fenton (2001). *The Strength of Poetry*. Oxford Lectures. New York: Farrar, Straus and Giroux. Salamander Press.

Kermode, Frank (1989). "Miserable Splendour." (Review of *Stirrings Still*) *The Guardian*, 19 March 1989: 28.

McHoul, Alec (1997). "Ordinary Heterodoxies: Towards a Theory of Cultural Objects."*UTS Review* 3.2 (1997): 7-22.

Nancy, Jean-Luc (1991). "The Unsacrificeable." *Yale French Studies* 79 (1991): 20-38.

Rancière, Jacques (2004). *The Flesh of Words: The Politics of Writing*. Trans. Charlotte Mandell. Stanford: Stanford University Press.

––––– (2010). *The Aesthetic Unconscious*. Cambridge: Polity Press.

Smith, Russell Beckett "Negativity and Cultural Value." *Samuel Beckett Resources*. [http://www.samuel-beckett.net/smith.html]

Wasson, Tyler (ed) (1987). *Nobel Prize Winners: An H. W. Wilson Biographical Dictionary*. New York: H. W. Wilson.

Wittgenstein, Ludwig (2009). *Tractatus Logico-Philosophicus*. Cosimo Books.

Wolosky, Shira (1991). "The Negative Way Negated: Samuel Beckett's *Texts for N*.

3. Mystical site: a stone for Stein

Agamben, Giorgio (1999) *Potentialities*. Trans. Daniel Heller-Roazen. Stanford, California: Stanford U.P.

Aitken, Robert (1991) *The Gateless Barrier*. North Point Press.

Alenier, Karren LaLonde (2009) "Gertrude as Buddha." *Scene 4 Magazine*. December 2009. [http://www.scene4.com/achives-qv6/dec-2009/1209/karrenalenier1209.html]

Bachelard, Gaston (1958) *The Poetics of Space: The Classic Look at How We Experience Intimate Space*. Trans. Maria Jolas. Boston: Beacon Press.

––––– (1971). *On Poetic Imagination and Reverie*. Selected, translated and introduced by Collete Gaudin. Putnam, Connecticut: Spring Publications, Inc.

Barthes, Roland (1968) *Writing Degree Zero*. Trans. Annette Lavers and Colin Smith. Hill and Wang

––––– (1975). *The Pleasure of the Text*. Trans. Richard Miller. Hill and Wang.

––––– (1977). *Roland Barthes by Roland Barthes*. Trans. Richard Howard. Hill and Wang.

——— (1978). *A Lover's Discourse: Fragments*. Trans. Richard Howard. Hill and Wang.

Blanchot, Maurice (1995). *The Writing of the Disaster*. Trans. Ann Smock. Lincoln & London: University of Nebraska Press.

Culler, Jonathan (2002). *Barthes. A Very Short Introduction*. Oxford: Oxford University Press.

Dydo, Ulla & Gertrude Stein (1993). *A Stein Reader*. Northwestern University Press.

Dydo, Ulla & Rice, William (2008). *Gertrude Stein: The Language that Rises*. Northwestern University Press.

Elias, Camelia (2004). *The Fragment: Towards a History and Poetics of a Performative Genre*. Bern: Peter Lang Publishing.

Gold, Michael (1936) "Gertrude Stein: A Literary Idiot." *The New Masses*. [http://writing.upenn.edu/~afilreis/88/stein-per-gold.html].

Hoy, David Couzens (1981). "Philosophy as Rigorous Philology? Nietzsche and Poststructuralism." Ed. Lawrence Kritzman. *Fragments: Incompletion and Discontinuity*. New York: New York Literary Forum.

Jabès, Edmond (1996). *The Little Book of Unsuspected Subversion*. Stanford: Stanford University Press, Meridian: Crossing Aesthetics.

James, William (2008). *The Varieties of Religious Experience: A Study in Human Nature*. Rockville, Maryland: Arc Manor.

Johnson, Anthony (2005). "Notes Towards a New Imagology." *The European English Messenger*, 14. 1.

Kritzman, Lawrence, ed. (1981). *Fragments: Incompletion and Discontinuity*. New York: New York Literary Forum.

Livingston, Paisley (1998). *Counting Fragments, and Frenhofer's Paradox*. Institut for Filosofi: Skriftserie No. 17. Aarhus: Aarhus University.

Mazzoni, Cristina (1996). *Saint Hysteria: Neurosis, Mysticism, and Gender in European Culture*. Ithaca: Cornell University Press.

Prokosch, Frederic (1983). *Voices: A Memoir*. Farrar, Strauss, Giroux.

Shaughnessy, N.C. (1994). "'When This You See Remember Me' – Three Plays by Gertrude Stein". Ed. Gabriele Griffin. *Difference in View – Women and Modernism*. London: Taylor & Francis.

Stein, Gertrude (1967). *Look at Me Now and Here I Am. Writings and Lectures 1909–45*. London: Penguin Books.

——— *How to Write* (1975). New York: Dover Publications, Inc.

——— (1985). *Lectures in America*. ("What Is English Literature?") Beacon Press.

——— (1995). *The Making of Americans*. Normal & London: Dalkey Archive [1925 edition].

——— (2001). *The Autobiography of Alice B. Toklas*. London: Penguin Classics.

——— (2004). *Everybody's Autobiography*. Exact Change.

Steward, Samuel (1984) *Dear Sammy. Letters from Gertrude Stein and Alice B. Toklas*. St Martins Press.

Stewart, Allegra (1957). "The Quality of Gertrude Stein's Creativity." *American Literature*, Vol. 28, No. 4 (Jan., 1957), pp. 488-506. Duke University Press.

4. Grace in sight: Lacan, O'Hara, Hofstadter, Rotman

Balakian, Anna (1959). *Surrealism: Road to the Absolute*. New York: Noonday.

Derrida, J. (1989). *Psyche: Invention of the Other. Reading de Man Reading*. (L. Waters & W. Godzich, Eds.). Minneapolis: University of Minnesota Press.

Felman, Shoshana (1982) "Psychoanalysis and Education: Teaching Terminable and Interminable." Yale French Studies, No. 63, *The Pedagogical Imperative: Teaching as a Literary Genre*.

Felman, S. (1987). *Jacques Lacan and the Adventure of Insight: Psychoanalysis in Contemporary Culture*. Cambridge, Massachusetts: Harvard University Press.

Goldblatt, Robert (1992). *Logics of Time and Computation.* Leland Stanford Junior University: Center for the Study of Language and Computation.

Hintikka, J. (1962). *Knowledge and Belief: An Introduction to the Logic of the Two Notions.* Cornell: Cornell University Press.

Hofstadter, D. R. (1979). *Gödel, Escher, Bach: An eternal golden braid – A metaphorical fugue on minds and machines in the spirit of Lewis Carroll.* London: Penguin.

Keynes, John Maynard (1942). "Newton, the Man." *Newton Tercentenary Celebrations, 1947.* (Posthumous address at the The Royal Society of London on the event to celebrate the tercentenary of Isaac Newton's birth in 1942. Due to the war the event took place in July 1946) [http://www-history.mcs.st-andrews.ac.uk/history/Extras/Keynes_Newton.htm – link last accessed on April 17, 2010.

Lacan, Jacques (1972). "Of Structure as an Inmixing of an Otherness Prerequisite to any Subject Whatever." *Structuralist Controversy.* Richard Macksey and Eugene Donato, eds. pp. 186-94. Baltimore: John Hopkins University Press.

Lacan, Jacques (1999). *On Feminine Sexuality, the Limits of Love and Knowledge:* The Seminar of Jacques Lacan, Book XX, Encore. Jacques-Alain Miller and Bruce Fink, eds. New York: WW Norton & Comapany.

Leibniz, G. W. (1996). *New Essays on Human Understanding* (Cambridge Texts in the History of Philosophy). Cambridge: Cambridge University Press.

O'Hara, Frank (1995). *The Collected Poems of Frank O'Hara.* Donald Allen, ed. University of California Press.

Rotman, Brian (2008). *Becoming Beside Ourselves: The Alphabet, Ghosts, and Distributed Human Being.* With a foreword by Timothy Lenoir. Durham & London: Duke University Press.

Shaw, Lytle (2006) *Frank O'Hara: The Poetics of Coterie.* Iowa City: University of Iowa Press.

Wittgenstein, Ludwig J. (1969). *On Certainty.* Oxford: Blackwell Publishing.

5. I cite cyborgs: Nietzsche, Melville, Acker, Zarathustra

Acker, Kathy (1992). "The Language Of The Body." CTheory.net. Eds. Arthur and Marilouise Kroker. [http://www.ctheory.net/articles.aspx?id=1].

Agamben, Giorgio (1999). "Bartleby, or On Contingency." Giorgio Agamben, *Potentialities: Collected Essays in Philosophy*. Trans. Daniel Heller-Roazen. Stanford: Stanford University Press.

Ahern, Daniel (1995). *Nietzsche as Cultural Physician*. Pittsburgh: Penn State University Press.

Benesch, Klaus (2002). *Romantic Cyborgs: Authorship and Technology in the American Renaissance*. Amherst, MA: University of Massachusetts Press.

Copjec, Joan (2002). *Imagine there's no woman*. Cambridge, MA: The MIT Press.

Evens, Aden (2006). "Object-Oriented Ontology, or Programming's Creative Fold." *Angelaki. Journal of Theoretical Humanities*. Vol. 2. Nr. 1. April.

Foucault, Michel (1977) "Nietzsche, Genealogy, History." *Language, Counter-Memory, Practice: Selected Essays and Interviews*. Ed. by D.F. Bouchard. Ithaca: Cornell University Press.

Gasset, Ortega y, J. (2002). *Toward a Philosophy of History*. Chicago: University of Illinois Press.

Goldberg, Natalie (2005). *Writing down the Bones: Freeing the Writer Within*. Boston and London: Shambala.

Guattari, Félix (1995). *Chaosmosis: An Ethicoaesthetic Paradigm*. Trans. Julian Pefanis. Bloomington: Indiana University Press.

Haraway, Donna (1991). "A Cyborg Manifesto: Science, Technology, and Socialist-Feminism in the Late Twentieth Century." *Simians, Cyborgs and Women: The Reinvention of Nature*. New York; Routledge.

Hegel, F. W. (1975). *Aesthetics: Lectures on Fine Art. Vol. I (Aesthetics)*. Trans. T.M. Knox. Oxford: Oxford University Press.

Kochhar-Lindgren, Gray (2005). *TechnoLogics: ghosts, the incalculable, and the suspension of animation*. Albany: SUNY.

Marion, Jean-Luc (2001). *The Idol and Distance: Five Studies.* Issue 17 of Perspectives in continental philosophy. New York: Fordham University Press.

——— (2007). *The Erotic Phenomenon.* Chicago: University of Chicago Press.

Melville, Herman (1853). "Bartleby, the Scrivener: A Story of Wall-Street." [http://www.bartleby.com/129].

Mules, Warwick (2006). "Creativity, Singularity and Techne: the making and unmaking of visual objects in modernity." *Angelaki. Journal of Theoretical Humanities.* Vol. 2. Nr. 1. April.

Nietzsche, F. (1964). *Beyond Good and Evil: Prelude to a Philosophy of the Future.* Trans. Walter Kaufmann. New York: Vintage Books.

——— (1979). *Ecce Homo. How one becomes what one is.* Trans. R. J. Hollingdale. Middlesex: Penguin Books.

——— (1961/1984). *Thus spoke Zarathustra. The Portable Nietzsche.* Trans. & ed. Walter Kaufmann. New York: Penguin Books, 103-439.

——— (1984b). From: *The Gay Science. The Portable Nietzsche.* Trans. & ed. Walter Kaufmann. New York: Penguin Books, 93-102.

——— (1984c). *Twilight of the Idols. The Portable Nietzsche.* Trans. & ed. Walter Kaufmann. New York: Penguin Books, 463-563.

——— (1997). *Untimely Meditations.* Trans. R. J. Hollingdale. Ed. Daniel Breazale. Cambridge: Cambridge Texts in the History of Philosophy.

Olivier, Bert (2007). "Nietzsche, immortality, singularity and eternal recurrence." *South African Journal of Philosophy.* 26 (1).

6. Epistemologists of site: Markson and Codrescu

Bakhtin, M.M. (1986). "The Problem of Speech Genres." *Speech, Genres and Other Late Essays.* Ed. Caryl Emerson and Michael Holquist. Trans. Vern W. McGee. Austin: University of Texas Press.

Barthes, Roland (1995). "The Death of the Author." *Authorship – From Plato to the Postmodern.* Seán Burke, ed. Edinburgh: Edinburgh University Press.

Benveniste, Emile (1971). *Problems in General Linguistics.* Trans. Mary Elizabeth Meek. Coral Gables: University of Miami Press

Burroughs, William (1970). *The Last Words of Dutch Schultz.* Cape Goliard.

Codrescu, Andrei (1973). "De Natura Rerum." *Great American Prose poems from Poe to the Present.* 2003. Ed. David Lehman. New York: Scribner Poetry.

——— (1977). *The Lady Painter.* Boston: Four Zoas Press.

——— (1993). *Road Scholar: Coast to Coast Late in the Century.* Photographs by David Graham. New York: Hyperion.

——— (1999). "Zeitgeist: Making Up America – Optimism at all costs is the price we pay for prosperity." *American Demographics.* Jan 1999; 21. 1.

——— (1999b). "What is American about American Poetry?" *Poetry Society of America.* [http://www.poetrysociety.org/codrescu.html]

——— (2000). *A Bar in Brooklyn.* Santa Rosa: Black Sparrow Press.

——— (2001). *An Involuntary Genius in America's Shoes (And What Happened Afterwards).* Santa Rosa: Black Sparrow Press.

——— (2003). "Geographers at Mardi Gras: An Address to the American Geographers' Association Annual Meeting in New Orleans, March 4, 2003" [http://turnrow.ulm.edu/AndreiCodrescu.htm] .

Clark, Brian Charles (2001). What We Bear: A Study of Surphysical Narrativity. [On line] http://www.class.uidaho.edu/narrative/theory/what_bear.htm.

Empson, William (1973). *Seven Types of Ambiguity.* London: Chatto and Windus.

Fried, Debra (1986). "Repetition, Refrain, and Epitaph". *EHL.* Vol. 53. Issue 3. (pp. 615-632). Johns Hopkins University Press.

Gessen, Keith (2001) *Writing for No One* [On line] http://www.kraus99.com/english/noone.htm.

Ginsberg, Allen (1956). *Howl and Other Poems.* San Francisco: City Lights Books.

Jameson, Frederic (1981). *The Political Unconscious: Narrative as a Socially Symbolic Act.* Ithaca: Cornell University Press.

Lehman, David (ed.) (2003). *Great American Prose poems from Poe to the Present*. New York: Scribner Poetry.

Lyotard, Jean François (1994). *Lessons on the Analytic of the Sublime*. Stanford: Stanford University Press.

Markson, David (1988). *Wittgenstein's Mistress*. Illinois: Dalkey Archive Press.

——— (1996). *Reader's Block*. Chicago: Dalkey Archive Press.

——— (2001). *This Is Not a Novel*. Washington, DC: Counterpoint.

Mills-Courts, Karen (1990). *Poetry as Epitaph: Representation and Poetic Language*. Baton Rouge and London: Louisiana State University Press.

Murphy, James J., ed. (2012). *A Short History of Writing Instruction: From Ancient Greece to Contemporary America*. London: Routledge.

Paschen, Elise & Mosby, Rebekah Presson (2001). *Poetry Speaks: Hear Great Poets Read Their Work from Tennyson to Plath*. Sourcebooks Mediafusion: Book & CD edition.

Rajan, Tilottama and Wright, Julia M., eds. (1998). *Romanticism, History, and the Possibilities of Genre*. Cambridge University Press.

Riffaterre, Michael (1983). *Text Production*. New York: Columbia University Press.

Schlegel, Friedrich (1991). *Philosophical Fragments*. Trans. Peter Firchow. Minneapolis: University of Minnesota Press.

——— (1957). *Literary Notebooks 1797-1801*. Toronto: University of Toronto Press.

Silverman, Hugh J. (1994). *Textualities: Between Hermeneutics and Deconstruction*. New York and London: Routledge.

Taylor, Mark C. (1997). *Hiding*. Chicago: University of Chicago Press.

6. Epistemologists of creative writing: axiomatic redux

Elias, Camelia (2009) *Eight Senses Plus Two*. EyeCorner Press.

——— (2010). *The Logician*. EyeCorner Press.

About the author

Camelia, PhD & Dr.Phil. (habil.) is a professor of English and Chair of American Studies at Roskilde University. Her research is in comparative literature, literary theory, and visual manifestations of the occult as a cultural text. In her spare time she makes art, practices divination with cards, and writes prose poems.

www.ingramcontent.com/pod-product-compliance
Lightning Source LLC
Chambersburg PA
CBHW031326230426
43670CB00006B/252